UNDERSTANDING
Hamlet

A STUDENT CASEBOOK TO ISSUES, SOURCES, AND HISTORICAL DOCUMENTS

Richard Corum

The Greenwood Press
"Literature in Context" Series
Claudia Durst Johnson, Series Editor

GREENWOOD PRESS
Westport, Connecticut • London

Library of Congress Cataloging-in-Publication Data

Corum, Richard.
   Understanding Hamlet : a student casebook to issues, sources, and
historical documents / Richard Corum.
      p.   cm.—(The Greenwood Press "Literature in context"
series, ISSN 1074-598X)
   Includes bibliographical references (p.   ) and index.
   ISBN 0-313-29877-7 (alk. paper)
   1. Shakespeare, William, 1564-1616. Hamlet—Sources.
   2. Literature and history—England—History—16th century—Sources.
   3. Denmark—In literature—Sources.   4. Princes in literature—
Sources.   I. Title.   II. Series.
PR2807.C67   1998
822.3'3—dc21   98-12147

British Library Cataloguing in Publication Data is available.

Library of Congress Catalog Card Number: 98-12147
ISBN: 0-313-29877-7
ISSN: 1074-598X

First published in 1998

Greenwood Press, 88 Post Road West, Westport, CT 06881
An imprint of Greenwood Publishing Group, Inc.

Printed in the United States of America

The paper used in this book complies with the
Permanent Paper Standard issued by the National
Information Standards Organization (Z39.48-1984).

10 9 8 7 6 5 4

P

In order to keep this title in print and available to the academic community, this edition
was produced using digital reprint technology in a relatively short print run. This would
not have been attainable using traditional methods. Although the cover has been changed
from its original appearance, the text remains the same and all materials and methods
used still conform to the highest book-making standards.

For Morgan, Nathaniel, and Louise

Contents

Illustrations

Introduction

If Shakespeare's works are the Himalayas of literature, *Hamlet* is his Everest: "the world's most famous play by the world's most famous writer," not to mention the world's longest, most complex, most demanding, most discussed, and most influential literary text—"the masterwork that remains the heart of the heart of Western culture" (*Newsweek*, 1997). Who has not made its acquaintance, even if only in the sanitized versions one reads as a child or sees on most stages? Who has not once spoken at least one of its famous lines? And who has not found it difficult to understand?

When *The Tragicall Historie of Hamlet* (the title of the early Quartos) first opened in 1599 at the Lord Chamberlain's Men's new Globe Theatre just across London Bridge in Southwark, the city of London, rapidly becoming an urban metropolis, was experiencing far-reaching change. Its population and political power, as well as the number of its poor, had vastly expanded since Henry VIII divorced England from continental Catholicism in the early 1530s. Classical texts in English translations were appearing virtually monthly at the booksellers' stalls in the portico of St. Paul's Cathedral. Inflation was rampant as early modern forms of capitalism gradually replaced feudal economic practices. Business and trade were prospering because peace had reigned, and because the powers that be had been sympathetic to innovation since Queen Elizabeth I assumed the throne in 1558. Beginning about 1576, professional theatres like The Theatre and The Curtain came to be built in "liberties" outside the city's walls—areas of freedom safe from the jurisdiction of the city fathers and from conservative efforts to silence the new knowledge that was emerging in these theatres. Social mobility was a possibility for many of London's middling classes, and, despite such opportunities (or, more likely, because of them), suicide rates throughout England were setting new records. Adolescents, delayed longer and longer from marriage (until twenty-eight, on average, for men, and twenty-six for women), were gaining greater presence in the culture and its literature, if not also greater political power. And on the south bank of the Thames, the recently erected Globe Theatre (half owned by Shakespeare and six of his fellow actors), competed with other venues for the city's increasing leisure wealth, offering London's citizens and tourists, particularly adolescent ones, opportunities for delight, instruction, and assembly unavailable elsewhere.

As an apprentice or a shop girl in 1599 London, you would have had a variety of ways to spend your free time and your excess pennies. You could take a boat upstream to a holiday spot on the Thames, shop in the city's markets and stalls, or walk out one of its thoroughfares to look at a stake that had been driven through the heart of a recently buried suicide. You could spend your time at a tavern or a cockfight, or go to a brothel, a gambling den, or the bear-baiting arena. Along with crowds of sensation seekers, you could take in a hanging or beheading at Tyburn or Wapping Marsh, walk to Bethlem Hospital (Bedlam) and gawk at the insane, or try to catch a glimpse of the queen or an aristocrat entering or leaving the Tower of London. Or you could go to the Globe in the afternoon and stand in the cockpit under an open roof and watch a new play like *The Tragicall Historie of Hamlet*.

Presumably you would go to the Globe and watch *Hamlet* because it was the newest play by the best playwright in London, and Richard Burbage, the best actor, was playing the lead; because you knew Shakespeare had rewritten an ancient legend you'd recently read in translation; because you knew that *Hamlet* was the latest instance of a genre, revenge tragedy (modeled on recent translations of the classics), you particularly liked, a genre, moreover, that was scarcely older than you or the public theatres that had come into being during your lifetime; or because the Globe and the plays it offered provided you with something unavailable to you anywhere else in London: the equivalent of a secular university education.

If you went to the Globe and watched this new play, you would soon recognize that *Hamlet* is a play about adolescents and, more particularly, what adolescents do when they lose a powerful and commanding father. On the stage of the Globe, you would see seven adolescents—Hamlet, Ophelia, Laertes, Fortinbras, Horatio, Rosencrantz and Guildenstern (four of whom lose a father)—struggling to overcome melancholy by taking one of the dead-end options offered them by their parents and/or their culture.

Watching *Hamlet*, you would also see that this play is about fathers—particularly the demands fathers make on their adolescent children, the knowledge and advice they hand down to these adolescents, and the adequacy of such demands and knowledge. You would see the terrible consequences of obeying certain parental demands, and the equally terrible consequences of not being able to figure out what to do other than merely disobey such demands. Watching *Hamlet*, you would learn about the ways parents manipulate and use adolescents to further their own desires, not to mention the tragedy that frequently results from such use and manipulation. And you would leave the Globe wondering about the sufficiency of your parents' knowledge, as well as questioning the advisability (if they were) of allowing them to go on controlling and manipulating your life. Moreover, you would see how difficult it is, and how necessary it is, for you to become independent and set out on your own. In short, if you watched *Hamlet* at the Globe and saw all seven of its adolescents end up dead by the time the play's action is finished, you would understand that Shakespeare's company was staging a play about how the lives of adolescents like yourself come to be wasted. In fact, you would see that *Hamlet* is a play about how certain kinds of parents and/or certain kinds of cultures tragically squander the lives and energies of its adolescents, and what these adolescents must do if they are not to be blasted [to wither or fall under a blight] "in the morn and liquid dew of [their] youth" (1.3.41). Thus, just as London gave you options about how you might spend your free time and your excess pennies, *Hamlet* gave you options with respect to how you might live your life.

But, as modern readers, we are not Elizabethans, so we face significant obstacles in the way of understanding *Hamlet* and seeing these options. The language of the play, even when modernized, is not our language, nor is the culture of the play's original audiences our culture. With the exception of one or two productions at the beginning of the nineteenth century, the *Hamlet*s audiences saw, and that critics interpreted from 1660 until 1980, were so altered or butchered (by cutting lines, speeches, scenes, characters) that they had little or nothing to do with the play Shakespeare wrote and staged at the Globe. Moreover, Shakespeare's theatre, a quasi-illegal activity on the margins of society, had a different form and function than theatres have tended to have since 1660 when they first joined hands with church and state. Moreover, like theatre, literary tragedy also functioned differently in 1599 than it often does now.

Thus, up against an Everest of a text to understand and the obstacles that stand in the way of understanding it, this book begins by illustrating the historical, contextualizing method it will use throughout in terms of a brief scene between Polonius and Reynaldo (2.1) that has been cut from virtually every production of *Hamlet* for the past 300 years, and from every movie prior to the four-hour film Kenneth Branagh directed in 1997. The question asked in this first chapter is not so much "What is the best knowledge to use in reading this scene?" but, "If the best knowledge of the past three centuries found this scene worthless, then what knowledge will allow us to understand why Shakespeare included it in this play?" In light of this test case, the second half of Chapter 1 proposes that there are always at least four different kinds of best knowledge circulating in any culture at any point in time, which means, among other things, that in Shakespeare's own time, *Hamlet* was understood in at least four radically different ways.

Chapter 2 deals with two other historical contexts crucial to an understanding of *Hamlet*: the popular public theatres in which Shakespeare and his company first produced *Hamlet*, and the genre—tragedy—in which it is written. The assumption in this chapter is that an understanding of the theatre in which *Hamlet* was staged and the literary genre in which it is written is crucial to an understanding of *Hamlet*.

Having reached base camp with the equipment assembled in these first chapters, we will then stop in Chapter 3 ("Literary Analysis: Hamlet's Options"), get out a telescope, and survey at some length the route we will be climbing to get a sense of the crevices and glaciers, the faces and clefts that lie ahead. After extended literary analysis, we will then tackle, in four subsequent chapters, the rugged and majestic terrain we have surveyed, following Hamlet's route from melancholy (Chapter 4), to ghost (Chapter 5), revenge (Chapter 6), and antic disposition (i.e., Hamlet's pretended madness) (Chapter 7). The views are exhilarating and the going is sometimes difficult, but working our way across these diverse terrains will allow us first-hand experience of the complex materials from which the brilliant play we are seeking to understand was constructed. From this vantage point we will then look at Gertrude (Chapter 8) and Ophelia (Chapter 9)—two major figures in this text who have long been seen far too exclusively from Hamlet's point of view. The conclusion takes up the pressing question of what route Hamlet and the other adolescents in the play could have taken that would not have led to tragic death or a stage littered with dead bodies.

The argument of this book is that if we get ourselves out of the center of London, across the Thames and into the public theatre in which *Hamlet* was initially produced, if we know what is meant by a literary tragedy, and if we have access to a wide range of early modern thinking about melancholy, ghosts, revenge, antic dispositions, suicide, men and women, then, like the play's early audiences, we will be able to understand the *Hamlet* Shakespeare's company staged in 1599.

As is clear from this brief account, tragedy and comedy, especially in high places, are matters of knowledge, the best knowledge amounting finally to whatever knowledge enables one to avoid tragedy and generate comedy. In this light, the thesis of this book is that it is precisely this kind of knowledge that Shakespeare's *The Tragicall Historie of Hamlet* offers us as a play, even though it is also precisely this knowledge that Hamlet and the other adolescents, as characters in this play, so thoroughly lack. Thus, as a modern reader, you have a choice that perhaps you did not think you had: you do not have to follow Hamlet's path or that of any of the other adolescents you see on stage as they write tragical histories for themselves; rather, you can learn from Shakespeare's play how to avoid reduplicating such terrible disasters. If, having seen or read *Hamlet*, you do not have a clear sense of what created the tragic pile of dead bodies that litters the court at Elsinore, or what must be done if you are to avoid such a lethal conclusion, then you have not understood *Hamlet*.

In each chapter a variety of materials, many not readily accessible elsewhere, are excerpted from Elizabethan and classical sources as contexts for understanding this play: essays, poems, plays, histories, scriptural passages, treatises, official documents, stories, religious tracts, homilies, engravings, memoirs, village records. In addition to such documents and the text introducing them, each chapter also contains an introductory discussion, study questions, topics for written and oral discussion, and a list of suggested readings.

Hamlet quotations are from the 1604 second Quarto, though occasionally this text has been modified by reference to the 1623 first Folio. All quotations are keyed parenthetically to the Oxford text as reprinted in *The Norton Shakespeare*, edited by Stephen Greenblatt (1997).

Except for titles and epigraphs, quotations from the play, and excerpts from supporting documents have been modernized by the author. In the longer abridged excerpts, ellipses within sentences and paragraphs have not been indicated, and quotations marks have been added to increase clarity.

Like others who work on this play, my debt to the hundreds of essays and books that could not be acknowledged below is enormous, as is my gratitude to the staffs of the rare book collections of Cambridge University, the Huntington Library, the University of Minnesota, and the University of California at Santa Barbara. I would also like to thank my Shakespeare classes in the College of Letters and Science and the College of Creative Studies at UCSB; Robert Gedeon, Edward Yang, and Korina Jochim, research assistants from heaven; Peggy Kirk, an unfailing source of insight and encouragement; Barbara Rader of the Greewnwood Press for supporting this project; Professor Claudia Durst Johnson of the University of Alabama, whose editorial suggestions have been unfailingly helpful and deeply appreciated; and Louise Fradenburg, without whose knowledge, conversation, friendship, and support this book would have been less clear, less interesting, and much less fun to write.

SUGGESTED READINGS AND WORKS CITED

Gates, David. "Dead White Male of the Year: Shakespeare." *Newsweek*, 6 January, 1997, p. 87.

Greenblatt, Stephen, ed. *The Norton Shakespeare*. New York: W. W. Norton, 1997.

THE
Tragicall Hiſtorie of
HAMLET,
Prince of Denmarke.

By William Shakeſpeare.

Newly imprinted and enlarged to almoſt as much
againe as it was, according to the true and perfect
Coppie.

AT LONDON,
Printed by I. R. for N. L. and are to be ſold at his
ſhoppe vnder Saint Dunſtons Church in
Fleetſtreet. 1604.

Title page of the 1604 Quarto, commonly known as the "Good" Quarto.

1 ⎯⎯⎯⎯⎯⎯⎯⎯⎯⎯⎯⎯⎯⎯⎯⎯⎯⎯⎯⎯⎯⎯⎯⎯⎯

Method and Social Geography

METHOD

> . . . to catch behind the smooth surface of the text, a subtle interplay of threats and fears, of attacks and withdrawals.
>
> —Carlo Ginzburg

Before turning to the central characters and action of *Hamlet*, it is helpful to illustrate the method used throughout this book with what may seem an altogether unimportant test case: the seemingly insignificant scene between Polonius, councilor to the king, and Reynaldo, his man servant (2.1). Hated by T. S. Eliot ("not by Shakespeare!"), cut from virtually all productions and films (not in Olivier's or Zeffirelli's *Hamlet*, and done badly in Branagh's), and largely ignored by critics, this scene, when it is produced, is used to depict Polonius as an obsessive father trying to keep tabs on his son, Laertes, by the questionable method of having Reynaldo spy on him in Paris. When produced, this scene contributes to the goal of having Polonius serve as comic relief. In fact, having Polonius absentmindedly bumbling about in this scene, as generally throughout the play, has long been the right, the professionally successful, and the audience-pleasing way to stage Polonius, just as in the academic criticism influenced by this long-standing stage tradition, this is the right way to understand Polonius. However, if we switch the context for our understanding of Polonius and this scene from this performative/critical tradition to the political realities of Shakespeare's time—if, instead of understanding Polonius as comic relief, we understand him as part of his audiences' sociopolitical reality—we would understand Polonius in a very different way. To facilitate such a move let us turn to a passage from Niccolò Machiavelli's (1469–1527) best known work, *Il Principe* [*The Prince*] (1532), a text avidly hated by church/state authorities, and just as avidly read by anyone with ambition who knew Italian because Machiavelli was the first in print in the West (although not in print in English until 1640) to replace idealistic myths with brilliantly acute realism. In this passage Machiavelli analyzes men in high places who, like Polonius, work for men in even higher places. If it were not for the fact that the first English translation is (and perhaps had to be) exceedingly inaccurate, it would be cited instead of Russell Price's modern translation from *Machiavelli: The Prince*, edited by Q. Skinner.

FROM NICCOLÒ MACHIAVELLI, *THE PRINCE*
(1532; English trans., Cambridge: Cambridge University Press, 1988) 80

Chap. XXII. Touching Princes Secretaries.

The choosing of ministers [state secretaries] is a very important matter for a ruler: whether or not they are good depends on whether he is shrewd. The first indications of the intelligence of a ruler are given by the quality of the men around him. If they are capable and loyal, he should always be taken to be shrewd, because he was able to recognize their ability and retain their loyalty. But if they are mediocre and disloyal, a low estimate of him will never be mistaken, because the most important error he has made is to choose them. . . . For if a ruler shows judgement in discerning the worth of what another man says and does (even if he himself lacks originality of mind), he can discern the good or bad deeds of his minister, and reward the former but punish the latter. And since the minister realizes that he cannot deceive his master, he is careful to behave well. There is an infallible way for a ruler to weigh up a minister. If you realize that he is thinking more about his own affairs than about yours, and that all his actions are designed to further his own interests, he will never make a good minister, and you can never trust him. For a man who governs a state should never think about himself or his own affairs but always about the ruler, and concern himself only with the ruler's affairs.

In later cultures where kings and their secretaries no longer had real power (or were in the process of having their power taken over by parliaments), and where as a consequence public feeling for kings and their ministers, when not contempt, was idealistic sentimentality, Polonius perhaps makes sense as a long-winded, ridiculous cartoon figure. But in early modern cultures (e.g., Renaissance England), where kings and ministers of state were laboring to monopolize power, it is difficult to believe that Polonius would have been staged utterly bereft of power or presence. To say this does not mean that early modern theatre did not satirize the powerful; it did. Nor does it mean that a historically believable Polonius would not have had idiosyncratic mannerisms, would not perhaps have gone out of his way at times to appear to be forgetful and long-winded; but in early modern England, only a very naive person with no knowledge of court intrigue and no exposure to the ambitions of those in power would have taken a man like Polonius, whatever his mannerisms, merely at face value. Those with their wits about them would have assumed that beneath whatever dutiful pose he has fashioned, Polonius could not be other than shrewd. So one question to ask is what ends of his own is he up to behind his mask of dutiful servant? Another is how those in early theatre audiences would be able to see the invisible ambitions they would have taken, it is suggested, for granted?

Figuring out how Polonius's actions are designed to further his own interests and yet not seem in the least to be doing so requires that we consider first what his plans are with respect to Ophelia. The usual view is to assume that, functioning as a loyal state servant, he is doing exactly what he seems to be doing: heavy-handedly keeping his daughter in her proper subordinate place and mindful of her lower social status. Thus, the minute he hears of her relationship with Hamlet, he steps in and ends a relationship that cannot be, making Ophelia toe the social line at whatever cost to her hopes and desires. But this is not, of course, the half of it. With the death of the old king, Hamlet Sr., things have changed in Denmark. Technically, there is no upward social mobility in a hierarchical society since everyone is in (and can only be in) their proper place, yet Claudius has in effect married up, and this has (or could be seen as having) opened up new possibilities for those willing to take risks. Polonius—clever, intelligent, and ambitious—is rushing to exploit this new situation to better his children's circumstances, most particularly by deciding to plot a marriage between Ophelia and Hamlet despite the danger such an ambition entails. But how to succeed in a situation where visible pushing would cost him his job if not his life? By what indirect method (to use his own terms) will he find this "direction" out (i.e., get what he wants)? Before the play begins, he has dangled Ophelia in front of Hamlet (later in the play he says he will "loose" her to Hamlet [2.2.163], loose having the barnyard sense of making a female animal available for copulation) until Hamlet, well worked up, is just about to bite, and then, pretending to notice for the first time what is going on, Polonius suddenly yanks her out of Hamlet's reach: "I went round [directly] to work / And my young mistress thus I did bespeak [address], / 'Lord Hamlet is a Prince out of thy star [above your sphere] / This must not be' " (2.2.139–42). Surely the intended effect is to make Hamlet desire Ophelia so much that he will press for a marriage Polonius cannot press for at all.

The brilliance of this strategy is that there is no strategy at all in the eyes of anyone watching. No one, including Ophelia, can find Polonius out because nothing indicates that he is doing anything other than serving the interests of the king. So, paradoxically, it is the absence of any explicit evidence of what he is doing that proves Polonius's brilliance. In fact, only if overt evidence were available would he be the fool we have taken him to be.

In this context it can now be seen that, more generally, Polonius is not simply being tedious to think Hamlet love mad when Hamlet is acting mad: "And he, repulsed . . . / Fell . . . / Into the madness wherein now he raves" (2.2.146–47, 150). Hamlet love mad is precisely what Polonius had planned for and, in his mind, has effected. Polonius's problem is that he doesn't know, and can't know, that Hamlet's desires have been derailed, and that the madness Polonius reads as love madness is in fact an antic disposition (feigned madness). Polonius's strategy has not taken, and, reasonably speaking, could not have taken into account such a turn of events. Nevertheless, Polonius knows that something is not right. He suspects that Hamlet's condition isn't love madness, though he continues to act as if it were, still hoping in this way to help his marriage plan along. Thus, in several brilliant scenes with Hamlet, Polonius probes and spies, trying to figure out what is going on with Hamlet at the same time that Hamlet, also probing and spying, is similarly trying to figure out what is going on with Polonius. In at least one later scene, this mutual testing takes the form of insinuation and attack. Consider, for example, the notoriously difficult "camel, weasel, whale" scene:

POLONIUS: My lord, the Queen would speak with you, and presently.

HAMLET: Do you see yonder cloud that's almost in shape of a camel?

POLONIUS: By th' mass, and 'tis, like a camel indeed.

HAMLET: Methinks it is like a weasel.

POLONIUS: It is backed like a weasel.

HAMLET: Or like a whale.

POLONIUS: Very like a whale.   (3.2.344–51)

It is possible, of course, to read this as a scene in which a Prince humiliates a servant by forcing a servant to agree with him. It is also possible to read it as a scene in which Polonius is humoring a man he thinks temporarily mad. In either case *camel, weasel,* and *whale* will probably be understood as nothing more than antic (mad) nonsense. Each term is individually meaningful, of course, but the sequence, applied to a cloud, has proven difficult. However, if we understand this scene in the context of a Machiavellian intrigue, it seems clear that, among other things, Hamlet is using *camel, weasel, whale,* and *cloud* to attack Polonius under the cover of his feigned madness. Assuming that a loyal state minister should not have the fickle properties of a shape-changing *cloud,* Hamlet is in effect saying: Polonius, you pretend to be a faithful beast of burden, a *camel,* but, like a *cloud,* you really don't have a fixed shape. In fact, now that I look closely at your shenanigans, I see that you really are a vicious little *weasel* slinking about in pursuit of your own interests, or, stop to think of it, a *whale* lethal to anyone who imagines you to be nothing more than you appear.

Since these *cloud, camel, weasel,* and *whale* terms are metaphors that are not tied to one specific object, they can also refer to persons other than Polonius—Gertrude, for instance. Hamlet is on his way to her closet [private room] and it seems likely that her "fickleness" is as much on his mind as Polonius's. Angry that, *cloud*-like, she can be one thing, and then change and be something else, and then change again, he is venting his anger at the alleged abnormality her shape-shifting produces: a woman of virtue (a *camel*, beast of burden), who, despite appearances to the contrary, is (he has concluded) a sneaking, adulterous whore (a *weasel*), if not also a monstrously cold-blooded murderess (a *whale*, a creature equated at the time with Satan and/or death).

Moreover, because Hamlet, simulating madness, is himself caught up in the same shape-shifting vice he is accusing Polonius and/or Gertrude of practicing, his use of these terms cannot help but take on a degree of self-reference, threatening, if not boasting, that the *camel* they mistakenly take him to be will shift *weasel*-like and speak daggers, and then shift again and, *Leviathan*-like, kill, which is exactly what we see him do in the following closet scene.

Imagine now the difference this kind of Machiavellian Polonius would make in a stage production. Instead of watching Hamlet getting easy laughs by scoring cheap shots off a senile old man, we would see two brilliant tacticians, each wearing a fake disposition, each trying to maintain his own cover while exposing that of the other, and each, cramped by his own fraud, unable to expose the other's fraud except by the sort of indirect tactics we find here. Instead of comic relief we would have an exceptionally skillful and dangerous game in which two master tacticians, both playing for very high stakes, would return the other's serves with powerful cross-court volleys. Which understanding of these scenes, it might be asked, would appeal more to audiences, the historical Machiavellian possibilities we have just reconstructed, or the bumbling-fool stage version to which we have long been witness?

If, to return now to the Reynaldo scene with which we began, we set aside the tradition that has characterized this scene as worthless, and similarly historicize it in the context of Machiavellian policy, it, too, becomes a fascinating addition to the play. Consider Polonius's instructions to his man Reynaldo, in the context of Polonius's relation to his son Laertes, and particularly in relation to the earlier scene in which Polonius and Laertes say farewell (1.3). Despite appearances to the contrary, Polonius is not gearing up conventional fatherly advice simply to insure that Laertes will be a proper, well-behaved young man while abroad in France, though this is precisely what his behavior would allow an observer to think. Nor is the point of having Polonius mouth these platitudes to teach universal human truths. Nor (shifting to 2.1) is Polonius sending Reynaldo to Paris to see if Laertes has been obeying his father's commandments, though again such a conclusion is available to anyone overhearing their conversation. Rather, the point of the earlier "platitude" scene is to get Laertes off to Paris in customary fashion so as *not* to raise suspicions. And the point of the later Reynaldo scene is likewise to get Reynaldo off to Paris in a way that also will not raise suspicions. The conventional is Polonius's cover, not his goal. Let us assume, then, that Polonius is not sending Reynaldo to Paris to *get* information by means of Reynaldo's insinuations about the direction Laertes' Parisian behavior *might be* taking (though this is what Reynaldo thinks he will be doing, and as far as he knows, what he will be doing). Rather, Polonius is sending Reynaldo (without Reynaldo being aware of it) to *send* information to Laertes that will, by indirections, determine the direction Laertes' behavior *has* to take while Laertes is in France. This strategy is necessary because Laertes, left to his own devices, would listen to his father's platitudes, go to Paris, work hard to be the proper young man his father seems to desire ("neither a borrower nor a lender" [1.3.75], etc.), and would come back to Denmark an older version of the dutiful plodder he was when he left. But this sort of son isn't at all the son Polonius desires. What he needs is not a plodding bourgeois Laertes, but a proud and powerful aristocrat who can stand by Ophelia when she becomes queen. To produce this sort of son out of the son he in fact has, and to do so without losing his or his son's life, Polonius has to get Laertes abroad, and then has to figure out a way of making sure that the platitudes he issued upon Laertes' departure from Denmark will be forgotten by Laertes. Clearly the only way he can make sure that Laertes will forget them is to create an indirect demand that will encourage Laertes to do things that would normally be altogether out of his sphere. Polonius's method, then, is not just to have Reynaldo make inquires about Laertes, or just to spread false gossip about Laertes to see what Reynaldo can get in the way of response; rather, it is to use Reynaldo's slanders to create in the minds of the Danes in Paris an aristocratic image of Laertes that will float in the air of rumor like a ghost:

POLONIUS   . . . And there put on [attribute to] him
     What forgeries [fictions] you please . . .

> . . . such wanton, wild, and usual slips
> As are companions noted and most known
> To youth and liberty. . . .
> That they may seem the taints of liberty,
> The flash and outbreak of a fiery mind,
> A savageness in unreclaimed [unchecked] blood . . .
> (2.1.20–36)

By floating in the Parisian air an image of a fiery, aristocratic Laertes freely indulging in swearing, gambling, drinking, and brothel-going, Polonius puts Laertes in the position of choosing between living up to an as yet imaginary aristocratic reputation, or repudiating this reputation by remaining the petty plodder plotted by Polonius's platitudes. As we see later, Laertes acts the part Reynaldo's imaginary "bait of falsehood" scripts for him by becoming, among other things, an expert at sword play. And though he returns to Denmark (in act 4) the aristocrat Polonius desires, Laertes also returns to a social theatre that now lacks the sister heroine for whom he was meant to be chief supporting actor.

But why go to such lengths, such trouble, such indirections to cast Laertes in an aristocratic role? Why not just conspire with him, or let Reynaldo in on the game? Two early modern texts explain why. First, from Erasmus: "kings have many ears and many eyes. . . . They have ears that listen a hundred miles from them; they have eyes that spy out more things than men would think" (1545, vols. iiii–v). Second, from Ecclesiastes, the biblical source for this commonplace wisdom: "Wish the king no evil in thy thought, nor speak no hurt of him in thy privy chamber; for the bird of the air shall betray thy voice, and with her feathers, shall bewray thy words" (10.20). If Reynaldo were privy to Polonius's objective, he could use this information to gain power over Polonius for his own gain, or sell it to the king for profit or promotion. Moreover, were Laertes aware of such a plan, it and the conspiracy creating it would cause too much self-consciousness, if not too much guilt and fear, for him to be able to pursue it successfully.

Polonius's plan must and does proceed indirectly; yet by being so indirect as to be invisible, the question arises as to how it can be proven to exist, since Polonius leaves and (if he is to succeed) can leave no evidence. The only evidence there is, given Polonius's shrewdness, is a collection of traces written in the white ink of his private thoughts, traces we would not see, little less look for, were we not looking at this scene in the context of Machiavelli's *Prince*, and were we not willing, by virtue of this context, to allow Polonius devious ambitions and significant power in his own right that he must keep absolutely invisible if he is to keep his job and his head.

In the following passage, a particularly difficult one for modern readers to understand, Shakespeare writes two such traces in white ink (in addition to others in the rest of the scene):

> POLONIUS . . . You laying these slight sullies on my son,
>   As 'twere a thing a little soiled with working,
>   Mark you, your party [partner] in converse, him you
>   would sound,
>   Having [Asking him if he has] ever seen in the prenomi-
>   nate [aforesaid] crimes
>   The youth you breathe of guilty, be assured
>   He closes with you in this consequence,
>   "Good sir," or so, or "friend," or "gentleman,"
>   According to the phrase [manner of speaking], or the ad-
>   dition [title]
>   Of man and country.
> REYNALDO Very good my lord.
> POLONIUS And then, sir, does a [he] this, a does, what was I
>   about to say?
>   By the mass I was about to say something,
>   Where did I leave?
> REYNALDO At "closes in the consequence."
> POLONIUS At "closes in the consequence," ay, marry,
>   He closes thus, "I know the gentleman. . . ."   (2.1.40–55)

What are these traces? The first is the break in Polonius's concentration; the second is the triple repetition of "he closes with you in the consequence" (interpreted in the *Pelican* edition as: "he follows your lead to a conclusion"). I am suggesting that two trains of thought simultaneously occupy Polonius's mind. One, written in black ink, is the instruction Polonius is publicly communicating to Reynaldo. The other, written in white ink, Polonius alone is privy to. What happens is that, caught up thinking about the second of these while speaking the first, Polonius momentarily slips and lets his unspoken thoughts disturb his spoken ones. This disturbance, taking the form of a break in concentration and a repetition, is our evidence that the line "he closes with you in the consequence" [follows your lead to a conclusion] signifies both the action the Danish person listening to Reynaldo in Paris will do when he hears Reynaldo's insinuations (i.e., follow Reynaldo's lead to the alleged conclusion), and what Polonius hopes Laertes will do when Laertes hears these insinuations echoing about Paris (i.e., follow Reynaldo's lead to the aristocratic conclusion Polonius is plotting). That is, the pronoun he (in "he closes . . ."), has a double referent in Polonius's mind—an anonymous Dane in Paris on the one hand, and Laertes on the other, both of whom are to follow Reynaldo's lead to the same conclusion (both are to "close with you in the consequence"), the one in thought, the other in action. Thus, rather than a senile clown so absent of mind that he needs a servant to keep track of his thoughts, Polonius turns out to be a cauldron of ambitions that lets out just enough wisps of his private purpose for a theatre audience to ascertain its presence unless, like Reynaldo, they are too dull witted to catch on to what is happening under their noses.

Because Machiavelli, Erasmus, and Ecclesiastes are not the only early modern contexts which are available for historicizing Polonius, one might ask why we are using these contexts rather than other possibilities. Had we used, for example, Thomas Becon's early modern *Catechism* on the duties of fathers and of "young unmarried men"—an early modern Puritan minister's religious conduct book—to understand these scenes, we would have had ample confirmation of the long-standing belief that Polonius, Laertes, and Reynaldo are doing nothing more than what they seem to be doing, though from Becon's middle-class puritanical perspective Polonius would not have been seen as a ridiculous old man, but as an earnest bourgeois father doing his dutiful best to be the loyal servant his job demands. To the question of why we choose Machiavelli instead of Becon, the next section offers an answer.

SOCIAL GEOGRAPHY

> The complexity of a culture is to be found . . . in the dynamic interrelations, at every point in the process, of historically varied and variable elements.
> —Raymond Williams

The method we are using is valuable because it allows us to understand *Hamlet* from more than one early modern perspective, but since this diversity can be confusing, it is helpful, in understanding the rich and complex territory we are mapping, to turn to distinctions offered by Raymond Williams, a modern British literary historian. Since these distinctions will be used throughout the rest of the book, it is important to explain them in some detail. Their chief value is that they will prevent us from thinking that early modern English culture was unitary [whole, undivided], and this will hopefully make it impossible to think that putting *Hamlet* in a historical context means putting *Hamlet* into just *one* context, since in early modern England, as in every culture before and since, there are always at least four significantly different contexts to contend with:

1. *residual* (what is left over from the past),
2. *dominant* (what is presently in control),
3. *transgressive* (what lies beyond the boundaries of the acceptable), and
4. *emergent* (what arises as new).

With respect to Elizabethan England, *residual* in part meant the Catholic religious establishment, which, though declared illegal in 1532, nevertheless hung on in memories, values, published texts, subversive practices, ruined or remodeled monastic buildings, as well as in a Europe where Catholicism was still primarily dominant. For Elizabethans residual also meant those early subversive reactions to the Catholic order mobilized by Wyclif, Hus, Melanchthon, Zwingli, and Luther, among others, linked in the public mind with Wittenberg and the 1521 Diet of Worms, and associated with Hamlet in the play. Residual also designated a wide spectrum of conservative social feelings based in agrarian resistance to economic and social change. In part, residual also marked that long traditional, blood-based hereditary aristocratic order which successive Tudor monarchical bureaucracies labored to disempower.

Dominant signifies the Protestant, monarchical, bureaucratic cultural formation that emerged with Henry VIII (1491–1547), and came into full power during the reign of Elizabeth I (1558–1603). Dominant also meant that the authority formerly vested in the Pope, Catholic tradition, and/or an oligarchic English aristocratic nobility, came to reside instead in a sovereign monarch, English common law, and parliament.

Transgressive means everything defined as illegal and/or sinful according to the laws of the dominant culture and/or the more general codes of the culture. In religious terms, transgressive activities included atheism, witchcraft, sodomy, prostitution, incest, and adultery; in political terms, treason, rebellion, sedition, and the like; in social terms, violations of, for example, sumptuary laws (laws that made it illegal for people to wear clothes that would elevate their social status or alter their gender). Though the transgressive is distinguished from the dominant and residual, it is a phenomenon that also occurs *within* each of these domains.

Emergent, to quote Raymond Williams, means the "new meanings and values, new practices, new relationships and new kinds of relationships [that] are continually being created" (123). These include the sorts of new knowledge a dominant order readily appropriates (i.e., takes over) as a way of strengthening itself, and the sorts of new knowledge that such an order regards as sufficiently threatening to contain or suppress.

Two simple examples from modern times: (1) messengers are a *residual*, telephones and the mail a *dominant*, graffiti a *transgressive*, and the Internet an *emergent* way of sending messages; (2) gossip is a *residual*, newspapers and magazines a *dominant*, zines and graffiti a *transgressive*, and television an *emergent* way of getting the news. Television, on its way to being the *dominant* news media (if it isn't already), is gradually pushing newspapers into *residual* status, and gossip, though no longer the chief way we get information, has been radically reempowered by the Internet.

From a dominant perspective, virtually all residual, transgressive, and emergent activities are viewed as *subversive*, though subversion is also, of course, present in the dominant itself. And, just as society as a whole is divided into at least these four domains, every cultural entity in such a society is also similarly divided. In other words, this four-part array replicates itself across the entire social order as well as in its smallest particles. Thus, individual consciousness, emotions, intentions, and the like are divided in ways parallel to the way the culture as a whole is divided. For this reason it is possible to say that though every cultural entity (person, text, critic, author, law, or cultural institution) is always in one domain, it is, paradoxically, never just in one domain. In short, Williams's terms are useful as a cultural telescope and as a cultural microscope because they allow us to see that difference, to whatever degree, is always present in every cultural entity.

In principal these terms are value free, meaning that each is neutral. In practice, however, they quickly become value laden for the reason that individual persons or groups are positioned within one part of the whole, and thus are never identical with the social order as a whole, even if this or that person or group thinks it is identical. This value-relative feature of cultural diversity is one way of understanding what Hamlet means when he says, "there is nothing either good or bad but thinking makes it so" (2.2.244–45). Much of the hard work of understanding the past, then, lies in figuring out where someone who is pronouncing values in a culture is standing, as well as the domain in which the object being evaluated is itself located. Consider the case of Machiavelli. From a residual perspective Machiavelli was reviled as an instance of the satanic other, and *The Prince*, demonized, was deemed worthy of instant destruction. From one dominant perspective he was criminalized as a subversive defending the usurpation of legitimate authority; but from another dominant perspective he was a heroic figure who wrote to liberate Italy from foreign rule. From one transgressive perspective, he was a tool of dominant power, since he dedicated *The Prince* to Lorenzo de Medici (ruler of Florence during part of Machiavelli's lifetime); yet from another, he was a subversive wit satirizing Medici rule. From an emergent perspective, however, Machiavelli was the first in western cultural history to publish a realistic analysis of power, and hence is the father of modern political science. It is this last fact which explains why Machiavelli's *Prince* offers a particularly valuable historical context in which to think about Polonius and *Hamlet*: because it was the first text to be published in the West that contains sufficient knowledge to understand Polonius's situation adequately, as opposed to the thousands of residual, transgressive, and dominant texts flooding the booksellers' stalls that did not have enough knowledge to do so. So, given the choice of viewing the Polonius/Reynaldo scene from the perspective of a residual text like Thomas Becon's *Catechism*, from that of a contemporary dominant text like the famous letter of fatherly advice Sir William Wentworth sent his son in 1602–1603, or that of an emergent text like Machiavelli's *Prince*, the choice is obvious: only the latter allows us to see Polonius's doubleness, and thus the internal difference (the self-promoting transgressive ambition Polonius disguises as a dominant act of self-sacrifice) that makes him an interesting early modern character, and not just a stereotypical bit of costume drama.

STUDY QUESTIONS

1. In what situations have you seemed to serve the interests of those above you (parents, teachers, employers, deity), but in fact were secretly serving your own interests instead?

2. How could parents give adolescents official public advice on the one hand, and contradict this advice with more powerful unconscious and unofficial advice on the other?

3. If you were asked to make a list of the ten most important emergent thinkers in the history of western culture, who would you include?

4. What examples of residual thinking come to mind with respect to present day America?

5. If you were to divide up what you know into residual, dominant, transgressive, and emergent categories, what would go in each?

6. Which of these four terms most adequately describes your relationship to society?

7. What kinds of conflict can erupt between these various social positions? What works to reduce, and what to increase, such conflict?

8. List the ways in which a high school can exhibit residual, dominant, transgressive, and emergent activities.

QUESTIONS AND TOPICS FOR WRITTEN AND ORAL DISCUSSION

1. Explain why the platitudes handed Ophelia by Laertes and Polonius, and those handed Laertes by Polonius are useless and impossible to follow even by someone determined to do so. Then explain why in everyday life fathers and brothers frequently impose such stuff on sons or sisters.

2. What other traces of Polonius's private ambition can be found written in white ink in act 2, scene 1?

3. Collect instances where Polonius explicitly presents himself as a loyal servant of the crown and then show how even these assertions of public duty provide evidence of Polonius's transgressive doubleness.

4. Write a dialogue in which a modern day parent hands an adolescent child some useless or impossible platitudes.

5. Write a skit for the classroom in which characters take dominant, residual, emergent, and transgressive positions on a current issue. Describe costumes that would emphasize these roles.

6. Create a display that shows residual, dominant, transgressive, and emergent forms of music and musical instruments.

SUGGESTED READINGS AND WORKS CITED

Howard, Jean E., and Marion F. O'Connor, eds. *Shakespeare Reproduced: The Text in History and Ideology*. New York: Methuen, 1987.

Jardine, Lisa. *Reading Shakespeare Historically*. London: Routledge, 1996.

Stallybrass, Peter, and Allon White. *The Politics and Poetics of Transgression*. Ithaca, NY: Cornell University Press, 1986.

Tavener, Richard, trans. *Prouerbes or Adagies . . . of Erasmus*. London: E. Whytchurche, 1545.

Williams, Raymond. "Dominant, Residual, and Emergent." In *Marxism and Literature*. Oxford: Oxford University Press, 1977.

2

Theatre and Tragedy

THEATRE

> . . . an inquiry into [Elizabethan theatre] *per se* would be non-sensical: such an inquiry could only obscure the phenomenon it was intended to elucidate, for by isolating [theatre] from social practices, it would conceal the sole context in which the [theatre] makes any sense—namely, the structure of [Elizabethan] polity.
> —David Halperin (borrowed from another context)

Like English society in general, early modern London was constructed of at least four conflicting parts. This chapter focuses on one of these parts, the emergent, and looks at one of several powerful new institutions that constituted early modern London's emergent sphere: its popular public, peripheral theatres. The second half of this chapter examines the chief instrument emergent playwrights developed in these theatres to critique the activities of English society's other three domains: literary tragedy, of which *Hamlet* is the most brilliant English exemplar. To understand *Hamlet* is in part to understand how these public theatres and this genre delighted and instructed early modern English audiences. One way to do this is to contrast these theatres with other forms

ST PAUL'S CATHEDRAL
The BEAR GARDEN and the GLOBE THEATRE

Detail from J. C. Visscher's *View of London* (1616).

of early modern theatre, and thus other forms of delight and instruction. The terms introduced above allow us to identify three other kinds of theatre (in a broad sense of the term) that were available to the inhabitants of Elizabethan England.

Residual Forms of Theatre

When Henry VIII divorced England from Catholicism in 1532, numerous forms of previously dominant theatre, declared illegal by Henry's courts of law, immediately became residual: actors such as Catholic priests, nuns, sinners,; plays such as mass, indulgences, mystery and morality plays, pageants and pilgrimages; and stages such as cathedals and convents.

Three things chiefly characterize residual forms of theatricality. First, each prohibits a person from being (in theory at least) a member of an audience in the modern emergent sense of this term. Everyone at mass, for example, is required to be onstage, in character, correctly costumed, speaking the right lines, and participating in the action. One cannot be a nonparticipant or get offstage without penalty, whether immediate or deferred, because to be offstage means one would be a heretic and/or an atheist, and thus damned. Second, the action that takes place in residual theatre is deemed real rather than fictional in the sense that (in theory at least) one believes (has to believe) that the stage set (heaven, earth, hell) was constructed by, that the script(ure) and roles (priest, penitent congregation, Pope) were written by, and that the action is being directed by a deity whose agents (Christ, the church, its clergy) are stage managing a one-and-only production. Third, all other forms of theatre are mere fictions or false illusions, and thus are demonized, banned, or rigorously contained. These three features of residual theatre were also common to the theatre written by archaic agrarian communities and ancient hereditary aristocracies, though in the latter case *traitor*, rather than *sinner*, would be used to describe those who step off the one-and-only "real" stage. Residual theatre functions to isolate power in a privileged elite, inscribe habitual behavior on the minds and bodies of subject populations, and guarantee cultural repetition (tradition) without significant difference.

Dominant Forms of Theatre

The dominant forms of theatre (again in the broad sense) that pushed Catholic, hereditary aristocratic, and agrarian modes into residual status also took a variety of forms:

> *Royal*: Elizabeth playing the role of queen on stages called royal palaces;
>
> *Aristocratic*: Robert Devereux acting his part as the earl of Essex on the stage of his manor house or at court;
>
> *Civic*: citizens performing the roles of Lord Mayor, alderman, merchant tailor in theatres called Guild Hall, Royal Exchange, Cheapside Market;
>
> *Religious*: men acting the parts of Anglican minister or archbishop of Canterbury in plays called church or funeral services on stages called St. Paul's Cathedral or cemeteries;
>
> *Domestic*: men playing the parts of good husbands and masters of apprentices, women acting the roles of silent, obedient wives, children reciting the lines of dutiful student or obedient apprentice—on stages called home, shop, school.

Like their residual predecessors, dominant forms of theatre worked to legitimize rule, consolidate power, and contain subversion by encouraging a populace to respect, love, and support monarch, nobility, church, city, and state. Dominant forms of theatre were produced day after day by citizens to convince themselves that they were (that they desired to be, that they had to be) in their proper roles playing their proper parts and speaking their proper lines in the larger play that constituted English sociocultural life. Consider the opening sentences of a 1559 state-produced homily on obedience entitled, *An exhortation concerning good Order, and obedience, to Rulers and Magistrates*, that was read in English churches on a regular basis throughout Elizabeth I's reign:

> Almighty God has created and appointed all things in a most excellent and perfect order.... In earth he has assigned and appointed kings, princes, with other governors under them, all in good and necessary order.... The Sun, Moon, Stars, Rainbow, Thunder, Lightning, Clouds, and all birds of the air, do keep their order.... And man himself also has all his parts in a profitable,

necessary, and pleasant order. Every degree of people in their vocation, calling, and office has appointed to them, their duty and order. Some are in high degree, some in low, some kings and princes, some inferiors and subjects, priests, and lay men, Masters and Servants, Fathers and children, husbands and wives, rich and poor, so that in all things is to be lauded and praised the goodly order of god, without the which, no house, no city, no commonwealth can continue and endure or last. For where there is no right order, there reigns all abuse, carnal liberty, enormity, sin, and Babylonical confusion. (69)

In order to assume the authority of the former Catholic/aristocratic/agrarian social order and replace it as dominant power, the Protestant church/state took over and freshly remodeled much of the stage set ("Sun, Moon, Stars"), special effects ("Thunder, Lightning, Clouds"), cast of characters ("kings and princes . . . Masters and Servants"), villains ("carnal liberty, enormity, sin"), direction ("assigned and appointed"), and plot ("most excellent and perfect order") which this former order had produced, and did so to make it as difficult as possible for anyone to produce rival sets, scriptwriters, casts of characters, heroes, villains, or plots.

Transgressive Forms of Theatre

Transgressive theatre and its thousand and one plots! A married craftsman, playing the roles of husband, father, merchant tailor in a play written by, and on a stage constructed by the dominant order is restless in these roles and this play, so he gets involved in a plot to overthrow Elizabeth I (who has been excommunicated by the Pope), and finds his life as a political subversive a more vital part in a more meaningful play. Or his wife, tired of the home stage set with its supporting cast of family characters, and sick of acting her mother and wife roles, gets involved in an affair in order to enjoy adventure, excitement, pleasure. Or their bored son spends his afternoons at taverns getting drunk and daydreaming. Or, thinking back to Chapter 1, Polonius scripts illegal roles and lines for himself and his children in order to alter the position of characters on the stage of Elsinore.

These transgressive forms of theatre fundamentally differ from residual and dominant theatre in the sense that they make people inescapably *doubles* (husband *and* subversive, wife *and* adulteress, son *and* daydreaming drunk, Lord Chamberlain *and* plotter) rather than, as in dominant and residual theatre, *single* (i.e., unitary), which is one reason why transgressive theatre is so hated and so envied by dominant and residual members of a culture, not to mention why it gives pleasure to those who pursue it. Moreover, in transgressive theatre, one performs not on one, but on two stages, so another crime and/or sin in the eyes of dominant and residual parties is that in plotting sedition one has gotten off the culture's dominant main stage. One has, in short, refused to keep the "comely course and order" one was "assigned and appointed."

Emergent Theatre

Residual, dominant, and transgressive forms of theatre clearly used up massive amounts of energy in early modern England; however, they did not satisfy a number of powerful desires:

1. the desire not always to have to play transgressive roles in the dark (the desire not to have to lie or be secretive);

2. the desire to decriminalize several of the transgressive roles one played;

3. the desire to move up socially and play roles one was not allowed to play before;

4. the desire not to have to play any role on any stage set with a supporting cast of characters, scriptwriter, director, or stage manager whom one had not chosen for oneself;

5. the desire to be able to invent and actualize at will roles, identities, stage sets, and actions that had never been seen before—the desire to be one's own scriptwriter, director, casting and stage manager, lighting, costume, hair and make-up designer to whatever extent one wanted; and

6. the desire to be able to participate vicariously in many of these roles, identities, and actions on a temporary, experimental basis by watching them acted by professional actors in public places where one did not have to feel like a voyeur, or be fearful of state/church persecution.

Thus, when certain conditions prevailed, a new secular theatre emerged to contest these residual, dominant, and transgressive theatrical strongholds. These new public theatres clearly satisfied desire number six in the list above, but the first five of these desires obviously were not wholly satisfied until a modern secular culture committed to this new theatre's radically subversive principle that "all the world's a stage" also emerged to replace such strongholds. Popular public theatre was not, then, just one of the sites in early modern culture where—as its opponents were well aware—modern secular culture was coming into being; rather, it was the principal blueprint on which modern secular cultures were built.

Let's look at two of the most important functions of these early modern public theatres. First, they provided places where one could get offstage and be audience in the sense both of being off the stage that is one's everyday life, and of not being on a stage where a fictional play is taking place. Having long had the freedom to move on and off the stage virtually at will, it is difficult to imagine what relief, what self-empowerment, what freedom, particularly from guilt, shame, and punishment, this ability to be offstage meant for an early modern person. In fact, being offstage was one of the principal causes of the delight early modern audiences received from emergent theatre. Second, public theatres provided a space where the action being performed is fictional, not so much in the sense that this action isn't happening or hasn't happened outside the theatre, but in the sense that it is not happening for real in the theatre. To say this is now a cliché, but the point of fictionality in early modern culture is likewise perhaps lost because it is taken for granted. One delight the fictional clearly had for early modern audiences was that by "holding a mirror up to nature" (i.e., by putting a fictional replication of what existed in the everyday world onstage), emergent theatre allowed individuals to look at their superiors whom they could not have looked at in the same way in the everyday world. To "look at" them in the sense of sitting in judgment, as a kind of audience-jury, analyzing whether monarchs, aristocrats, and a clergy, who for centuries had been proclaiming that the roles they acted and the plays they starred in were indispensable, were worth what they claimed to be, or not. Was it indispensability they saw when—sitting offstage safe from the power of these monarchs, aristocrats, and clergy—they were able to look at these figures *and these figures could not look back?* Not likely!

What fictional also means in an early modern context is the opportunity to liberate imagination, memory, and reason from the church/state institutions that had long dominated these mental faculties. So freed, emergent theatre audience members could vicariously live other lives in other worlds that might satisfy their desires, using emergent theatre to test these lives and worlds fictionally on a stage to ascertain how well they would fly before committing their selves, time, and energies to actualizing them in fact. In short, popular public theatre was the research and development branch of early modern culture, and a major accomplishment of this branch was not only to remodel or replace old plays (monarchy or religion) with new plays, but most important, to remove the old stages (cathedrals, courts, palaces, churches) on which these plays had been running for centuries without putting any specific new stages in their place. Popular theatre's brilliant innovation was to create a blank, neutral stage that served as a kind of all-purpose drafting table (a clean slate, a blackboard) for endless experimentation. Of course, the fundamental remodeling job here was the *removal* of heaven, hell, the inhabitants of such domains, and the scripts these inhabitants had written. To get nothing but empty sky above human heads and physical dirt beneath human feet (to have a open space to build in, and raw materials to build with) was the major retooling of the cosmos that characterized and empowered public theatre in early modern London. Being *on* this new stage (or seeing someone similar on it) was as much a delight for audiences as it was a delight to be *off* the old stage.

How popular were these emergent theatres? In the immediate decades on each side of 1600, approximately 4,000–6,000 Londoners were going, each day the theatres were open, to each of the four or five major public amphitheatres, and paying a penny to stand, or two or three times more to sit, to see one of the approximately 1,200 plays written or translated during this period. Each day the theatres were open, roughly two to four percent of the city was moving from dominant, transgressive, and occasionally no doubt residual sectors of the city into this emergent space, and continued to do so until the theatres were closed in 1642 by a residual Puritan backlash. To construct a modern analogy, we could say that several major rock concerts were taking place virtually every day in a London of approximately 200,000 inhabitants.

Up to this point we have been concentrating on the ways in which emergent theatres were designed to delight their audiences. In turning now to the ways in which they were also designed to instruct these audiences, we will be focusing on a technology that again, is virtually invisible because it goes without saying. To explain, let us return to a point mentioned above.

Emergent theatre cuts a specifically charged slice of life out of the everyday world and puts it onstage in front of an audience in almost exactly the same way, and for almost exactly the same purpose, that a biologist puts a slice of a plant stem under a microscope, a pathologist puts a diseased kidney under a microscope, or an astronomer trains a telescope on a slice of the night sky. This will no doubt seem a matter of course to us, but it certainly wasn't in early modern culture where a telescope, as Galileo discovered, threatened the status quo precisely because it allowed one to see too much. As noted, one effect of this process of "cutting out" and "placing before" is that it allows an audience to look at a slice of life with relative safety, since subjecting one's betters to one's gaze would have been offensive in the world outside the theatre.

Another consequence of this activity of "looking directly at" is that an audience would have been able to see considerably more of the object under its theatrical microtelescope (the royal court, for example) than it would have been able to see of this object outside the theatre. Indeed, audiences were able to see things inside the theatre most of them could not have seen outside it (and not just because they were frequently looking at historical objects from the past). It is not accidental that the word theatre comes from the Greek, *theatron*, "to see, or view."

An even more radical consequence is that the new public theatres allowed audiences to look at objects from an emergent perspective, meaning that public theatre provided them with new intellectual tools with which to analyze what they were looking at, much as a university biology department provides the analytical discourses (biology, chemistry, mathematics) as well as the tools and resources (a laboratory and its equipment) a biologist needs to analyze what he sees on a slide. Many Elizabethans got themselves to a public theatre, then, and paid a penny to stand for three to four hours in daylight under an open roof (rather than get themselves to a tavern, gambling hall, brothel, bear-baiting ring, cockfight, cathedral, or church), not just because they may have wanted to do some or all of the sinful things the antitheatricalists claimed they wanted to do, but because they wanted to get the equivalent of a modern secular university education, and for virtually all of them public theatre was their principal, if not their only, opportunity to get such an education. In short, popular public theatres played basically the same role in early modern culture that modern secular public universities play today. They gave their audiences relatively safe spaces in which to look directly at things they couldn't look at elsewhere, and they provided the knowledge with which—and an emergent perspective from which—these audiences could see and understand what they were looking at in radically new ways. Theatre gave its audience the instruction it needed to take on the role and act the part of secular students in a culture where this role was virtually impossible to act anywhere else. And we know that this was the case because, when modern secular universities came into being, they built their lecture halls, moot courts, dissecting rooms, laboratories, and observatories as, in effect, theatres. The antitheatricalists got one thing right. They recognized that people went to the theatres to learn. But these opponents of the public theatres had no idea what it was that these audiences were learning except that it meant the end of what they themselves were teaching. (It is perhaps needless to mention that being a student, like being a musician, engineer or artist, is a theatrical activity through and through. As a student one learns the lines, acquires the costume and properties, and acts the role until lines, costume, and role become habitual. Even at this point, however, this role is a constructed performance that must be repeated to be maintained.)

It is important to note that creating and disseminating new knowledge was not public theatre's only function any more than these activities are a modern university's only function. Divided internally like every other cultural construct, popular theatre was never solely an emergent phenomenon. To the extent that theatrical companies were officially licensed by the queen as part of her court theatricals and subject to the censorship of her Master of Revels, they clearly served a number of dominant ends, just as modern universities serve the needs of the state governments that fund them, even though this service is not their principal objective. Public theatres also served as—and for some of its audience no doubt served only as—a transgressive space, just as modern universities do for a number of their students (fraternity parties, for example). And, like universities, theatre was not in the business of forcing its audience to see or learn; indeed, many who go to college, happy with their current knowledge, do not want to acquire new knowledge either.

So what did emergent theatre audiences learn, and what resources and tools made popular public theatre, unlike virtually all other forms of theatricality in early modern England, an emergent cultural phenomenon rather than a residual, dominant, or transgressive one? To answer this question, let us continue to develop the theatre–university analogy. A student doesn't go to a university just to look at fossils, literary texts, or molecular structures (appreciation classes are phenomena of our recent past). A student goes to learn the discourses (not so much bodies of knowledge as technologies by which new knowledge is generated) that allow modern university disciplines (biology, women's studies, sociology, English) to keep producing new supplies of knowledge.

However, rather than divide itself up into various disciplines each of which utilizes relatively unique sets of emergent discourses, early modern theatre engineered itself as an alternative version of this same methodology both by removing old discourses (e.g., religious discourses) from its auditorium, and by confining these old discourses to various characters on its stage, thereby leaving a neutral space around these characters where any number of new discourses could emerge. By refusing to let dominant, residual, and transgressive discourses control its space (and by limiting such discourses to a character), early modern public theatre cleared a space where new discourses not only could emerge but had to emerge, since if they didn't its audiences would not have been able to see anything more significant about what was taking place on the stage in front of them than they could have seen outside the theatre. Unless it offered new discourses, and new perceptions (e.g., unless it could show a formerly idealized king, for example, to be an opportunistic tyrant), theatre would lose what gives it its critical difference. Moreover, it is precisely the limited and limiting knowledge in the heads of characters like Hamlet, Claudius, and Polonius that emergent theatre uses its new discourses to analyze, contain, and hopefully, replace.

The claim here is not that early modern audience members arrived at the Globe knowing subversive emergent discourses like Machiavelli's political science. Clearly, with few exceptions, they didn't (or they didn't know Machiavelli in a usable way). Rather, the claim is that many audience members came to the theatre to learn political science or some other equally useful new discourse, and that many of them did learn these discourses to the extent they didn't get distracted by identifying with those onstage or (which is the same thing) by maintaining identifications with dominant or residual authorities outside the theatre. If this process sounds difficult or impossible, it is no more difficult or impossible than what students do at modern universities where on- and offstage distractions (parents, religion, drugs) make it impossible for some students to learn new knowledge.

Why did early modern theatres want their audiences to learn elements of political science? One answer is because in the space of a theatre audiences are able to see that political science is a body of knowledge that the elite have monopolized under the cover of demonizing, criminalizing, and/or parodying it; and thus a body of knowledge which you, as a member of this audience, lack, and which a play like *Hamlet* gives you so you can see what this lack does to your life if, for example, you are in Ophelia's or Laertes' situations. As *Hamlet*'s audience you learn that authoritative efforts to eradicate or misrepresent Machiavelli are one of the ways the elite subjects you to their authority, as well as blinding you to their own Machiavellian manipulations.

Let us also acknowledge that Shakespearean theatre stages the Polonius/Reynaldo scene to provide its audience with emergent discourses other than political science, one of which is the discourse we now term psychoanalysis: that break in Polonius's concentration, that eruption of his subconscious thoughts into his conscious ones, that repetition of the way he voices his desire— effects Freud and Jacques Lacan (a twentieth-century French psychoanalyst) later analyzed and understood in the same systematic, expository fashion that Machiavelli analyzed political power. Why does *Hamlet* give its audience seemingly insignificant ripples like Polonius's repetition and both a context in which, and elements of a discourse with which, to understand them? Because, watching this scene in the context of this play, you learn that you are not wrong to think these ripples meaningful, even though someone in power like Polonius would no doubt tell you, were you to notice them, that they are totally meaningless. So, if nothing else, this scene empowers you to believe in your ability *to make meaning*, in contrast to being merely the bearer of meanings someone else makes, or fails to make, for you (Mulvey 1975).

Let's also acknowledge that the play does not give you the modern labels political science and psychoanalysis, or for that matter the modern name for another emergent discourse which, as I have been implicitly arguing, early modern theatre gives its audience, that is, *deconstruction* (by deconstruction, theorized by Jacques Derrida in Paris in the late 1960s, we mean, among other things, any activity that shows an allegedly perfect unitary entity—whether self, text, law, king, or deity—to be a construction made up of bits and pieces of rather ordinary and contradictory historically conditioned materials). Having and using these emergent modes of knowledge in Elizabethan England did not require knowledge of their modern discursive names. Indeed theatre, as we have been arguing, was deconstructing residual, dominant, and transgressive forms of theatre long before the modern term *deconstruction* was invented, or its most recent theorist, Jacques Derrida, developed this discourse in expository–argumentative terms instead of in Shakespeare's poetic–dramatic terms. Moreover, theatre could have gone on operating in these powerfully emergent ways even if the terms political science, psychoanalysis, and deconstruction had never been coined. In fact, one could say that the early modern name of each of these modern discourses was *theatre*, a phenomena as subversive in its time, and as subject to attack and misrepresentation, as deconstruction is in our own time.

From what has been argued above, it is clear that until recently what has been missing in modern understandings of *Hamlet* are the various emergent discourses that this play and its theatre offered their audiences. What has also been lost are numerous other ways *Hamlet* brings forth new knowledge to delight and instruct its audiences. To restore this instruction and hopefully some of this delight by reconstituting the emergent knowledge made available by Shakespeare's *Hamlet* is the project the rest of this book takes on, beginning, in the next section of this chapter, with the generic discourse of which *The Tragicall Historie of Hamlet* is a signal instance.

TRAGEDY

> ... the historical "task" effectively accomplished by tragic form was precisely the destruction of the fundamental paradigm of the dominant culture.
>
> —Franco Moretti

For the purposes of the argument that follows, imagine any number of entities: body, psyche, community, sports team, law firm, country club, corporation, dance band, nation. Fundamental to each of these entities are three objectives:

1. to prevent destructive things like SCUD missiles, poison, AIDS viruses, bullets, swords, claws, spies, ultraviolet rays, cholesterol, fat, or outsiders from entering its interior space and causing it inconvenience, pain, failure, disease, or death;
2. to keep things in this interior space from breaking down, mutating, suffering accidents, getting sick, dying; and
3. to maximize its happiness, profit margin, batting average, record sales.

When these objectives are met, life is a comedy; when they are not, it's a tragedy. So, it's a tragedy/comedy that the wings fell off/did not fall off her airplane, that his pacemaker malfunctioned/functioned, that they lived their whole life and never/frequently experienced moments of happiness.

Aware of this difference, an entity generally does what it can to keep things inside from rotting or falling apart, and to keep dangerous or lethal things outside from getting in. So, to keep things out, eyes blink shut, earplugs snuggle in ears, gates go up, sunscreen is applied, windows close. However, should something destructive get in or come into being inside, an entity does what it can to get these things out or to isolate them. Bodies vomit, menstruate, urinate, defecate. Penitents confess. Minds forget. Criminals are executed. Books are burned. *Catharsis* (from Greek *kathairein*, to cleanse, from *katharos*, pure): purification or purgation. *Purgation* (from Latin *purgare*, from *purus*, pure), a cleansing, a purification by separating and carrying off whatever is impure, heterogeneous, or superfluous; a clearing of guilt, or defilement, to cause evacuations from, especially the intestines. *Pure* (from Latin *purus*, pure): without alloy, stain, or taint; clear; unmixed; free from all that vitiates, weakens, or pollutes; free from moral defilement or guilt; hence, innocent; ritually clean (*Webster's New Collegiate Dictionary* 1961). What entities do to avoid tragedy and insure comedy.

But in some circumstances this process goes awry. Some of the things entities purge are not clearly or obviously dangerous, and in some cases what is kept out or thrown out to insure comedy produces tragedy instead. So there are differences of opinion, and, in free or relatively free societies, debate, since to the question, "Is *x* lethal, or is *x* necessary for a happy life?" different parts of a culture have different answers. Thus, much time and energy is spent in deliberation and/or conflict. Several such *x*'s from the recent past and present: Should women vote, travel, go to school, speak in public, teach or stay home, wear veils, be delightful, cook, keep silent, submit to male rule? Does the death penalty lead to cultural happiness and purity, or to torture and cultural rot? Should homosexuals marry, adopt kids, teach in school classrooms, serve in the armed forces, have happy lives like others of us, or be harassed, beaten, and executed as they were at Sodom and Gomorrah? Should contraception and abortion remain legal, or not? Should all members of a community be forced to attend church, or not? Should theatres and universities be closed down, or not? Should adolescents be sexually active, or not? In short, what must be kept out, what must be purged from, and what must be maintained if the society we are a part of is to avoid death, sustain life, and maximize happiness? Beyond the most obvious physical conditions, moreover, what do life, death, and happiness mean; or, rather, who decides what they mean? Who decides if the actions listed above cause comedies or tragedies? And, finally, how is that thing called a literary tragedy related to the fact that one person's comedy often requires (or is claimed to require) another person's tragedy?

Emergent literary tragedy enters the space of cultural debate when a dominant (and/or residual) element of a culture is absolutely sure that if the culture is to survive and have a profitable and happy life it must kill, throw out, incarcerate, ban, or prevent from entering someone who, or something which, an emergent element of the same culture feels cannot be killed, purged, banned, or prevented from entering if the culture is to survive and have a happy and profitable life. And because it usually has no other power than the pen, this emergent element writes a literary tragedy to argue its case. Dominant figures tend not to write literary tragedies, because in their minds everything they do is a comedy, and because, as the Nazis did, they don't write on paper or for a theatre stage, but on the stage of everyday life by (among other things) executing their opponents.

Consider in this respect an event which Alice, a former student of mine, experienced while working for the Peace Corps in the seventies. Stationed abroad, Alice's job was to teach English to local young women. And since the locality where she was stationed was pretty boring, she and her Peace Corps friends had private parties where, despite local laws, they danced, drank alcohol, flirted, and smoked—they wrote a comedy for themselves. After several months, one of the women in Alice's class found out about these parties and asked if she could come. After some hesitation and a lot of questions about how this student found out about the parties, Alice said she could come if she kept it absolutely secret. The young woman said not to worry since she understood the danger. So the next Saturday evening this young woman, pretending to go to her bedroom to sleep, climbed out her window and went to Alice's party. The next weekend she went to another, and in time she became a regular. At these parties she drank, danced, and after several weeks became friendly with one of the American men. When the parties were over, she would climb back into her room, go to sleep, and wake up the next day acting as if nothing were out of the ordinary. Prompted by the Shakespeare play Alice was teaching in class, she came to think of herself as Juliet. After continuing in this way for a couple of months, "Juliet" grew careless, forgot to wake up on time, and slept through the beginning of the family Sunday breakfast. Her father, wondering why she had not come down to eat, asked his younger daughter why her sister wasn't up. The younger girl, still angry about a fight she had had with her sister the day before, and jealous that she wasn't old enough to go to the American parties her sister had recently told her about, said that "Juliet" had been partying with the Americans.

Hearing this, the father asked a number of questions, sat perfectly quiet for a few minutes, then got up from the table, went to his gun closet, took out a shotgun, went upstairs, and shot his daughter while she was asleep in her bed. He then turned around, went downstairs, sat at the table, and finished breakfast with the rest of his family without anyone saying a word about what had just happened. When the community heard about this incident, the father was celebrated as having done exactly the right thing to purge his family from all that vitiates, weakens, or pollutes; to keep it faultless, free from moral defilement, hence, innocent; ritually clean (*Webster's New Collegiate Dictionary* 1961). In the eyes of at least the dominant segment of his community, this father was seen as having created a comedy by purging with his shotgun a daughter who could not continue to exist in his family if this family were (in his eyes) to sustain its life and maximize its happiness. In the eyes of my former student and her Peace Corps colleagues, all of whom were sent back to the States, this father was seen as having caused a terrible tragedy. So, given that the father's comedy was the daughter's tragedy, and that the daughter's comedy would have been the father's tragedy, do we conclude that the father's act was comedic ritual purification, or cold-blooded tragic murder? Clearly, one's judgment depends on where one is positioned, and whether one thinks that this young woman was leading a sinfully polluting transgressive life (the dominant view) or a dangerously courageous one (the emergent view). Clearly, it also depends on whether we think that we, as American outsiders, have a right to judge this father and his actions despite his judging and executing his daughter, and exiling her friends.

The literary question raised by such an incident concerns the genre in which this story was told. It was related as an instance of emergent tragedy. Were I one of the father's friends, however, I would have told the same incidents as dominant comedy. How would I or the father's friend have put this story onstage so that an audience would see it as comedy instead of as a tragedy? And, even more difficult to answer, how would I have put this story on stage as a tragedy in the father's country where his friends would censor what could appear onstage had their country a public theatre, which it didn't, because theatre was yet one more of those defiling American obscenities which the father and his friends were keeping out of their country to ensure its purity.

Before dealing with these questions it is useful to note that we will see a distant version of this story produced as a comedy in the first of the antitheatrical tracts reproduced in the document section below. The diatribe Phillip Stubbes writes about the effects of popular public theatre on its good, pure English audiences (a diatribe that could have led to Stubbes's blowing up a theatre and its inhabitants—see Stubbes document in this chapter) is parallel to a story "Juliet's" father might have written about the tragic effects of American parties on his otherwise good, pure daughter had he not written a "comedy" with his daughter's blood. In the last section an emergent account of early modern theatre was written against negative residual accounts like Stubbes's, whereas in this section, having been told an emergent version of "Juliet's" story, you are asked to think about the comedic form the father's dominant version of this story would take and how this comedic form would differ from the tragic form told to you. Clearly, one difference would be that the narrator of these events would support and vindicate "Juliet's" father, and would tell the story from his dominant point of view. The narrator would get you to identify with the father long before you knew about "Juliet." He would build the father up as a pillar of the community and a model of religious faith. He would present "Juliet" as a prodigal child even in the best of times, and celebrate the younger daughter as a model of young womanhood. He would show the father deliberating in his mind between his legal duty and the remnants of his feelings for his daughter, most of which would have already turned to hostility. And the narrator would paint the worst possible picture of the Americans and their evil parties. Against emergent representations of the father as a cold-blooded murderer, this narrator would represent the father as a heroic maintainer of religious family values. His themes? Exactly the same ones I used in the story I told you. Catharsis. Purgation. Life. Health. Happiness.

Let us simplify this discussion and say that the objective of literary tragedy, a genre that emerged in early modern England as the principal and most powerful instrument of the new popular public theatres (and emerged only when these theatres emerged and existed only as long as they existed), can be summarized in a formula: In emergent tragedy certain past necessities are shown to be present crimes, and certain past crimes are shown to be present necessities. That is, the very thing a dominant order thinks absolutely necessary (e.g., the code that calls for death when sacred law is transgressed), emergent tragedy ("Juliet's" story) is just as certain must itself be seen as a crime and thrown out. And the crime this dominant order thinks must be thrown out (i.e., "Juliet's" behavior), emergent tragedy is just as certain must be kept in.

The questions this discussion leads to are the ones the rest of this book will attempt to answer: "What past necessities does Shakespeare's *Hamlet* show to be present crimes?" and "What past crimes does it show to be present necessities?"

Following are excerpts illustrating how residual, dominant, and transgressive citizens reacted to the popularity of the new London theatres, and how, with the discourses available to them, these citizens understood and represented the delight and instruction offered by such theatres.

DEMONIZING EMERGENT THEATRE

For an example of the legions of residual diatribes aimed at emergent theatre, consider the following excerpt from an extremely conservative puritanical tract authored by Phillip Stubbes in 1583. To prove theatre evil, Stubbes demonizes its educational effects, a strategy that denies theatre any redeeming qualities, and thus locates public theatre (in his mind) firmly in transgressive space next to brothels and taverns. For Stubbes everything fits on either one or the other side of a good/evil binary, a rigidity specifically designed to defend against the possibility that he might learn anything new, since any knowledge he does not already have can only be satanic error.

FROM PHILLIP STUBBES, *THE ANATOMIE OF ABUSES:*
CONTAYNING A DISCOVERIE, OR BRIEFE SUMMARIE OF SUCH
NOTABLE VICES AND IMPERFECTIONS, AS NOW RAIGNE IN MANY
CHRISTIAN COUNTREYES OF THE WORLDE
(London, 1583)

[T]here is no mischief, which these plays maintain not . . . Do they not draw the people from hearing the word of God, from godly Lectures and sermons? . . . Do they not maintain bawdy, insinuate foolery, & renew the remembrance of heathen idolatry? Do they not induce whoredom and uncleanness? nay, are they not rather plain devourers of maidenly virginity and chastity? For proof whereof, but mark the flocking and running to Theaters & Curtains [i.e., two of the first professional theatres in early modern London], daily and hourly, night and day, time and tide, to see Plays and Interludes; where such wanton gestures, such bawdy speeches, such laughing and fleering [sneering], such kissing and bussing, such clipping and culling [hugging], such winking and glancing of wanton eyes, and the like, is used, as is wonderful to behold. Then, these goodly pageants being done, every mate sorts to his mate, every one brings another homeward of their way very friendly, and in their secret conclaves (covertly) they play *the Sodomites* [homosexuals], or worse. And these be the fruits of plays and interludes for . . . if you will learn falsehood . . . ; if you will learn to deceive; if you will learn to play the Hypocrite, to cogge [deceive], lie, and falsify; if you will learn to jest, laugh, and fleer [sneer], to grin, to nod, and mow [grimace]; if you will learn to play the vice, to swear, tear, and blaspheme both Heaven and Earth: If you will learn to become a bawd, unclean, and to aevirginate Maids, to deflower honest Wives: if you will learn to murder, flay [plunder], kill, pick [pockets], steal, rob, and rove [become a beggar]: If you will learn to rebel against Princes, to commit treasons, to consume treasures, to practise idleness, to sing and talk of bawdy love and venery [pornography]: if you will learn to deride, scoff, mock, & flout, to flatter & smooth [talk]: If you will learn to play the whoremaster, the glutton, Drunkard, or incestuous person: if you will learn to become proud, haughty, and arrogant; and, finally, if you will learn to contemn [despise] God and his laws, to care neither for heaven nor hell, and to commit all kind of sin and mischief, you need to go to no other school, for all these good Examples may you see painted before your eyes in interludes and plays.

CRIMINALIZING EMERGENT THEATRE

If we turn now to how dominant Londoners felt about popular theatre, we find that they sought to suppress it as a source of civic disorder—as a threat to their dominance. A particularly interesting text illustrating their position is one of many antitheatrical petitions the Lord Mayor and the Aldermen of London submitted to Queen Elizabeth's Privy Council over the course of several decades. The city fathers' strategy (not altogether dissimilar to Stubbes's) is to criminalize theatre as a breeder of subversive activities, thereby scapegoating theatre for the socioeconomic problems dominant culture itself created, and which it could not solve without considerable personal financial loss, as those city fathers well knew. So, rather than deal with the actual causes of, or work out viable solutions for the socioeconomic problems they humbly identify in their petition—solutions that would cut deep into their wealth and power—these far from humble citizens are more than eager to attack theatre, even while profiting from the "mere humble servant" theatrical role they themselves are playing.

FROM AN OFFICIAL PETITION SUBMITTED BY THE LORD
MAYOR AND THE ALDERMEN OF THE CITY OF LONDON TO
QUEEN ELIZABETH'S PRIVY COUNCIL 28 JULY 1597
(London: Malone Society *Collections*, 1907) i, 78

To the Lords against Stage Playes

Our humble duties remembered to your good Lordships and the rest. We have signified to your H[onors] many times heretofore the great inconvenience which we find to grow by the Common exercise of Stage plays . . . being persuaded (under correction of your Honors' judgment) that neither in polity nor in religion they are to be suffered in a Christian Commonwealth, specially being of that frame and matter as usually they are, containing nothing but profane fables, lascivious matters, cozening [cheating] devices, and scurrilous behaviors, which are so set forth as that they move wholly to imitation & not to the avoiding of those faults and vices which they represent. Among other inconveniences it is not the least that they give opportunity to the refuse sort of evil disposed and ungodly people, that are within and about this City to assemble themselves and to make their matches for all their lewd and ungodly practices; being as heretofore we have found by the examination of divers apprentices and other servants who have confessed unto us that . . . Stage plays were the very places of their Rendezvous. . . . For avoiding whereof we are now again most humble and earnest suitors to your honors . . . for the . . . final suppressing of the said Stage Plays, as well at the Theatre, Curtain, and bankside as in all other places in and about the City. . . . And so most humbly we take our leaves. From London the xviij [18] of July. 1597. Your Honors' most humble.

MISREPRESENTING EMERGENT THEATRE

That owners of taverns, brothels, bear-baiting arenas, and gambling halls also wanted to do away with the competition created by public theatres is an assumption supported by the sentence that concludes the passage excerpted below. This quasi-transgressive, quasi-dominant take on theatre defends playgoing as a social safety valve capable of piping off vast quantities of excess male energy which, Nashe asserts, would otherwise be put to worse abuses. Particularly striking about his argument is that Nashe uses the same discourse to defend theatre that the city fathers use to denounce it.

FROM THOMAS NASHE, *PIERCE PENILESSE HIS SUPPLICATION TO THE DIUELL*
(London, 1592)

[I]f the affairs of the State . . . cannot exhale all these corrupt excrements [i.e., create enough occupations to keep the riffraff busy], it is very expedient they [this riffraff] have some light toys [trifles] to busy their heads withall . . . which may keep them from having leisure to intermeddle with higher matters. To this effect, the policy of Plays is very necessary, howsoever some shallow-brained censures . . . might oppugne [condemn] them. For whereas the afternoon, being the idlest time of the day; wherein men that are their own masters . . . do wholly bestow themselves upon pleasure, and that pleasure they divide . . . either into gaming, following of harlots, drinking, or seeing a Play: is it not then better . . . that they should betake them to the least, which is Plays? Nay, what if I prove Plays to be no extreme, but a rare exercise of virtue? . . . In Plays, all cosonages [deceits], all cunning drifts over gilded with outward holiness, all stratagems of war, all the cankerworms that breed on the rust of peace are most lively anatomized [cut open and exposed]: they show the ill-success of treason, the fall of hasty climbers, the wretched end of usurpers, the misery of civil dissension, and how just God is evermore in punishing of murder. . . . As for the hindrance of Trades and Traders of the City . . . that is an Article foisted in by the Vintners, Alewives, and Victuallers, who surmise, if there were no Plays, they should have all the company that resort to them lie bowzing [drinking] and beer-bathing in their houses every afternoon.

STUDY QUESTIONS

1. If husband *and* political subversive, and wife *and* adulteress are *double* roles from dominant and residual perspectives, why isn't the role of wife/mother or husband/father *double* as well?

2. Is the "play" that has been written for you and in which you have been cast sufficient? Could you write the play that will be your life in a better way? What resources would you need to engage in such creative (re)writing?

3. In the modern world, who defends public education in terms virtually identical to the ones Nashe is using to defend early modern theatre? And who attacks public education with almost exactly the same terms Stubbes attacks Elizabethan theatre?

4. Does one person's comedy always require another person's tragedy?

5. Could it be said that perspective is one of the most important pieces of instruction early modern theatres offered their audiences? If so, how does theatre teach us to see things from a vantage point other than those offered by dominant and residual institutions?

6. In what way is psychotherapy like theatre? What do these seemingly very different instructional technologies have in common?

QUESTIONS AND TOPICS FOR WRITTEN AND ORAL DISCUSSION

1. If antitheatricalists were able to demolish the emergent domain and its theatres, could they force audiences back on the old "stages" and back into the old "plays"? In this context, consider the news reported by Rod Nordland and Tony Clifton in the October 14, 1996, issue of *Newsweek*:

> The Mullahs who took over last week in Kabul, the conquered capital of Afghanistan, made Iran's ayatollahs look like Western playboys. The fundamentalist Taliban movement issued decree after decree through its six-member ruling council, the Shura. Television stations and movie theatres were shut down, and music was banned from the radio. Kabul's 1 million people were ordered to pray five times a day—including two visits to the local mosque, where attendance would be taken. Criminals were threatened with beatings, mutilation and death. Men were given 45 days to grow proper Muslim beards—which are left untrimmed—and were told to shed their Western clothes

in favor of traditional Afghan dress. Women were chastised even more severely. They were sent home from their schools and jobs and were instructed to veil themselves from head to toe. . . . Violators of the female dress code were beaten on the streets by Taliban fighters.

Compare this to the early modern antitheatricalists' arguments that "filthy" players and theatregoers "are worthy death," and that a holy war alone would be able to purge England's present rotten state.

2. Discuss the similarities between the extracts printed above and a city ordinance reproduced in an "Angry Poodle" column of the May 11, 1995, Santa Barbara *Independent*:

> Twenty-five years ago, the Santa Barbara County supervisors launched a preemptive strike designed to prevent any Woodstock-like celebrations from occuring within the county's borders. They did what any elected official does when confronted with peril: They passed a new law. The ordinance language deliciously describes the dangers of "rock" concerts. "Many of the participants arrive in stolen automobiles and abandon such automobiles at the outdoor festival. . . . Participants in rural areas have slaughtered all of the cattle on adjoining properties. . . . Many participants in such rock and roll festivals sleep out in the open. . . . Others drive automobiles and run over those so sleeping." If you think that's funny, guess what? The ordinance is still on the books.

Think about ways in which a rock concert like Woodstock is different from, as well as similar to, early modern theatrical productions of plays like *Hamlet*.

3. Why is Stubbes terrified of being in any play, or speaking any script other than the one written and produced by his deity? What does this religious play possess that, in Stubbes's mind, makes it infinitely better than the plays and lines written by an individual like Shakespeare?

4. After reading the analysis of theatre offered in this chapter, were you tempted (and why would you be tempted) to attack it from a dominant/residual perspective? Why is a discussion of emergent theatre as threatening, and as open to attack, as this mode of theatre itself is?

SUGGESTED READINGS AND WORKS CITED

Beckerman, Bernard. *Shakespeare at the Globe, 1599–1609*. New York: Macmillan, 1962.

Belsey, Catherine. *The Subject of Tragedy*. London and New York: Methuen, 1985.

Dollimore, Jonathan. *Radical Tragedy*. New York: Harvester Wheatsheaf, 1984.

Douglas, Mary. *Purity and Danger: An Analysis of the Concepts of Pollution and Taboo*. London and New York: Routledge, 1966.

"An Exhortation concerning good Order, and Obedience to Rulers and Magistrates." In *Certaine Sermons or Homilies appoynted to be read in Churches, In the time of our late Queene Elizabeth*. London: Iohn Norton, 1633.

Garber, Marjorie. "*Hamlet*: Giving Up the Ghost" [a deconstructive reading]. In *William Shakespeare: Hamlet*, edited by Suzanne L. Wofford, 297–331. Boston: St. Martin's Press, 1994.

Gurr, Andrew. *Playgoing in Shakespeare's London*. Cambridge: Cambridge University Press, 1987.

Moretti, Franco. "The Great Eclipse: Tragic Form as the Deconsecration of Sovereignty." In *Signs Taken for Wonders*. London: Verso Editions and NLB, 1983.

Mullaney, Steven. *The Place of the Stage: License, Play, and Power in Renaissance England*. Chicago and London: The University of Chicago Press, 1988.

Mulvey, Laura. "Visual Pleasure and Narrative Cinema." *Screen* 16 (1975), 6–18.

Murfin, Ross C. "What is Deconstruction?" In *William Shakespeare: Hamlet*, edited by Suzanne L. Wofford, 283–296. Boston: St. Martin's Press, 1994. This introductory essay also includes a useful selected bibliography on deconstruction.

Williams, Raymond. *Modern Tragedy*. London: Chatto & Windus, 1966.

Detail from Olaus Magnus, *Carte Marina* (1572), showing "sledded pollax." Reprinted with permission from the James Ford Bell Library, University of Minnesota.

_____

3

Literary Analysis: Hamlet's Options

To be ignorant of causes is to be frustrated in action.
—Francis Bacon

. . . and now remains
That we find out the cause of this effect,
Or rather say, the cause of this defect . . .
—Polonius (2.2. 100–102)

To understand what Hamlet does and, as importantly, what causes his behavior, it is helpful to begin with the events that took place in Elsinore during the two months separating Hamlet Sr.'s death and Hamlet's encounter with the ghost. Bringing this context into focus will protect us from seeing the events of this play solely from Hamlet's extremely inadequate perspective.

"OUR MOST VALIANT BROTHER"

For several decades the Denmark of the play was ruled by Hamlet Sr., a quasi-pagan, quasi-Catholic, Scandinavian soldier-king out of Anglo-Saxon, Viking legend who spent his time in camps of war and on battlefields, defeating old Norway in single combat and smiting "sledded pollax" [probably Polacks (Poles); possibly a

pole-axe] "on the ice" (1.1.62; see illustration), activities structured by an aristocratic code of military honor. Apparently Queen
Gertrude was not happy in this heroic, patriarchal world, and the
king's brother, Claudius, reading the signs of her discontent, saw
an opportunity and, when the time came, presumably offered what
she must have desired: not drinking bouts and recitals of battle
legends, but activities that would help create a space where culture, not war, would be the focus of Denmark's social energies,
and Gertrude would be a center of power. Thus, when Hamlet Sr.
dies, Claudius and Gertrude begin replacing his heavy-drinking,
fighting-man's world of the epic outdoors with something closer
to a Mediterranean culture's interiors, moving the locus of power
from the battlefield to the rooms and closets [private chambers]
of the castle.

For a time Hamlet lived in this paternal, masculine world. But
by going to college at Wittenberg, he seems also to have sought to
distance himself from this world and from the differences separating his parents. And he apparently found in Germany something
of what he desired: not the interiorities of a romance culture, but
the classical texts, the finer intellect, the larger degree of personal
agency (specifically, the freedom to make choices for himself), the
moral heights and historical range offered by a Protestant humanist
subjectivity. By virtue of this distance and the tenuously balanced
ambivalence it afforded, Hamlet seems to have maintained something like love for both an overwhelming father and a discontented
mother.

As the play starts, Hamlet's father's funeral is two months in the
past. His mother and stepfather are in the midst of instituting a
new cultural formation in Elsinore. Nothing, we are told, is "dis-
joint . . . [or] out of frame" (1.2.20), and everyone seems to be
happily prospering "in the sun" (1.2.67) of Gertrude and Claudius's court except Hamlet, who, suffering from the traumatic loss
of his father and his father's world, and angry that his hopes of
being king have been crushed by the new reign, is standing dis-
gruntled on the sidelines. Moreover, these losses and dislocations
are happening to him at the age of thirty, the age, Sir Thomas
Browne tells us, when a man is at the height of his powers and
abilities: "Some Divines count *Adam* 30. yeares old at his creation,
because they suppose him created in the perfect age and stature
of man" (1643). So questions arise. What is the effect on a thirty-

year-old prince who has long expected and is ready to take over power when he is suddenly confronted with the loss of a masculine paternal world and the legacy of the royal identity that went with it? And what happens when such a prince finds himself sidelined by a new dominant regime in which he has no identity other than being "too much in the sun" of Claudius's royalty/paternity and Gertrude's happiness?

On Hamlet the signal effect of being marginal to two antithetical worlds is, of course, *melancholy*, that sinking into the darkness of the earth that occurs (in the terms of ancient humoral psychology) when massive amounts of one's elements of air and water have been dissipated by loss, and there is no way to mitigate the resulting depression (earth/black bile) because, after the flames of anger (fire/choler) rage and burn out, there is little left of oneself except black bile (see Chapter 4).

So the play begins when the known world is fading and the old positions in it have collapsed, when a handful of soldiers prove uneasy, when a servant like Polonius is getting ideas, and the prince of the realm—displaced, angry, and depressed—is in disarray. In his out-of-joint situation and the unease that accompanies it, we wonder, of course, what Hamlet, the noblest and brightest young man in his culture, can do, what he should do, and we anticipate seeing what he will do.

"HOW . . . UNPROFITABLE / SEEM TO ME ALL THE USES OF THIS WORLD"

The first thing this isolated and decentered prince does after he stops trying to conceal his sense of failure and mounting hostility is to restore something of the world he has lost, and articulate some of the anger he is feeling by wearing, months after his father's death, an inky [black] cloak and a face of grief throughout his mother's and stepfather's nuptial celebrations. In this costume and role, he will maim these rites and insult his mother in public as a way of punishing her and her new husband. He will utter snide, disrespectful, nastily ironic things to his new and hated stepfather, trying for the first of several times to make Claudius erupt into rage. Despite being thirty, he will act the part of a moody, sullen, withdrawn, clothes-inappropriate, angrily passive-aggressive adolescent. And though we are prepared, after his first scene, to consider him a villain, our sympathies, once his first soliloquy begins, draw us to his presence, his intense energy, his difference.

In surveying this first court scene (1.2) we see that for a while Claudius and Gertrude are willing to put up with Hamlet's transgressive behavior simply by ignoring it, letting Hamlet posture while they deal with Fortinbras's revenge plot and Laertes' return to Paris. They are not, of course, convinced that Hamlet's grief is real, nor do they feel guilty in the face of his assault. They sense his bad faith, as well as the power of the anger fueling his performance. Finally, no longer willing to tolerate such an affront to their majesty and happiness, not to mention the peace of the court itself, they close out one of the initial options Hamlet is electing by issuing what is in effect a royal command: Be a good son (or else)! Things have changed, and you must change as well! So put aside your grief, and live in this world, not in the one that has passed—"cast thy nighted color off, / And let thine eye look like a friend on *Denmark* [i.e., your stepfather]. / Do not for ever with thy vailed lids / Seek for thy noble father in the dust" (1.2.68–71). Behind this demand the early modern audience hears a commonplace biblical subtext from *The Proverbs of Salomón* (*The Geneva Bible*, 1560): "My son, hear thy father's instruction, and forsake not thy mother's teaching. For they shall be a comely ornament unto thine head, and *as chains* [jewelry] for thy neck" (1:8–9).

Forbidden to persist in his antiparental behavior and altogether unwilling to obey a demand that would script him as an ideal son, Hamlet immediately tries a third option. Like Laertes, he will return to school. However, his stepfather and mother close this out as well: "for your intent / In going back to school in Wittenberg / It is most retrograde to our desire"; "I pray thee stay with us, go not to Wittenberg" (1.2.112–13, 119). No reason is given.

In the months separating Hamlet Sr.'s death and the first scenes of the play, Hamlet has been pursing yet another option: he has involved himself with Ophelia and, isolated from the parental "sun," has tried to make their little room of erotic pleasures an everywhere. When kingship and delinquency prove impossible, and the hope of returning to Wittenberg dies, this transgressive prospect reasserts its numerous advantages: "Doubt thou the stars are fire, / Doubt that the sun doth move," Hamlet's love lyric to Ophelia argues, "But never doubt I love" (2.2.116–17, 119). But despite Hamlet's costuming himself for this role with "stockings fouled, / Ungartered, and down-gyved [acting like fetters] to his ankle" (2.1.80–81), Polonius's refusal to let Ophelia have further intercourse with Hamlet closes this door, one Hamlet locks in the nunnery scene from disgust at what he takes to be Ophelia's betrayal. So, with the door sealed that might have opened onto love and marriage, Hamlet will lose all desire in this line: "go to, I'll no more on't" (3.1.145).

Looking around, there is yet another option closed out that could have offered Hamlet relief. Had his father's world still existed, he might have led an army against the "lawless resolutes" Fortinbras has "sharked up" to revenge his own father's death at the hands of Hamlet Sr. But a military "enterprise / That hath stomack in 't" (1.1.98–99) is made impossible by Hamlet's uncle's new regime's reliance on diplomacy—on the ambassadors, Valtemand and Cornelius, who, proving successful, make war and whatever heroic identity Hamlet might have had in this line a futile fantasy.

Though it does not follow his inclination, Hamlet might also have spent time drinking with his father's soldiers, and in this way kept close to that disappearing world, not to mention piping off some of his anger in "heavy-handed revels." But his uncle and now stepfather king, presumably in order to ingratiate himself with soldiers demoralized by the loss of their former heroic leader, if not also by the turn of events that are remaking the Danish Court, closes out this possibility by getting there first. And listening from the sidelines to the "trumpet . . . bray out" as Claudius "drains his drafts of Rhenish" (1.4.12–13, 11), Hamlet rejects this option in disgust, since to participate in such a scene would subject him to further exposure from Claudius's hated "sun."

Looking ahead, other options are or soon will be closed out as well. Presumably Hamlet could have resigned himself to philosophic observation, his "blood and judgment . . . so well comingled [mixed], / That they [would not be] a pipe for Fortunes finger / To sound what stop she please" (3.2.62–64), but Horatio's arrival cancels any chance of Hamlet becoming a stoical stone.

Once Rosencrantz and Guildenstern arrive, no doubt Hamlet thinks about spending time while at loose ends male-bonding with these friends until their admission that they are spies paid by his parents to find him out—"My Lord, we were sent for" (2.2.284)—shuts this door forever.

Under the surface of Hamlet's "I am too much in the sun," we discover yet another option Hamlet seems to have contemplated before he encounters the ghost. Certainly he could get himself out of the sun, end his "heart-ache" and at least one of "the thousand natural shocks / That flesh is heir to" (3.1.64) simply by killing his new stepfather king. But given that the almighty has fixed his canon firmly against subjects, however princely, eclipsing a divinely anointed king, such an act would "blur the grace and blush of [Hamlet's] modesty, / Call [his] virtue hypocrite," and turn Hamlet himself into a "lawless resolute." Moreover, were he to commit such a rash act in the wake of Gertrude's remarriage, what would he say to his mother as she contemplated the slain body of her new husband, a king who, in her eyes and those of the Court, was doing everything a good king ought to be doing? Indeed, what does Claudius do in public that could possibly be construed as tyrannical, tyranny being the only grounds that would allow Hamlet to execute his king legitimately?

Therefore, given that every viable means of fashioning himself seems closed out, Hamlet contemplates, and perhaps would commit in high Anglo-Saxon, Roman fashion the heroic option of "not to be" had Wittenberg's and the new Danish order's Christian deity not also "fixed / His canon 'gainst self slaughter" (1.2.131–32). To be sure, the play keeps Hamlet's thoughts on this subject of not being in the sun theoretical and general (and to Hamlet himself) so as to keep him available as a hero, since, were he were to make his suicidal musings explicit and personal, he presumably would be too questionable for many in any audience to maintain their belief in his heroic potential.

In short, Hamlet is stymied. He needs to act, to do something that will fashion a viable identity for himself, but every mode of action his culture offers him—every door out of his melancholic space of traumatic loss and disarray—is closed except the impossible demand, "be an ideal son," that he won't and can't obey. If Hamlet were to take any of these options, act any of these roles, force open or walk through any of these closed doors, there would be no hero and no plot of the sort this play requires since clearly none of these options suffice. None are heroic. None would "denote [Hamlet] truly" (1.2.83). Moreover, as audience, we haven't come to the Globe just to see a prince take one or another conventional trajectory in such a situation, and, most assuredly, we haven't come to see Hamlet become an ideal, dutifully obedient son (we're in Southwark, not the City, and this is a popular emergent tragedy, not a church/state pageant). We want to see what a *hero* will do in what is a virtually hopeless dilemma. And if asked why we want to see what Hamlet will do when all the ordinary options prove impossible, we might say that we do so because historically speaking such a situation is one of the most difficult and important moments we ourselves face, given that the situation Hamlet is in is not just one in which many of us have failed, but one in which some of us would presumably like not to fail again. So up against difficult circumstances, his melancholy deepening, what, then, is Hamlet to do if he is not simply to go around in circles taking up arms against closed doors or lamenting the assaults of (in his mind) the outrageous fortune to which he has been subjected? What will he do to keep his melancholy from sinking him into despair and madness, or turning him to regicide, or ending his life by a far from heroic form of self-slaughter? By situating Hamlet in a space where the usual doors are shut and the screws tightened ("Denmark's a prison"), the play asks if Hamlet will be able to create an opening in a wall where one has not previously existed. After all, what is lacking in the array of options outlined above is new knowledge, a new option, and surely it is a hero's task (or at least a modern hero's task) to supply such a lack. At this point in the play a new step must be taken, but whether it will lead to comedy or to tragedy is, of course, the question.

"BE THOU A SPIRIT OF HEALTH, OR GOBLIN DAMNED"

Up to a certain point in the preceding paragraphs many critics would be in considerable agreement with what has been sketched in, and though some would see no reason why Hamlet can't be a dutiful son and in this way avoid the tragedy his actions unfold, most would agree that he can't, that what happens next makes the play, and that what happens next is, of course, the ghost, not to mention the chief cause of most of the incompatible understandings we have of this play. Horatio, encountering a silent apparition and unable to reach a conclusion about the status of this "thing," remains cautious, fearful, suspicious. But, having more to work with and powerful desires pushing him, Hamlet (like critics, actors, directors) must draw a conclusion; he has to decide, he has *to*

Henry Fuseli, *Hamlet and the Ghost* (1796). Courtesy of the Davidson Library, University of California, Santa Barbara.

know who or what this questionable apparition is because, unlike Horatio, he, as hero, has to *act*.

Over the long history of *Hamlet* criticism, knowledge concerning the ghost has taken three principal forms (with, of course, intermediate positions between them). For archaic or residual identified critics who know that this ghost is the *soul* of Hamlet's dead father returning from a pagan underworld or a Catholic purgatory or hell, the ghost is *real*, meaning that it exists as an independent entity in its own right. It is also real for dominant critics who know that it is a demon (a "goblin damned") come from hell despite the fact that it may speak the truth (and though Hamlet opens up a third possibility—"a spirit of health . . . from heaven" [1.4.21–22]—this angel possibility quickly drops out of the play and the literature about it). For another, emergent group of critics the ghost is a *fantasy* object— a psychic hologram, a hallucination—fabricated, however unconsciously, by Hamlet's and his colleagues' imaginations.

Let us consider first the older, archaic/residual assumptions that the ghost is the returning soul of Hamlet's dead father. Critics who take this position accept the ghost, and expect Hamlet to accept it, as a legitimate authority figure. Thus, to the extent that Hamlet exists in the residual world of his father, the ghost (his father's soul) is his final authority figure. And since there is no higher authority, the ghost's answers to questions, statements of fact and deductions are truthful and can be believed and acted upon implicitly. Hamlet, in short, must regard the ghost's demands—remember me! revenge me!—as law, and he must obey this law. Moreover, since this world makes no distinction between revenge and justice—revenge being the name of the action that enforces justice—and since if there were no revenge there would be no justice, who is better qualified or more likely to enforce revenge than a son? From these premises a traditional residual understanding of *Hamlet* follows:

1. Hamlet, hearing the ghost, knows what happened to his father and has sufficient legitimate evidence to convict Claudius of being a traitorous regicide.
2. No one else needs to be convinced of, or has any say in, determining Claudius's guilt.
3. Hamlet *knows* that it is his duty to obey his father's (ghost's) command.

4. He knows that if Gertrude were a good wife she would accept his word on the matter of Claudius's guilt and welcome the execution of her new husband.

5. However, despite this knowledge, Hamlet procrastinates, coming to his senses and proving obedient only at the last possible moment.

6. For this mistake, he must die, a death that is tragic because, had he obeyed earlier, he would have lived.

Let's turn now to a dominant reading of the ghost. In this model

1. Hamlet knows the ghost is real, but in time comes to see that it is a demonic spirit disguised as his father's soul (the soul of a pagan dead person come from under ground demanding revenge would also be considered demonic from this perspective).

2. Hamlet knows that even if this demon is telling the truth about Hamlet Sr.'s death (though of course there is no way he can know whether it is or not) such a fact is irrelevant, since demons often tell their victims the truth if that is what it takes to lead them to hell.

3. He knows, too, that despite its claim of having accurate knowledge, a demonic apparition is not a legitimate authority figure and that its remember/revenge commands are illegitimate and evil.

4. He knows that the only legitimate authority figure in his world is the church/state and the Christian deity who authorizes this church/state, and that the law of this deity—"Vengeance is mine, saith the lord"—makes revenge a crime.

5. He knows that, even if this ghost were the soul of his dead father, there are two fathers—a mortal, fallen, dead natural father and an immortal, living, divine one—and that a man, though son to both, must obey the latter whenever these two fathers (or their substitutes) issue contradictory commands. Consider Thomas Becon's *Catechism: "Father.* But what if the father command the child to do that thing which is contrary to the word of God? *Son.* Here the child oweth unto the father no obedience. For 'we must obey God more than men' " (1564, 358).

6. Hamlet knows, then, that he should stay in his place "in the sun" where his deity placed him, and obey Claudius as his divinely anointed king.

7. He recognizes that having made himself, as far as crime goes, identical to Claudius, he, too, must atone for his sin by dying.

Although these antithetical readings of the ghost have long shaped the culture's understanding of this play, and have obviously contributed to its fame, they do not and will not suffice because they are the effects of a conflict with respect to authority between those who identify with the older style aristocratic/feudal/quasi-pagan/quasi-Catholic rule that is now residual in Elsinore (and in Elizabethan England), and those who identify with the newer style monarchical/bourgeois/Protestant rule that is now dominant in Elsinore (and in Elizabethan England). Indeed, each of these understandings of *Hamlet* is correct within the terms of its own historical system, but incorrect within those of its rival. So if a critic uses the former system, the ghost *is* the soul of Hamlet's dead father and is not a demon! But if a critic uses the latter system, it *is* a demon and is not a dead father's soul! Moreover, there is no way to adjudicate between these two systems except to choose one instead of the other: there is no way to prove that the ghost is soul or demon. Thus, given that, as a result of cultural changes taking place in Elsinore (and in Elizabethan England), both codes are available to Hamlet (and to his audience), it is not accidental that he uses both to understand the ghost, or that using both, his understanding of the ghost gets very confusing. Nor is it accidental that following his lead, audiences and critics have done likewise. Indeed, much of the older criticism about this play writes large outside the play one or the other side of the conflict that is taking place onstage in Hamlet's head: is this the soul of my dead father, or is this a demon? So what is irresolvable onstage becomes too easily resolved and yet never resolved offstage because critics who identify with part of what is happening in Hamlet's head ignore the other part *and* the dilemma these contradictory parts create. In fact, both of these views of the ghost are unhelpful in understanding the play since they only give conflicting, inadequate knowledge with respect to the ghost that is in Hamlet's head and in his culture's dominant/residual database. They give us nothing of the emergent knowledge that Shakespeare's early modern theatre is encouraging us to acquire with respect to this matter, knowledge that, among other things, will help us understand why such a conflict is taking place in Hamlet's head and why such a conflict is being staged. To limit our knowledge of Hamlet's ghost merely to the dominant or residual codes available onstage (and circulating in early modern England) would be to erase from our critical equation Shakespeare, his theatre, and whatever emergent knowledge exists in such a theatre. And this would be to misunderstand *Hamlet*.

As such a misunderstanding will not do, it is necessary to see how the ghost functions in this play if, whatever its appearances to the contrary, it is regarded not as something real that happens to Hamlet, but as something *fictional* that Hamlet causes to happen; just as it was necessary to understand, despite appearances and longstanding authority to the contrary, that (as Copernicus and Galileo recognized) the earth does not stand still but moves around the sun. So, we ask again, what does Hamlet elect to do when his other options run dry? One emergent answer is that he "seizes the night" by *creating* a ghost of his dead father (or, if one prefers the weak version of this argument, he *uses* a ghost previously created by a handful of disaffected soldiers who have also been sidelined by the new reign and who are likewise longing for a return of the old order). In other words, a ghost doesn't just happen to show up to get Hamlet out of a tight spot; rather, to use Horatio's terms, Hamlet "waxes desperate with imagination" (1.4.64). And what pops up as a result of this "lunacy" (in the sense of moon-like waxing) is a ghost whose knowledge may simply indicate that Hamlet's "imaginations are as foul / As Vulcan's stithy" [smithy] (3.2.76–77).

For Hamlet there are clearly numerous advantages and disadvantages of creating/using such an apparition, but before discussing these, it is important to note that from an emergent perspective Hamlet *is* the authority figure in the sense that, since he creates the ghost, he can construct it in whatever shape, use it in whatever way, and make it say whatever he desires. So, if he needs the apparition he has created to be his dead father's soul, it *is* his father's soul—if he chooses to activate the codes of a former dominant, now residual, Danish epic culture that make the ghost a higher authority than himself, then *he* has chosen to put himself in the position of having to obey its demand. Likewise, if at a later point he needs this apparition to be a demon from hell, then it *is* a demon, since, by choosing to activate the codes of the now dominant Danish culture that subject him to the higher authority of a Christian deity, he is choosing to put himself in the position of not having to obey the ghost he has created. Likewise, if he chooses to see this ghost as a fiction (or a fraud), it *is* a fiction (or a fraud), since by activating emergent codes, he becomes the authority figure of last resort. In short, Hamlet chooses, however consciously, to have the ghost be one thing at one moment, another thing at another, or any other thing he wants it to be: invisible in the closet scene with Gertrude, for example, or altogether absent and unthought of at the end of the play.

"BETWEENE . . . MIGHTY OPPOSITS"

As we saw above, Hamlet is stymied. The new regime offers him nothing that is commensurate to what he has lost (father, father's world, kingship, centrality in the culture as well as in his mother's life). In his mind there is nothing he can do to be powerful, much less heroic, and, unable to return to school or act in masculine fashion, he finds himself in an infantilized position where his only option, he thinks, comes down to being suicidally depressed in the "sun" of Claudius's and Gertrude's happiness. This clearly will not do. He must defeat his melancholy, and reverse his subordinate position. So, to fashion a different self and open a door out of his dilemma, Hamlet creates/uses a ghost. But how does a ghost solve his problem? What does it offer?

First of all, consolation. By flooding the black, melancholic space around him with the waxing and waning light of a dead father's ghost, Hamlet is able to activate a pagan version of the medieval dream vision, a *consolatio* in which a recently deceased loved object returns after his/her death to console the one who, left behind, is drowning in grief.

Then nostalgia. By reconstituting the most powerful part of a past world that is now fading—his father—Hamlet can once again be "son" to, and be in the "sun" of, a heroic warlord rather than (in his mind) an effeminized Claudius, not to mention reinstating, on the margin of the dominant space from which they have been exiled, the values, customs, and codes of this known and comfortable paternal world. In John-Joseph Goux's terms, Hamlet and ghost are the "neurotic individual" who has become the "symptom of the era left behind" (Goux, 1990).

Third, emotional vindication. Creating/using a residual ghost who can be made to speak of murder, adultery, and betrayal legitimizes Hamlet's desire to turn his dark rage against the bright new world his mother and stepfather are installing, a Denmark, if Hamlet's hunch is right (i.e., if the speeches he puts in the mouth of his ghost are right), he can now judge as being more "rotten" and "out of joint" than is his father's dead, putrefying, and very out-of-joint physical body.

And, of course, a heroic identity/role. Hamlet's ghost transforms what everyone else in Denmark regards as an accidental death into a murder, and Hamlet, appropriating the symbolic capital associated with such a crime, can fashion himself (however privately) as the solution to an absolutely central but an as yet unknown problem. If there were no ghost and no murder, there would be no need for a hero (or, for that matter, a detective), and Hamlet would have to hand the term hero to his mother and stepfather in recognition of their accomplishments in remodeling Denmark.

These are by no means, however, the only functions Hamlet's ghost's tirade performs. Much more important is the fact that by constructing a residual authority figure, Hamlet is able (however consciously) to subject himself to a second, rival, and equally impossible, paternal parental demand: remember me, forget everything else, revenge my death, sustain my world (i.e., be my ideal, obedient son [be like me!]). This demand Hamlet can then set against, and use to keep himself from obeying, the original of its ghostly mirror image, namely, the impossible demand recently issued by his mother and stepfather: obey us, forget your noble father, accept the new order, live in our world (i.e., be our ideal, obedient son [be like us!]). Creating a ghost is a necessary strategic move because, in addition to the functions itemized above, such a ghost allows Hamlet to establish the compelling new demand, heroic revenge, which he needs to countermand his mother's demand, but a demand that he also has no intention of obeying.

We now have a way to understand Hamlet's indecisiveness, and, in particular, to understand why, having constructed a residual ghost-soul, Hamlet sometimes constructs his apparition as a dominant ghost-demon, and at other times as nothing more than his overwrought mind's fantasy object. The point is that Hamlet runs through these changes in order to make it *impossible* to do the revenge he would have to do if the ghost were his father's soul, or the obedience he will have to do if the ghost is a demon or hallucination. That is, a residual ghost-soul makes revenge satisfyingly heroic but also terrifyingly necessary, whereas a dominant ghost-demon makes revenge, however deeply desired, a horrible, detestable crime; and an emergent fantasy-ghost erases the issue of crime altogether by reducing it to a figment of Hamlet's imagination. Thus, at any time he wants to, Hamlet can signify the ghost as imaginary and get rid of the whole "to be a revenger" or "not to be a revenger" obedience dilemma. But to do so has a cost: he would reduce himself once again to his previous infantilized position of powerlessness, identity confusion, alienation, rage, and grief—melancholic despair. Hamlet's ghost is "questionable" then, because Hamlet needs it to be a mixture of all three of these possibilities, since only in this way will it be (1) something he absolutely has to obey, (2) something he absolutely cannot obey, and (3) something he can write off as the nothing it in fact is if he is willing to retake the depressive position. By an act of stunning ventriloquism in which deeply introjected paternal discourse is heard coming from an apparition projected "over there," Hamlet, however consciously, creates a triple ghost and commits himself to triple business in order to suspend, paralyze, and distance himself from, and thereby restore a former ambivalence between, two mighty parental opposites.

To use Geoffrey Bateson's terms, we can say that Hamlet (however unintentionally) is putting himself in a version of a "double bind" by inverting its agency. (By double bind Bateson means a situation in which a parent unconsciously places contradictory demands on a child, insists that the child obey *both* of these mutually exclusive demands, and, at the same time, prohibits the child from discussing the fact that these demands are contradictory with anyone including the parent [Bateson, 1972].) So one reason Hamlet swears the soldiers and Horatio to a vow of silence concerning the ghost is that such a vow means that he will not have to discuss this ghost or its command with anyone in Denmark. And he seeks such silence because his ghost can only perform its triple functions as long as it and its knowledge/demand are not subjected to scrutiny in the public sphere. Thus, by constructing a situation that makes it impossible for him to obey either parent, despite having to obey both—a situation in which it is impossible for him to talk to either parent about the demand allegedly made by the other— Hamlet puts himself in a bind powerful enough to generate precisely the effect he wants, namely, *no exit* (to borrow the title of Jean-Paul Sartre's *No Exit*, a modern play indebted to this play).

"REVENGE HIS FOUL, AND MOST UNNATURAL MURDER"

But why does Hamlet ventriloquize through the ghostly apparition he creates, a story of murder and a demand for revenge (not to mention how Hamlet presumably hits on the fact that his father was murdered, if not also on something like the manner of this murder)? Not just because murder is what he suspects (since it is rather conventional in monarchical power structures), or because poison is legendary in cultures to the south, or that revenge is what he knows his father would have wanted (and would have wanted whether he had been murdered or not, since also offensive to a residual patriarch would be a hasty, incestuous remarriage of a wife to a brother), but because murder and revenge alone will serve Hamlet's turn. As a response to kin murder, revenge is absolutely demanded by the code of the pagan/aristocratic Father (as we saw above, it goes without question that in this residual world a son revenges his father's murder—as Fortinbras's, Pyrrhus's, and Laertes' actions illustrate). And (as we also saw) revenge is equally absolutely forbidden by the now dominant law of the new Christian/monarchical Father—" 'Vengeance is mine,' saith the Lord." So, if the biblical subtext reinforcing the mother's demand is "forsake not thy mother's teaching," the biblical subtext of the father's demand (reappropriated from the divine father by the natural father) is likewise from *The Proverbs of Salomón* (*The Geneva Bible*, 1560): "My son, keep my words, and hide my commandments with[in] thee. Keep my commandments, and thou shalt live. . . . Bind them upon thy fingers, and write them upon the tables of thine heart" (7: 1–3). Compare Hamlet's response to his pagan ghostly father's demand: "Yea, from the table of my memory / I'll wipe away all trivial fond records . . . / And they commandment all alone shall live / Within the book and volume of my brain / Unmixed with baser matter" (1.5.98–99, 102–4). Of course, one of the "trivial fond records" Hamlet is promising to erase is his divine ghostly father's injunction not to revenge, whereas the commandment he is writing, or finding, in its place is his mortal father's injunction to revenge. And this process of erasing and rewriting will continue to occupy Hamlet throughout much of the play because to live in each parent's world Hamlet must inscribe on the table of his memory exactly what in the other parent's world he must erase, since *to be* what one parent commands is *not to be* what the other demands. So as we saw above, these contradictory parental texts (reinforced by equally powerful and contradictory cultural codes and the zone of silence Hamlet constructs around them) have the effect of closing each other out, however temporarily, with the signal effect that Hamlet imagines that he not only will not lose either his father or his mother, or have to choose permanently between them, but, more to the point, he will not have to commit himself solely either to his mother's happy, sunny, sexually alive, but massively threatening world of interiorities (and among these the vulnerable ear and the allegedly mortal vagina) or to his father's angry, darkened, and fading, but customary world of seemingly safer and more predictable exteriorities (and among these the allegedly immortal pole-axe and the phallic dagger). This choice is as paralyzed by Hamlet's doubts about his mother's sexual fidelity as by his doubts about his father's immortality since he creates the fiction of the one's continuing existence as thoroughly out of the air as he does the fiction of the other's fickleness, and creates both in order to get his powerful parents in equally disadvantageous positions relative to himself.

"TO PUT AN ANTIC DISPOSITION ON"

Needless to say, *Hamlet* does not end once Hamlet invents an extremely clever yet hopeless sleight-of-hand solution to a problem that otherwise seems insoluble, if only because the create-a-ghost option he elects generates numerous problems in its wake. One of these is the form his deeply desired paralysis will take while he suspends himself between antithetical parental imperatives. What identity will he have, what role will he act, while he is trying to live simultaneously in mutually exclusive parental worlds and obey the contradictory laws of two ghosts, a paternal one and a holy one? Hamlet's solution to this problem is likewise historically conditioned, since just as his father's culture offers him a ghost to solve his melancholy, so it also offers him an *antic disposition* (feigned madness) to solve the problems created by this ghost.

To understand the various ways Hamlet's pretense of madness functions, we need to consider Shakespeare's source. In the Amløthi/Hamblet legend (see Chapter 7), the Claudius figure kills the Hamlet Sr. figure in public with the result that the Hamlet figure not only knows, as everyone else does, that a crime has in fact been committed, but, like everyone else, he also knows who committed it. Moreover, knowing that his uncle will have to kill him to prevent him from revenging his father's death at some point in the future, this nephew figure fakes idiocy *immediately* after his father's death to save his life and gain time to grow up and plan a way of effecting justice/revenge. To this plot, long popular in the west, Shakespeare (or perhaps the author of the earlier "Ur-*Hamlet*") made three crucial changes:

1. In *Hamlet* the nephew is thirty, not a child.

2. In *Hamlet* neither the nephew nor anyone else onstage (except Claudius) knows that Claudius killed Hamlet Sr. (i.e., as far as those onstage are concerned no crime has been committed, and as a consequence no one onstage regards the uncle figure as an evil tyrant until Hamlet, *two months later*, decides to do so).

3. In *Hamlet* the onstage culture is not an archaic/residual culture (as it is in the source) but a newly dominant early modern one.

Thus the antic disposition that is absolutely necessary in the sources *is not at all necessary* in Shakespeare's radically altered plot, since Shakespeare's Hamlet, unlike his predecessor, has no obvious reason to put on an antic disposition, not to mention doing so two months after the death in question. Clearly, Shakespeare has changed the motives for Hamlet's antic posturing since, in contrast to Shakespeare's source, it is, logically speaking, completely against Hamlet's interests to feign madness in Elsinore. As

Dr. Johnson put it two centuries ago: "Of the feigned madness of Hamlet there appears no adequate cause, for he does nothing which he might not have done with the reputation of sanity" (1765; 3:311). For Hamlet to play the fool, far from allaying whatever suspicion Claudius might be having, has the countereffect of creating suspicion: "Madness in great ones must not unwatched go" (3.1.187). So, we may ask, why does Hamlet antic himself, when doing so seems to accomplish nothing except put him in a position of unnecessary danger. Surely, had he his wits about him, the last thing he would do would be to pretend to have lost them in a situation where such a pretense, rather than hide his hunch, in fact works to advertise it. Clearly, the obvious and smart thing to do were Hamlet seriously pursuing revenge, would be to go on, business as usual, after he creates his ghost, since, in his situation, an appearance of normalcy would be a far more effective disguise than feigned madness, particularly since madness, especially in great ones, was greeted by early moderns, not with sympathy but with the reservations and fears associated with the suspicious, dangerous, and out of joint. So why play the fool when doing so makes one an obvious disturbance, if not a dangerous plotter, within the realm (Coddon 1994)?

By the logic of feudal masculinity, Hamlet puts on an unnecessary and in fact dangerous antic disposition—waving a red flag, as it were, in front of Claudius—to honor (and yet not to honor) chivalric code, not so much by warning (and not warning) Claudius, as by challenging (and not challenging) Claudius to a duel, but not to the duel of swords Hamlet Sr. would have preferred (though there is the fencing match with Laertes at the end of the play), but to a duel of wits that Hamlet is convinced he can win. The other reason, of course, that Hamlet is challenging Claudius in this oblique antic way is that he knows he has no evidence of Claudius's guilt. Thus, he needs to find a way of doing something like (yet not exactly like) what his father would have desired him to do.

By the logic of legal due process, such a disposition gives Hamlet time, not so much to figure out a way to kill Claudius, but to look for evidence that could convert his hunch into fact, not to mention giving him a means (a disguise) that enables him to spy in a way that is not as suspicious as spying would be if he were doing it as a prince. Of course, such a disposition also gives him a way of not being able to use any evidence he might get, since a mad person's testimony would have no evidentiary stature in an early modern royal court, or court of law.

By the logic of affect, Hamlet's pretense of idiocy allows him to vent anger and rage against those onstage whom he hates, and yet to do so under a sign of madness that in effect pulls his punches. Feigned madness lets him rage for real at Claudius and Gertrude if they are guilty, but it also lets him siphon off this rage as an effect of madness if they are not (a mode of raging and siphoning off Hamlet also uses in relation to Laertes in the graveyard scene in act 5). And, by a parallel logic of emotional honesty and/or economy, if Claudius and Gertrude are going to turn out to be guilty, Hamlet does not want to have put on a "pleasant disposition" in public, does not want to have "seemed" happy, does not want to have worn smiles in their presence. He wants to show his actual feelings even if these emotions are inappropriate under the circumstances, and nothing except a pretense of madness will allow such a transgressive display.

By a parallel logic of humor, feigned madness and the fool's license that goes with it lets Hamlet launch arrows of satire and ridicule at anyone in the new order he wants to hurt, but can't legitimately hurt since, by a logic of (non)communication, antic speech is a way of sending messages that by virtue of the condition of the sender, reach, but do not reach, their intended receivers.

By a logic of self-reflexivity, Hamlet's disposition is a kind of warning light that, so to speak, constantly blinks. In other words, feigned madness is Hamlet's way of reminding himself that he may in fact be mad to suspect his uncle and mother, not to mention a way of warning himself that it is probably best, and certainly safer, not to slip and let on what he suspects. By the logic of concealment, feigned madness is also, of course, the best way of resignifying any such slip as nonsense on the grounds that a mad person can be expected to say anything.

By a logic of parody, acting mad allows Hamlet to mimic in an outrageous and morally superior fashion what he suspects everyone else is doing—that is, being altogether other than they seem. So he can say, if only to himself, that although everyone including himself is a hypocrite, his hypocrisy at least is paying its way with the built-in punishment of reducing him to the status of the mad. He can also say to himself that although everyone else is also acting, he is a better actor than they are, since he suspects their fraud and they (he thinks) have no clue concerning his. So, by a logic of (non)exposure, Hamlet's antic disposition calls out by repeating in inverted form what he considers to be Claudius's, Gertrude's, Polonius's, Ophelia's, Rosencrantz's and Guildenstern's "sane dispositions," but does so in a way that forecloses any reception of, or resolution to, such a challenge. Antic behavior lets Hamlet act and enjoy the sizable benefits of the if-you-who-are-guilty-pretend-to-be-pure-I-who-am-sane-will-pretend-to-be-mad trope featured at the time in Erasmus's *Praise of Folly* (1509) and is indebted to the licensed fool and the world-up-side-down conventions of premodern as well as early modern cultures. The point of these conventions is a kind of magical threat: by acting mad/foolish I'll turn right side up the world you have turned upside down by really being mad/foolish. That is, two negatives make a positive! And thus, by a logic of audience appeal, Hamlet's disposition is one reason many like him, since it keeps him from doing two things they would not like as much: nothing, or slaughtering Claudius on first sight.

By a logic of filial obligation (as we saw above), such a disposition allows Hamlet a seemingly permanent way (and perhaps the only way) to defer making an irreversible decision, sustain his suspended, paralyzed position between, and to position himself as an irresolvable difference within, his parents' worlds. So, by the logic of self-preservation, Hamlet's pretense allows him to pursue and yet not pursue the revenge that he can't do, and that he must do. Moreover, it allows him to maintain, if not extend, his nighttime ghostly heroic self into his mother's and stepfather's daytime world in a way that prevents this self from fading away, as his ghost does, when the cock crows.

And by a logic of regression, feigned madness allows Hamlet to remain in an infantile position in which he does not to have to grow up. Thus, by a logic of temporality, his antic disposition allows him to play a role that cannot be permanent, one that, as it fades, cannot help but erode his ghost and his carefully contrived suspension, forcing him to reassert himself as a prince if and when he can figure out a better option to adopt than paralysis and antic posturing.

"THERE ARE THE PLAYERS"

Ghost and antic disposition are not, of course, the only ways that Hamlet's triple business structures the early and middle sections of this play. There is also his interaction with the traveling players to consider. Take, for example, Hamlet's use of a player and a play, "*Aeneas* tale to *Dido*," to embrace, and to reject, his desires to kill and not kill Claudius, to mourn and not mourn his father. Shortly after meeting the players, Hamlet recites a speech from a play that lives in his memory but "pleased not the million," and then watches as the troupe's master player finishes "there about of it especially where [Aeneas] speaks of Priam's slaughter" (2.2.427–28). As audience to this traveling player's performance of Grecian Pyrrhus's act of revenge, Hamlet relishes imagining his own sword biting through Claudius's head and shoulder: "And never did the Cyclops' hammers fall / On Mar's armour, forged for proof eterne [eternal protection], / With less remorse than Pyrrhus' bleeding sword / Now falls on Priam" (2.2.469–72). But at the same time that Hamlet desires to embrace this scene of bloody revenge, he also desires to defer it, and distance himself from it, by handing it over to the player to finish, and, as importantly by forcing himself and the actor to act this instance of revenge in the version that is told by Trojan Aeneas (Pyrrhus's enemy) to Dido, a version that deprives Pyrrhus of heroic stature by demonizing him: "Black as his purpose [he] did the night resemble / . . . . Head to foot / Now is he total gules [red], horridly tricked [decorated] / With blood of fathers, mothers, daughters, sons, / . . . That lend a tyranous and a damned light / To their lord's murder" (2.2.433,436–39). So, Pyrrhus's comedy is Priam's and Aeneas's tragedy, and like Hamlet's midnight ghost and its dark purpose, Hamlet's Pyrrhus theatrical is a triple piece of work: an inspiring model of revenge Hamlet embraces, a "tyrannous and damned" bit of brutality he rejects, and in either case, a fiction to boot.

And what is true of the player scene is true as well of the play-within-the-play, *The Murder of Gonzago*, since it is in Hamlet's production of this inner play that the triple business occasioning ghost, antic disposition, and Hamlet's exploitation of the players becomes most visible. One problem Hamlet wants to solve by producing this inner play is, of course, his lack of hard evidence. And evidence is a problem not only because Hamlet doesn't have any, and can't do without any, but also because he can't really get any, since, were he to get solid evidence of Claudius's treachery, he would have to side with his father, act his father's revenge desire, and, as a consequence, destroy his mother by destroying her happiness, since revenge would kill her lover and thus her. However, if Hamlet does not get something very much like evidence, he will have to side with his mother, act the good son desire of his mother, and abandon his father to oblivion since there is not a lot left in Hamlet's mind of the actual Hamlet Sr. for Hamlet to hold on to except the vindictive rage and the punitive blood-for-blood code that surfaces in the Hamlet–ghost scene. So, desiring to do both and neither, Hamlet has to get and cannot ever get such evidence, which means that he has to destroy whatever "evidence" he creates, just as eventually he destroys the ghost he creates.

"I'LL HAVE GROUNDS / MORE RELATIVE THAN THIS"

In this context we may now consider three allegedly solid bits of evidence critics and performances have long handed Hamlet, and in doing so have massively simplified this complex, brilliant play by reducing his action to tedious procrastination in the face of obvious knowledge based on indisputable evidence:

1. the ghost,
2. Claudius's reaction to the mousetrap play, and
3. the "the grand commission" Hamlet finds in Rosencrantz and Guildenstern's "packet" at sea (5.2.15–18).

Each of these is commonly taken to prove—and to give Hamlet knowledge of—Claudius's crime. However, none of these do so unless a critic or director grossly and erroneously constructs them to do so. Let us begin with the last.

The Grand Commission

To be sure, the commission is Claudius's way of getting rid of the one person he suspects of knowing his guilty secret, but this motive is known to no one but Claudius, and it cannot be legitimately inferred by those onstage from any of Claudius's actions. From the perspective of those at court, were they somehow to learn about it (and they don't since Hamlet shares this information only with Horatio), this death writ would be seen as what any king would have to do once the mad son of his queen stabs an innocent state secretary though a castle tapestry—once Hamlet criminally transgresses dominant code by acting as though the interiority of the queen's closet were a battlefield outside the castle. What Claudius is doing, if viewed from a contemporary perspective other than his own, is finding a way of solving the Hamlet problem without creating massive grief for Gertrude, though, from his own perspective, of course, he is countering the madness he suspects to be feigned with a feigned vacation. So, to send Hamlet temporarily off to England with two of his best friends in order to protect him and the state, but to let it secretly be a voyage from whence, due to sleight of hand, Hamlet will never return, is hardly evidence of guilt in the matter of Hamlet's father. In fact, once Hamlet has killed Polonius, evidence like the death commission, were it exhibited, would point in the direction, not of Claudius's unknown murder, but of Hamlet's actual one.

Moreover, were Hamlet's story of cunning theft, sealed commission, and substitution of names told in public, wouldn't the court regard this story as further evidence of Hamlet's earlier madness? Indeed, doesn't Hamlet present his narrative in such a way that it will appear even to Horatio as evidence of something like madness? Hamlet needs this evidence, and he needs Horatio to accept it as evidence, but he also needs to undermine it as evidence, so he couches his telling of it in such a way that will push it just beyond even his only friend's capacity to believe in it, with those capable of testifying to the contrary dead in England. In short, massive damage is done to the play if in this case we believe without question what Hamlet tells us, or if we give our offstage hindsight (particularly what we overhear in the prayer scene) to Hamlet, since by doing so we remove the *lack* of knowledge that creates Hamlet's dilemma and generates his various solutions to this dilemma.

The Mousetrap Play

Like the death writ, *The Murder of Gonzago* mousetrap play also is and is not evidence because Hamlet manipulates this inner play just enough to create something like "evidence" and, at the same time, to destroy the validity of any "evidence" so created. In other words, the mousetrap play has to convict the king, and yet it can't actually convict the king. Two instances follow.

Apparently Hamlet either rewrites *The Murder of Gonzago* so that it is the Player King's nephew, not his brother, who pours poison in the Player King's ear, or, alternatively, he chooses this play from the players' repertoire because of this difference. Thus Claudius, watching a nephew pouring poison in an uncle's ear, would have to be a very secure king not to take such a scene as a threat of assassination given that this inner play is produced by his nephew. Nor does it help that while the players are performing *The Murder of Gonzago* Hamlet meddles with what he sets up as a disinterested experiment by interpolating asides of his own between the players' speeches. One of these consists of lines Claudius would also find difficult not to take as possibly prefacing a plot to kill him: "Begin murderer, leave thy damnable faces and begin. Come, the croaking raven doth bellow for revenge" (3.2.230–32), especially since in Thomas Kyd's *The Spanish Tragedy* (c. 1589) the revenger's play-within-the-play is lethal to its observers.

Still, Claudius does rise, and says, "Give me some light, away" (3.2.247), so it is necessary to realize that, in the minds of those who have no reason to suspect anything, there are at least three reasons why Claudius would rise and speak in this situation (in addition to his fear that what is happening on the inner stage to the Player King is about to happen to himself).

1. He is deeply insulted by being threatened in a public manner by his obnoxious nephew, and, being a sovereign, puts an end to Hamlet's insults.

2. He reads "nephew" in the players' text as a transparent substitution for "brother," and is angered by being accused publicly of being a murderer.

3. Or, as a king, he does not want to see a Player King murdered on a theatrical stage in his great hall if only because such fictions give people ideas, and kings nightmares. It is highly unlikely then, that Claudius's rising and/or his cry, "Give me some light, away," would be read by an onstage court or an offstage Globe audience as signifiers of guilt. Rather, Claudius's reaction would most likely be read as the

very least a sovereign king would do in such a situation to protect his life, save his dignity, and put an end to one or another kind of public humiliation in a way that does not insult his queen.

As Hamlet well knows, his mousetrap play would produce viable evidence of Claudius's guilt only if it provoked Claudius into making a full confession of his crime before his court and queen, and this it obviously does not do. And even if the reaction Hamlet's experiment generates is a guilty one, and even if this reaction were perceived as a guilty one by court or queen (perceptions actors and directors need not insure), such as a reaction would still not prove Claudius guilty of Hamlet Sr.'s death, since it could be argued in Claudius's defense that he is reacting to the fact that at some point in the past he had had *thoughts* of doing such a horrid thing to his brother, and that merely seeing these former thoughts acted in a play awakens his memory and the guilt accompanying it, and causes him to put an end to Hamlet's play. It is important to note that Horatio, seeing what the audience sees, does not agree (to the extent that prudence allows) with Hamlet on this issue. The crucial point, however, is not that Horatio does not agree with Hamlet, but that Hamlet's meddling with the players' performance is designed in part to make certain that Horatio cannot agree with him despite the heavy pressure Hamlet places on Horatio to do so both before and after this inner play.

So Hamlet gets no evidence from *The Murder of Gonzago*. More to the point, he has no intention of getting any, since to do so would prove his hunch correct and force him to do what he does not want to do—act according to his father's and against his mother's desire. So Hamlet stirs up the king by doing what he knows would stir up any king, and like the death writ, this stirring up proves (1) that Claudius is a treacherous murderer, (2) that Claudius is an above average good king with problems to solve, and (3) that it is impossible to choose between these two possibilities. (There is at least one other reason why Hamlet both stages and undermines the play-within-the-play. Though part of him wants to celebrate the older marital values and loyalties figured forth in this antique pageant, part of him also hates this pageant, its out-of-date values and its equally out-of-date poetry.)

The Ghost

So we are left with this question: "Is the ghost's testimony evidence of anything?" In taking up this issue let us assume, for the sake of argument, that the ghost isn't merely a grandly dramatic echo of Hamlet's suspicions reverberating back from the night sky and a waxing moon. Instead, let us assume that the ghost is real and that it's narrative is completely accurate. We may then ask if the story the ghost tells Hamlet at night and in private could convict Claudius in an early modern court or court of law. Imagine this scenario: Hamlet believes the ghost and, on the basis of its testimony, kills Claudius without hesitation (and without having put on an antic disposition). He then shows Claudius's dead body to his mother and the court (we're assuming here that he doesn't do something despicable like killing Claudius and making it look, à la *Macbeth*, as though servants had done the dirty work). In this situation what is Hamlet going to say to a mother who does not see ghosts (as we learn in the closet scene), or to a court that clearly would not accept the hearsay word of a ghost as sufficient evidence on which to kill a divinely anointed king, especially by a nephew who is known to have had his eye on the throne, is known to be angry that Claudius got in the way, and is next in line? Is Hamlet really going to say, "A ghost told me to kill Claudius!"? Obviously Hamlet is far too intelligent to imagine such an argument would work unless he were able to back it up with supporting evidence or brute force. More important, would Gertrude believe him? Clearly not, given what she says in the closet scene when Hamlet claims merely *to see* his father's ghost: "Alas he's mad," and "This is the very coinage of your brain, / This bodiless creation ecstasy / Is very cunning in" [your madness (ecstasy) is very clever at producing a hallucination (bodiless creation)] (3.4.96,128–30). If she says this in that situation, is it at all likely that she would think Hamlet less mad if he told her he had killed Claudius at the behest of a ghost? In fact, part of the point of creating a ghost to speak his hunch is precisely that Hamlet knows he cannot produce it before this queen or in this court, because, were he to do so, they would reject it. (The question of how Horatio and the soldiers see this ghost is discussed in Chapter 5.)

Despite powerful evidence, then, that the ghost is "the coinage" of Hamlet's brain, critical/performative tradition, long overidentified with Hamlet, has nevertheless taken it to be real on the ground that dominant/residual Elizabethans believed ghosts to be real, even though (as we shall see in Chapter 5) it is altogether unlikely that most early modern theatregoers would have done so. More to the point, isn't it clear that Hamlet sets his ghost up so that even those, including himself, who might be inclined to believe it real will find it difficult not to regard it, as Horatio is inclined to do, as a demon that has put on a "Hamlet Sr. disposition" (at midnight, in the dark, temporarily released from purgatory, demanding revenge, silencing everyone afterwards, and particularly the old-mole-under-the-stage vice-figure farce lifted from medieval morality plays [see 1.5.148ff, especially 162]). Moreover, to see just how little evidentiary value it has, consider the sorts of evidence the play could, but does not, offer Hamlet: an eyewitness who saw Claudius pouring poison in Hamlet Sr.'s ear (evidence like that on which Heironimo bases his right to revenge his son's death in Kyd's earlier and exceptionally popular *The Spanish Tragedy*), a group of individuals (Horatio, Barnardo, and Marcellus, say) who hear such an eyewitness and prod Hamlet to act—the list goes on and on. The point of such a list is that, of the various possibilities, a ghost's testimony is the only form of evidence (other than a hunch in and by itself) that is totally *useless*, and yet at the same time totally compelling to whatever degree Hamlet wants it to be compelling. Nothing else could produce such a perfect double bind. In brief then, the "kill Claudius on the word of a Ghost" option, though extremely useful in the ways outlined above, is finally no different, legally or ethically speaking, from Hamlet's earlier and abandoned "kill Claudius because I want him out of the way" option.

"THE KING IS A THING . . . OF NOTHING"

In the first half of the play we watch Hamlet fight off despair and death by paralyzing himself between two parental worlds. Up to the end of the mousetrap play (3.2), Hamlet's life is tragic in the sense that suffering the pain of a terrible loss, he suspends himself between equally hopeless options. Beginning with the prayer scene (3.3.35–98), however, as everyone who writes about this play recognizes, things change significantly, and the question is: What does Hamlet do in the second half of the play (3.3 to the end)? What option does he finally take, and what is the value of what he does? To answer these questions we can work in two directions: from the end of the play in light of what eventually transpires—eight people are dead—as well as from what Hamlet does next: kill Polonius. In either case, what happens is death. And though death is a tragedy from the perspective of *The Tragicall Historie of Hamlet*, from Hamlet's point of view it is a special kind of "comedy."

Despite the energy Hamlet puts into maintaining a paralyzing position between opposing parental demands, various forces begin eroding this position almost as soon as it is built. On the general inability of the species to sustain equilibrium between contrary desires, Montaigne comments, "In my opinion, it might rather be said, that nothing is presented unto us, wherein there is not some difference, how light so ever it be: And that either to the sight, or to the feeling, there is ever some choise, which tempteth and drawes us to it, though imperceptible and not to be distinguished" (1604, xiv, 355). For similar reasons, Hamlet does not hang endlessly between patient obedience and revenge, if only because the benefits of doing so become less and less satisfying. His melancholy continues, and it cannot be lost on him that positioning himself in such a way as to obey contradictory parental demands is not only infantilizing, but doubly so. So in time, a desire to grow up and become the powerful man he thinks he would have been had he been king overwhelms his desire to maintain his double bind.

That Hamlet chooses his father's world is clear; however, what he does thereafter has seemed unclear and confusing. Is he becoming more and more befuddled, or is he moving towards a clear goal by means of various circuitous indirections? In taking up this problem, perhaps it will help if what Hamlet does is viewed as a series of phenomena, related not so much to what he intends to do or knows he is doing, but to what transpires whether his hand is visible or not. We do not need to assume Hamlet is altogether conscious of what he is doing after he abandons his mousetrap production. In fact, the play is more tragic if he is seen to be following a parental script he is not altogether conscious of following—if what is inscribed on the tables of his memory is seen to direct the role he plays. From such a "reading back from what transpires" perspective, Hamlet's life is a series of seven Herculean labors. ("Herculean" is an adjective justified by the numerous allusions Hamlet makes to Hercules throughout the play.)

HAMLET'S HERCULEAN LABORS

First Labor: Self-Criminalization

The point at which Hamlet first makes perceptible the choice that "tempteth and drawes" him is, of course, the closet scene where he kills Polonius, and thus acts in irreversible fashion for the first time in the play. Hamlet's way of breaking out of his suspended position of ambivalence is to criminalize himself in his mother's world because he knows, however consciously, that such an act will force him to align himself with his father's world since the only way he can decriminalize himself after such an action is to reinstate this paternal world. In such an world (or at least in Hamlet's fantasy of it) killing Polonius is not a crime (as his expression, "a rat," indicates), whereas in his mother's dominant world it is inescapably murder.

Second Labor: Father Idealization

The second of Hamlet's labors is to resurrect, if only in his own mind, his father's diminished and presently rotting body/world into an image perfect enough to embrace wholeheartedly. Hamlet does this by de-idealizing his uncle:

> Look here upon this picture, and on this,
> The counterfeit presentment [pictorial representation] of two
>   brothers.
> See what a grace was seated on this brow [i.e., Hamlet Sr.'s],
> Hyperion's [the sun god's] curls, the front [forehead] of Jove
>   himself . . .
> A combination, and a form indeed
> Where every god did seem to set his seal
> To give the world assurance of a man.
> This was your husband, look you now what follows,

> Here is your husband like a mildewed ear,
> Blasting his wholesome brother . . .   (3.4.52–64)

Of course this contrast is inherently self-contradictory since the miniature portraits Hamlet holds in his hands (or the Hamlet Sr. miniature he holds and the Claudius miniature hanging from a chain around Gertrude's neck [later stage tradition enlarged these to framed wall portraits; see illustration]) create a visual sense of equal smallness and sameness that cannot help but undercut Hamlet's hyperbolic rhetoric of absolute difference. This contrast is also self-contradictory in the sense that the images Hamlet asks Gertrude to envision (images echoing his earlier "Hyperion to a Satyre" juxtaposition of father and uncle [1.2.140]) have nothing in common with the uncle or the ghostly replica of the father witnessed on stage (unless, of course, director/actors construct them to do so.)

Thus, if we recognize the problems created by Hamlet's excessive praise and blame, and ask why Hamlet needs such a strategic, misrepresentative, propagandistically overextended binary fiction, the answer would be that such a lie is necessary not only to the task of idealizing his father's world, but to his third Herculean task.

Third Labor: Negation of Women

Like the killing of Polonius, Hamlet's portraits are a backlash against Gertrude's and Claudius's new order (a backlash anticipated by the tongue-lashing to which he subjects Ophelia in the earlier nunnery scene). The goal is to raise his father's world to a position of hyperideality, not just by demonizing Claudius, but also—and this is his third Herculean labor—by degrading his mother and her world to the status of garbage: "have you eyes? / Could you on this fair mountain leave to feed, / And batten on this moor?" (3.4.64–66). In other words, Hamlet tilts the world he carefully balanced throughout the first half of the play ninety degrees in order to

1. end his double bind;
2. decriminalize himself;

Frontispiece for Nicholas Rowe's 1709 edition of *Hamlet*. In this edition (the first to contain illustrations), the "counterfeit presentation of two brothers" takes the form of wall-mounted portraits of Hamlet Sr. (mostly hidden) and Claudius. Reprinted with permission from Special Collections and Rare Books, Wilson Library, University of Minnesota.

3. restore patriarchy;

4. phallicize himself;

5. defend against the mortal realities and limitations of his inadequate father and his rather petty actual past world;

6. deny everything valuable about his mother's world; and

7. persuade her to leave her world and join him in the idealized fictionalized past that is going to be their future.

In short, Hamlet's long tirade in the closet scene is designed to persuade Gertrude to accompany him back to the future.

How does Hamlet try to seduce his mother not to get into bed with him instead of Claudius, but to return to the past perfect with him instead of staying in the present with Claudius? First, as we saw above, this prince, who is utterly opposed to women's "paintings," paints Gertrude and her sensuality "base" (ignoble, inferior), her new world more base, her new husband most base. Thus, for her to return to an idealized paternal past is to live, whereas to stay in a de-idealized present is to die.

Having established a vertical binary with his mother's negated world at the bottom and his father's idealized one at the top, Hamlet, playing the role of "scourge and minister," then offers Gertrude a way she can rise from her fallen position as fickle whore and redeem her "good wife" status. She can leave her present husband's "moor" (an area of wasteground) and her goatish nature and climb up to her former husband's "mountain": "O throw away the worser part" of your cleft heart, Hamlet instructs her, "And live the purer with the other half" (3.4.148–49).

What is more, Hamlet's seduction/instruction seems to be working. Gertrude is wavering: "O Hamlet speak no more, / Thou turn'st mine eyes into my very soul" (3.4.78–79). Strangely, however, just as Hamlet's rescue mission appears to be succeeding, it crashes and burns. So, if the question is, What happens to cause such a massive and nearly successful labor to come to nothing? the answers are: "*Enter* GHOST" (3.4.93), and *the mission we think Hamlet is on is not the mission he is in fact on.* Despite appearances and perhaps desires to the contrary, Hamlet knows he cannot bring his mother with him into a purified paternal ark. Therefore, to make it impossible for her to heed the sermon he is preaching, or practice the penance he is suggesting, he must figure out a way to turn Gertrude into a pillar of salt while nevertheless appearing to be doing everything he can do to save her. To achieve this contradictory objective of seeming to redeem Gertrude while actually consigning her to oblivion, Hamlet evokes a ghost, knowing, first, that Gertrude cannot see it because in fact there is nothing to see, and second, that any allegation of its presence will make her think him mad and thus cause her to reject his instruction as merely an effect of his insanity.

Like Lot's wife leaving the "moor" of Sodom and Gomorah to dwell "in the mountain" (*Gen.* 19: 26, 30), Gertrude looks back, or, rather, is made to look back. The effect is to make sure that, like Lot's wife, she does not get to the mountain. Why? Because in Hamlet's mind Gertrude is responsible for Hamlet Sr.'s death despite the fact that Hamlet exonerates her of having had anything to do with the actual fact of it. Were he to let her enter the ark of his future past perfect world, she would (he is convinced) destroy this new improved world just as surely as she destroyed its predecessor. Thus, like Lot's wife, Gertrude cannot be allowed to redeem herself. Hamlet's sermon cannot succeed. Gertrude cannot leave her moor. She must fail to see or hear, and go on failing. And with this objective in mind, what better strategy can Hamlet use to ensure Gertrude's failure than to put her in a situation where she can't possibly see an imaginary manifestation of the immaterial world she cannot enter, despite Hamlet's extensive but counterproductive efforts to make sure she does see: "On him, on him, look you. . . . Do you see nothing there? . . . Nor did you nothing hear? . . . Why, look you there, look. . . . Look . . ." (3.4. 116–25)? The closet scene, then, is that moment in the play when Hamlet turns his back on his mother and abandons her world.

Why does Hamlet believe his mother would destroy the hyper-idealized paternal world that is scheduled to be Denmark's patriarchal future? Because scriptural wisdom of the sort found in *The Proverbs of Salomón* (*The Geneva Bible*, 1560), and written on the tables of Hamlet's memory since before his age of consciousness, remains deeply engraved and powerfully active no matter how energetically he or his mother have tried to detoxify such patriarchal introjects:

When wisdom enters into thine heart, and knowledge delights thy soul, *Then* shall counsel preserve thee, and understanding shall keep thee. . . . And shall deliver thee from the strange woman. . . . Surely her house tends to death, and her paths unto the dead. All they that go unto her, return not again, neither take they hold of the ways of life.

Hear me now therefore, o children, and hearken to the words of my mouth. Let not thine heart decline to her ways: wander thou not in her paths. For she has caused many to fall down wounded, *and* the strong men *are* all slain by her. Her house is the way unto the grave, which goes down to the chambers of death. (II: 10–11, 16, 18–19; VII: 24–27)

Desiring to take "hold of the ways of life," Hamlet not only puts this misogynistic wisdom into practice with respect to Ophelia and Gertrude, but does so because doing so "delights [his] soul."

Fourth Labor: Peripheral Vengeance

After killing Polonius, idealizing his father's world, and leaving Gertrude and Ophelia turning into pillars of salt, Hamlet's fourth Herculean labor is to direct his purging and purifying rage against a number of the (in his mind) peripheral vermin plaguing Elsinore, speaking daggers to some, and executing others. So he engages in a duel of wits with Rosencrantz and Guildenstern that turns lethal in much the same way an earlier duel of wits does with Polonius. Back from England, he joins in verbal battle with two gravediggers and then with Laertes and Osric to "expose" a sickness that (in his mind) is seen to range from the dirt of skulls and the mire of a suicide to the feathery affectations of an effeminized court. In short, in duels of wit that culminate in a murderous fencing match with Laertes, Hamlet scourges a Denmark that (in his mind) has grown upside-down and rotten in the four months following his father's death.

Fifth Labor: Self-purification

Hamlet's fifth labor establishes his true identity through six acts of self-purification:

1. Self-purification by symbolically casting himself in the sea, and then by resurrecting from this "baptismal" water a purified image of himself as his father's true son and heir, and thus the rightful king of Denmark: "This is I / Hamlet the Dane" (5.1.241–42).

2. Self-purification by landing "naked" on "High and mighty" Claudius's kingdom (4.7.42). Naked in this context does not mean "without clothes, nude," nor does it merely signify the literal fact that Hamlet is temporarily "destitute," "unarmed," "defenseless," "without a following"; rather, it underlines the fact that, "stripped of all disguise or concealment," he is now a dangerous challenger, since, as is said of a sword or other weapon, his metal is no longer "covered by a sheath." As a naked, phallic weapon, Hamlet is ready at last to insert his sword into Denmark's body to lance its alleged hidden rot (*OED*, 1971, s.v. naked).

3. Self-purification by removing his antic disposition (one effect of landing naked), and by incorporating his father's ghost within himself as his true self by taking the ghost he projected "out there" back within himself as, so to speak, his Platonic form. Consider the logic of this incorporation. His king/father is dead. In the presence of his father's dead body, a body that is physically rotting away, Hamlet faces (he thinks) the options of following his father's rotting corpse into the grave, keeping his dead father (as he has been doing) alive "out there" as a ghost, or (the option he now adopts) materially incarnating this dead father's ghostly essence with, and as, his own body. This incarnation allows Hamlet to take back the "sun" Claudius stole, and proves, as Hamlet has long maintained, that he has "that within which passeth show" (1.2.85). Hamlet's objective then, is to rephallicize himself, and he does this by materializing the ghost he imagines rising up out of his father's rotting corpse, not with thickened air of imagination, but with his own body and blood. In this way he brings this ghost alive as himself, and himself alive as this ghost, making it and himself once again a powerful physical *sun/son* capable of restoring Denmark's health.

4. Self-purification, in the graveyard scene, by purging his worldly ambitions and human vanities; his narcissistic ego; all of mortal, fallen life's empty "quiddities" and "quillities" (subtleties

G. Goldberg, *Hamlet and Yorick's Skull* (late nineteenth century). Courtesy of the Davidson Library, University of California, Santa Barbara.

and nice distinctions); all "gibes," "gambols," "songs," and "flashes of merriment"; all of his father's gross mortality and ridiculous folly for which Yorick's jawless skull is a symbolic surrogate (as Osric's affectations are for Claudius's court); and, finally, whatever hopes Hamlet had for worldly glory and something like Alexander's fame. In the graveyard scene, Hamlet splits himself in the same binary fashion he is splitting everything else: into the mortal garbage now being consigned to a grave, and the immortal essence that is his ideal self. (The root *rick* in Yorick and Osric [spelled Osricke in the Folio, Osricke in the second Quarto] carries the sense of king [from Celtic *rix* = Latin *rex*; (*OED*, 1971, s.v. rich]; however, with these prefixes (*os* signifies bone or mouth), *rick* indicates sovereignty inflected not in the direction of the king's ideal, second body, but of his mortal, first body. In other words, Osric marks Claudius as a mouth- and/or bone-king, just as Yorick symbolizes the corrupted physical body of Hamlet Sr. that is now "a thing of nothing.")

5. Self-purification by apologizing to Laertes in a way that allows Hamlet to separate his phallic, royal self from the mad, unpurged Hamlet whose antic disposition "sheathed" his true, "naked" metal: "Was't Hamlet wronged Laertes? never Hamlet. / If Hamlet from himself be tane [taken] away, / And when he's not himself, does wrong Laertes, / Then Hamlet does it not, Hamlet denies it, / Who does it then? his madness" (5.2.170–74).

6. Self-purification prior to battle and death by stoically handing himself over to a mixture of pagan fatalism and Catholic providentialism: "If it be, 'tis not to come, if it be not to come, it will be now, if it be not now, yet it will come. The readiness is all" (5.2.158–60)—early modern versions of "when your number's up," and "be prepared" clichés that echo battlefield slogans from the killing fields of his father's past.

Sixth Labor: Regicide and Matricide

Having completed five labors, Hamlet's sixth is to finish cleansing Denmark by purging the sources of infection, Claudius and Gertrude, who allegedly brought plague into his father's world, a plague symbolized by the poison Claudius allegedly poured into Hamlet Sr.'s body, and by the poison Claudius now pours into a chalice. Hamlet lets his mother drink this poisoned wine so her body will reabsorb the cause of Denmark's sickness. He stabs Claudius with the rapier Claudius has tainted to wipe clean and restore the purity of this phallic steel by an act that simultaneously destroys its unphallic opposite. And, in a kind of anti- or reverse-sacrament, Hamlet then pours the poison that did not go down Gertrude's throat down Claudius's.

Seventh Labor: Self-Slaughter

Hamlet's last labor is to die—to put the last remnant of the poison left in the body of Denmark (i.e., his own body) in a grave. Having incarnated the ghost of his father long enough to accomplish his objectives, Hamlet finally will "melt, / Thaw, and resolve" himself "into a dew," and thus, like the ghost he imagines, will no longer be trapped in the "too too solid flesh" of a physical body (1.2.129). Or, one could say, Hamlet chooses rather to accompany his father's immaterial ghost into the realm of the invisible than stay in Denmark and follow its rotting corpse into a grave where, like Alexander, he would end up "stopping a bunghole" (5.1.189). Hamlet's ideal self suicidally chooses *not to be* trapped any longer in a grotesque, mortal body so as to become the immortal self he desires more than anything else *to be*.

By seven heroic labors (self-criminalization, father idealization, negation of women, peripheral blood vengeance, self-purification, regicide and matricide, and self-slaughter), Hamlet finally defeats his melancholy, destroys the (allegedly) plaguey opposite that was his mother's world, gives birth (he thinks) to a patriarchal utopia, and becomes, in Horatio's mind at least, something like a saintly ghost as angels sing him to his rest in the bosom of his ghostly, phallic father. In short, Hamlet's "success" is to mark out a compromise option between suicide, revenge, and patience that accomplishes all three under the guise of purgation, purification, and self-phallicization (see figure):

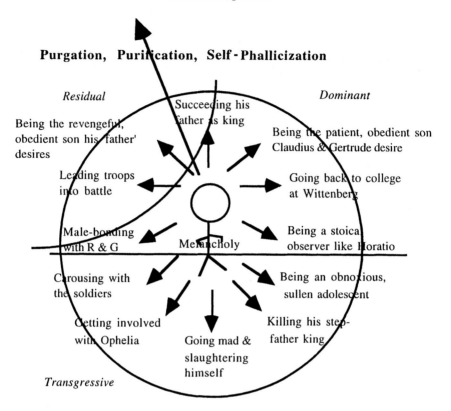

Purgation, Purification, Self-Phallicization

Residual   *Dominant*

Succeeding his father as king

Being the revengeful, obedient son his father' desires

Being the patient, obedient son Claudius & Gertrude desire

Leading troops into battle

Going back to college at Wittenberg

Male-bonding with R & G   Melancholy

Being a stoical observer like Horatio

Carousing with the soldiers

Being an obnoxious, sullen adolescent

Getting involved with Ophelia

Going mad & slaughtering himself

Killing his step-father king

Transgressive

"CARNAL, BLOODY, AND UNNATURAL ACTS"

Despite his success, the idealized Hercules role Hamlet acts in the last half of the play is often regarded as a failure. Why? Because, where Claudius killed one person, Hamlet is responsible for the deaths of eight (if not shortly nine): Polonius, Rosencrantz, Guildenstern, Ophelia, Laertes, Gertrude, Claudius, himself (and Horatio). Because the hero of the play and everyone he presumably intended to save are dead. Because the stage we are looking at, once filled with life, is now littered with dead bodies. Because the country Hamlet imagined as being out of joint is now wholly disjointed. Because the Danish royal line is extinguished. And because Fortinbras gets everything he desired without a fight. Hardly what one expects, many have said, of a hero!

So it is important to see first, that, despite appearances and negative judgments to the contrary, the "quarry" [pile of dead bodies] Hamlet constructs in Elsinore is not a failure in his mind, but precisely what he was taught to do, what in the end he desires to do, and what moreover he does brilliantly: *he gets rid of eight people, including himself, and he puts Fortinbras on the throne of Denmark!* In addition to seeing this "quarry" as a tragic mistake from our vantage point as audience, we must also see that, from Hamlet's onstage perspective, this bloody carnage, or, rather, this fruit of purgation and purification, is precisely how Hamlet writes a "comedy."

Second, it is also important to see that this pile of dead bodies is the product of Hamlet's revised plan to destroy Claudius. Rather than trying (and not trying) any longer to *expose* Claudius *as* a murdering tyrant as he did in the recent past, Hamlet, at least as early as the prayer scene (3.3), and certainly with the murder of Polonius (3.4), decides to do whatever he can to *force* Claudius to *become* such a figure in the present. Why else kill Polonius in Gertrude's closet? Why else the mousetrap play and later the insulting jokes concerning Polonius's dead body (4.3.17–20, 32–36)? Why else the salutation, "Farewell, dear mother," Hamlet addresses to Claudius as he leaves for England (4.3.51)? In short, though he failed to prove Claudius a tyrant in the first half of the play, he does what it takes to provoke Claudius to play this role in the second.

And third, it is important to see that Hamlet is following what he takes to be logical steps to get to the conclusion that it is absolutely necessary to destroy Denmark in order to save it.

1. My father is dead and I and Denmark are suffering a terrible traumatic loss.

2. For this tragic loss and the melancholy that accompanies it there is a cause.

3. So, I ask, what is the cause of this defect?

4. I know it is not my father, a man far too powerful and perfect to die. And I also know that finally it cannot be Claudius, a man far too weak to be more than an instrument.

5. Thus, it has to be a woman! Gertrude, a fallen woman, caused the relationships and loyalties between men to be

tainted, the rites between man and woman to be broken. She caused my father to be vulnerable in a garden. She drove Claudius to do what he did, and Ophelia to do what she did. She made me weak, depressed, paralyzed, infantile. She created the new social order that is obliterating the one founded by her rightful lord and master.

6. For this destructive cause and its tragic defects—for this woman whose "house is the way unto the grave, which goes down to the chambers of death" (*The Proverbs of Solomón* [*The Geneva Bible*, 1560] 7:27)—there is but one solution. I must purge her and Ophelia from the kingdom.

7. As important, I must purge every man she has infected, including myself, from Denmark's royal court.

8. I must then hand the purified Denmark I have created over to the only phallic man I know who is uninfected (and "unpenilized") by woman: Fortinbras (*strong-in-arm*). And I must hand this purged Denmark over to this solitary phallic exemplar by means of the one Dane whose blood and judgment has not been comeddled by [i.e., has not been mixed with] woman, Horatio.

9. And I must do all of this—get rid of these eight people and hand Denmark over to Fortinbras—because this is the only way I know to achieve catharsis, purgation, purity (from Latin *purus*, pure): without alloy, stain, or taint; free from all that vitiates, weakens, or pollutes; free from moral defilement or guilt; hence, innocent; ritually clean (*Webster's New Collegiate Dictionary*, 1961).

From a patriarchal perspective then, Hamlet is heroically successful not only because he models himself after Hercules, but because he imitates virtually every other heroic/mythic script enshrined and worshipped by dominant/residual cultures. He is a Moses figure who gets to, but not across the river, beyond which lies the land of milk and honey. He is a terrible flood cleansing Elsinore of everyone but a better (because an unwomaned) version of Noah. He is a Samson figure bringing down death on his enemies and himself. He is a John the Baptist figure clearing the way for a kind of Fortinbras-Christ. He is a Christ figure sacrificing himself to purge and redeem the sins of his people. And he is a deity figure who sends seven angels to pour out the purifying wrath of an apocalyptic last judgment on alleged sinners and the complex everyday world in which they live in order to hand a kind of heaven over to a purified, patient, obedient, and minuscule elect. Given then, that Hamlet acts out some of the most deeply inscribed and most profoundly revered heroic scripts Western Christian culture owns ("for he himself is subject to his birth" [1.3.18])—the scripts, in short, of this culture's divine comedies—how can his bloody apocalypse not be a comedy, or at least a tragi-comedy (i.e, a comedy enabled by its hero's death)?

"'I' HAVE SEEN WHAT I HAVE SEEN, SEE WHAT I SEE!"

Hamlet's cathartic action is a tragi-comedy from the perspective of its hero and from this hero's deeply reactionary masculine plot (a plot which Shakespeare did *not* write, but, as will be seen in Chapter 7, was authored by successive dominant/residual western Christian cultures and canonized by Shakespeare's source as the quintessence of *culture*). However, from the perspective of early modern theatre, Shakespeare's play, and the genre of literary tragedy, the *necessity* that piles up the dead bodies that litter the stage (like the *necessity* that caused "Juliet's" father to shoot "Juliet" while sleeping in her bed) is shown and seen to be a terrible *crime*. From the perspective of emergent popular theatre, in other words, Hamlet's alleged purgation/purification of Denmark is shown/seen to be no less and no more than a powerful reactionary backlash that Hamlet designs to destroy everyone who struggles against male dominance in one of its most conservative and virulent forms. And from this perspective, it is Hamlet himself, a prince who holds out for a time against such infection but in the end succumbs to its power and becomes the "scourge and minister" of its annihilating revenge justice, who is shown/seen to be the cause of this play's tragic defects. From this perspective, Hamlet's plan to force Claudius to become a tyrant is shown/seen to be deeply tyrannical; the logical steps by which he indicts woman as the cause of death is shown/seen to be not just hopelessly illogical and mysogynistic but violently and hysterically lethal; and the Herculean labors by which he tries to purge Denmark of plague and death are shown/seen to be the principal causes of plague and death in Denmark. Moreover, from such a perspective, far from getting rid of the mole, defect, fault, blemish, complexion, and habit, and dram (1.4.18ff) that corrode Denmark's noble substance from within,

Hamlet's actions are themselves shown/seen to be this mole, defect, blemish, complexion, habit, dram, just as his ghost is literally shown/seen to be an "old mole" beneath the stage of the Globe theatre (1.5.164). So rather than identify Hamlet's mother's social order as a cancerous "dram of eale [evil?]" within Hamlet's father's world (as Hamlet and the *plot* argue), Shakespeare's *play* reveals that this patriarchal Hamlet would be a lethal "dram of eale" in any modern world.

The emergent labors Shakespeare's play undertakes as a literary tragedy, then, are absolutely opposed to the residual/dominant ones Hamlet undertakes as its patriarchal hero. That is, the *play* is designed to

1. erase, to whatever degree necessary, its audience's previous patriarchal education;
2. redirect whatever is left of this audience's reactionary desires into emergent activities;
3. delegitimize the catharsis-by-violence option Hamlet elects to pursue when all other onstage options are closed out;
4. keep the *plot* of this play and its alleged hero from pouring any more poison into the *play's* audience's ears; and
5. purge from this audience's minds and culture that mole of "Hamlet" and the even older mole of his ghost that, if kept alive and imitated, would annihilate all nonpatriarchal human existence.

The play's objective, then, in contrast to Hamlet's, is to keep people like Polonius, Ophelia, Laertes, Gertrude, Rosencrantz, Guildenstern, Claudius, and Hamlet alive, and to get them completely out of their residual past, if not also well beyond where Gertrude and Claudius have tried to get them. Put in formal terms, the function of this emergent Shakespearean play is to contain and reduce to "nothing" its chief dominant/residual adversary—patriarchy's purge/purify ideology—by showing that what was a heroic necessity in the past is nothing but a tragic crime in the present.

As a literary tragedy then, *Hamlet* closes out *all* of the options apparently available to Hamlet in his own world, a foreclosure that encourages the understanding that although Hamlet does the wrong thing, none of the other options potentially available to him onstage would have been better, if only because none of them hold out against the power of his patriarchal inheritance, the "forms" and "pressures past," inscribed on the tables of his memory. In other words, a viable option/role/identity for Hamlet to act is not available in his Denmark, which is the principal reason why it is a tragic space. The new knowledge that is needed has yet to be invented. And what is worse, Hamlet, for one, has failed to invent it. Until a new option is invented, however, there can be no comedy from the perspective of Shakespeare's theatre, though had this new knowledge not been invented by 1600, there would have been no audience to watch, no theatre in which to act, and no Shakespeare to write *The Tragicall Historie of Hamlet* in 1600.

STUDY QUESTIONS

1. Why do Gertrude and Claudius prevent Hamlet from returning to Wittenberg? How would it change our perception of Hamlet if we didn't know he wanted to return to college?

2. "Drink it like a man!" is allegedly what five-year-old Raymond Giffin of Ft. Worth, Texas, was told by friend, Anthony Jimmeson, 21, before the child drank ten ounces of 90-proof liquor, causing him to lapse into a coma and die (*Newsweek*, March 12, 1990, 17). What does this incident have in common with *Hamlet*?

3. Is it likely that Hamlet's theory about how his father died is correct? Do we ever learn how Hamlet Sr. died? Do we need to know? Does Claudius supply details in the prayer scene?

4. What techniques do all-male military academies like The Citadel (Charleston, SC) use to purge women from their midst and thereby (allegedly) purify their masculine space?

5. On the subject of the validity of the ghost's testimony, consider the following:

> You are a student in my English class, and, like everyone else in the class, you turn in a *Hamlet* paper the third week of the term. A week later I hand your papers back, and announce, without mentioning names, that three members of the class plagiarized their papers. I also mention that since I can't prove this, I had to give these three people the grade they would have gotten had I not been suspicious. Nevertheless, since I am certain they did not write their own papers, and since I can't legally flunk them, I am going to get even by doing everything I can (behind their backs) to destroy their academic careers. I will pass on my suspicions to every other teacher they have this year, and I will, in the future, do likewise with every teacher they will take while they are at this school. If any school or college they apply to in the future asks me for a letter of reference, I will voice the same suspicion in print, though these students won't, of course, have any idea I will be doing so. In brief, I will get my revenge slowly and patiently and, I trust, quite successfully, and the beauty of my method is that they won't know whether I'm doing this to them or not (obviously they can't ask me if I suspect them). Any attempt on their part to prevent me from doing what I am going to do will be read as a confession of guilt. And if they want to know how I know that they plagiarized, I don't mind telling them a

ghost came to me last night at midnight and gave me their names.

What do you think about this strategy? Would you accept a ghost's testimony as valid evidence in such a case? What alternatives to revenge—what other options—would you offer this teacher?

6. What value would Hamlet's father give the purge/purify option Hamlet follows? Would he be angry to learn that Hamlet hands Denmark over to Fortinbras? If so, why? If not, why not?

7. In a recent issue of the *New York Review of Books*, Jason Epstein writes that "people become conservatives when they experience 'the horrible feeling' that a society they took for granted might suddenly cease to exist" (October 16, 1996, 31). Is this what Hamlet is experiencing?

8. How difficult is it to oppose deeply inscribed cultural demands? To what extent is purge/purify written on the tables of your memory?

9. Can one imitate Moses, an angry Yahweh, Samson, John the Baptist, and/or Christ and *not* end up playing Hamlet's lethal purge and purify role, or producing tragic effects?

10. Is Hamlet really responsible for all these deaths? Does he, for example, actually have anything to do with the death of his mother? Does he know that the cup is poisoned?

11. If Hamlet's death is accidental, how could it be part of a program of self-purification? How might his death be staged to indicate that it is not accidental?

12. Is the United States' view that during the Vietnam War it was destroying Vietnamese villages to save them, similar to Hamlet's view of his actions in Denmark?

QUESTIONS AND TOPICS FOR ORAL AND WRITTEN DISCUSSION

1. What is the point of Laertes' advice to his sister (1.3.1–51), particularly his tirade against passionate erotic love? You also might raise the question of Laertes' relation to women and sexuality. Why, for example, does he represent sexuality as warfare?

2. To what extent is Hamlet's instruction to the players (3.2.1 ff) censorship of the sort that Shakespeare's theatre company could not possibly have accepted and remain a successful popular professional company? To what extent do we see Hamlet purposefully *destroy* the capacity

(or at least radically *maim* the ability) of these traveling players to do anything like professional theatre in Elsinore? How would professional theatre threaten the option Hamlet is presently acting?

3. What is going on between Hamlet and Ophelia just before the mouse-trap play? (3.2.109 ff). Why does Hamlet add pornographic material to this theatrical event?

4. Why would dominant and residual critics, directors, and readers reject many of the arguments offered in this chapter? What would they lose if they didn't reject these arguments?

5. Numerous critics argue that the Hamlet found in act 5 is an increasingly healthy specimen of Christianity's premier virtues. They speak of a "regenerate" Hamlet, of his "achieved serenity," his "beautiful disinterestedness." Are they correct in a sense they do not intend?

6. It is often argued that the ghost's demand that Hamlet taint not his mind (1.5.85–86) is "a riddling impossibility." From a Christian perspective, why is it? From a patriarchal one, why isn't it?

7. One of Hamlet's desires is to emulate Hercules—to be a Danish Hercules. The question is whether this ambition is in fact laudable. We read in the April 1998 issue of *Esquire* magazine, for example, that Hercules "fathered more than fifty illegitimate children, killed countless men who had simply annoyed him, and murdered his own wife and children in a blind rage. But he is remembered instead for some mightly unbelievable accomplishments and was once considered the greatest hero ever" (The "Esky" editorial column, 21). Discuss why Hercules was once regarded "the greatest hero ever."

SUGGESTED READINGS AND WORKS CITED

Adelman, Janet. "Man and Wife Is One Flesh: Hamlet and the Confrontation with the Maternal Body." In *Suffocating Mothers: Fantasies of Maternal Origin in Shakespeare's Plays*, Hamlet *to* The Tempest. New York: Routledge, 1992. Chapter reprint in Wofford. See below.

Alexander, Nigel. *Poison, Play, and Duel: A Study in "Hamlet."* London: Routledge and Kegan Paul, 1971.

Barber, C. S., and Richard P. Wheeler. *The Whole Journey: Shakespeare's Power of Development*. Berkeley: University of California Press, 1986.

Bateson, Geoffrey. *Steps to an Ecology of Mind*. New York: Ballantine, 1972.

Becon, Thomas. *Catechism*. London: J. Day, 1564.

Browne, Thomas. *Religio Medici*. London: Andrew Crooke, 1643, sections 38, 88.

Calderwood, James. *To Be and Not to Be: Negation and Metadrama in Hamlet*. New York: Columbia University Press, 1983.

Cavell, Stanley. "Hamlet's Burden of Proof." *Disowning Knowledge*. Cambridge: Cambridge University Press, 1987.

Coddon, Karin. " 'Suche Strange Desygns': Madness, Subjectivity, and Treason in *Hamlet* and Elizabethan Culture." In *William Shakespeare: Hamlet*, edited by Suzanne L. Wofford, 380–402. Boston: St. Martin's Press, 1994.

Garber, Marjorie *Shakespeare's Ghost Writers: Literature as Uncanny Causality*. New York: Methuen, 1987.

Goux, John-Joseph. *Symbolic Economies: After Marx and Freud*. Trans. Jennifer Curtis Gage. Ithaca, NY: Cornell University Press, 1990.

Greenblatt, Stephen. *Renaissance Self-Fashioning: From More to Shakespeare*. Chicago: University of Chicago Press, 1980.

Hattaway, Michael. *Hamlet*. London: Macmillan, 1987.

Johnson, Samuel. *The Plays of Shakespeare*. Vol. 3. London: S. and R. Johnson, 1765, 311.

Leverenz, David. "The Woman in Hamlet: An Interpersonal View." In *Representing Shakespeare: New Psychoanalytic Essays*, edited by Murray M. Schwartz and Coppélia Kahn, 110–28. Baltimore and London: The Johns Hopkins University Press, 1980.

Levin, Harry. *The Question of* Hamlet. London: Oxford, 1959.

Luckacher, Ned. *Demonic Figures: Shakespeare and the Question of Conscience*. Ithaca, NY: Cornell University Press, 1994.

Mack, Maynard. "The World of Hamlet." *Yale Review* 41 (1952), 502–23.

Miller, Alice. *The Drama of the Gifted Child: How Narcissistic Parents Form and Deform the Emotional Lives of Their Talented Children*. New York: Basic Books, 1981.

Montaigne, Michel de. *The Essayes, or Moral, Politike, and Militaire discourses*. Trans. J. Florio. London: V. Sims, 1603.

Rose, Jacqueline. "*Hamlet*—the *Mona Lisa* of Literature." *Critical Quarterly* 28 (1986), 35–49.

———. "Sexuality in the Reading of Shakespeare: *Hamlet* and *Measure for Measure*." In *Alternative Shakespeares*, edited by John Drakakis, 95–118. London: Methuen, 1985.

Wofford, Susanne L. ed. *William Shakespeare: Hamlet*. Boston: St. Martin's Press, 1994.

A TREATISE OF MELANCHOLY.

Contayning the caufes thereof, and reafons of the ftraunge effects it worketh in our minds and bodies: with the Phificke cure, and fpirituall confolation for fuch as haue thereto adioyned afflicted confcience.

The difference betwixt it, and melancholy, with diuerfe philofophicall difcourfes touching actions, and affections of foule, fpirit and body: the particulars whereof are to be feene before the booke.

By T. Bright Doctor of Phificke.

Imprinted at London by Iohn VVindet,
1586.

Title page of Timothy Bright's *A Treatise of Melancholy* (1586). This item is reproduced by permission of The Huntington Library, San Marino, California, RB 53266.

4

Man, Melancholy, and Suicide

> ... melancholy betrays the world for the sake of knowledge.
> But in its tenacious self-absorption it embraces dead objects
> in its contemplation, in order to redeem them.
> —Walter Benjamin

To analyze the malady Hamlet calls "my weakness and my melancholy" (2.2.578), we will catalog the knowledge available in the heads of various characters on stage. This knowledge, however dominant in its own time, is radically, if not tragically, inadequate, and was coming to be seen as such in early modern England. Indeed, Shakespeare's audiences were being asked to reject such dominant knowledge because, despite its ability accurately to catalog the effects of melancholic conditions, such knowledge neither understood the actual causes of melancholic illnesses nor could it prevent or cure such illnesses—major reasons, no doubt, why new knowledge on this subject was emerging in the popular theatres as well as in other contemporary venues to combat what, by 1599, had been a long-standing, exceptionally detailed, and massively textualized tradition, a battle not dissimilar, in fact, to the one taking place in Italy between the rival cosmologies of Galileo and the Catholic church. Despite overwhelming odds, however, this new psychology, like Galileo's new astronomy, was on its way to victory, as the preface of a 1607 text by one of the last advocates of the old "humoral" knowledge, Thomas Walkington, defensively acknowledges in *The Optick Glasse of Humors*: "I know the Parascelsian will utterly condemn my endeavor for bringing the four Humors on the stage again, they having hissed them off so long ago" (1607, 10).

To understand this older "humoral" view of melancholy it is necessary to begin with the alleged fact that "Man . . . the head and chief of all that ever God wrought . . . the portraiture of the universal world . . . a marvelous and cunning piece of work" (Laurens 1599), did *not* suffer melancholic diseases in his Edenic past. And given that early modern men frequently wrote about the pleasures and vicissitudes of their everyday existence under the guise of cosmic allegories, we may extrapolate, from various accounts of man's prelapsarian (pre-fallen, Edenic) centrality in a Christian cosmos, a sense of how Hamlet may be remembering the situation in which he previously existed, a royal space he surely regarded as being created and preserved for himself, and in which he would remain central despite his differences and distancings with respect to this world in the past. In other words, Hamlet's view of his previous situation at Elsinore duplicates on a smaller scale the picture of man's position in the cosmos depicted by Pierre la Primaudaye, an early modern French philosopher:

> When I direct my flight now and then . . . even unto the heavens, and with the wings of contemplation behold their wonderful greatness . . . when I withdraw my spirit lower into the elementary region, to admire and wonder at the situation and spreading of the earth amidst the waters . . . when I admire the diversity of times and seasons, the continual spring of fountains, the certain course of rivers, and generally, so many wonderful works under the cope of heaven, I cannot marvel enough at the excellency of Man, for whom all these things were created, and are maintained and preserved in their being and moving, by one and the same divine providence. (1594, I:i, 4–5)

But if man and Hamlet held such privileged positions in the past, obviously neither do so in the present, and of the early modern treatments of man's displacement from cosmic centrality to the melancholic condition of his present radical decenteredness, none, perhaps, is as evocative as the first section of Robert Burton's massive *Anatomy of Melancholy*. Burton was by no means the first to detail the erosion of man's excellence, but few texts in the period allow us to catch in such brief space what Hamlet must have felt after the devastating collapse of his father's Denmark and his place in that paternal order. Burton's massive, encyclopedic text was published years after *Hamlet* was written; nevertheless, by collecting knowledge commonplace throughout the preceding century, it provides access to the archetype shaping Hamlet's sense of the "pitiful change" that makes it impossible for him to marvel any longer at the excellence of man or the heavens:

Man, the most excellent, and most noble creature of the World . . . a model of the World, Sovereign Lord of the Earth, and sole Commander and Governor of all the Creatures in it . . . created to God's own Image, to that immortal and incorporeal substance, with all the faculties and powers belonging unto it, was at first pure, divine, perfect, happy . . . free from all manner of infirmities. . . . But this most noble creature . . . O pitiful change, is fallen from that he was . . . [and has] become . . . a castaway, a caitiff, one of the most miserable creatures of the World. . . . [Because of him] the earth [is] accursed, the influence of stars altered, the four elements, Beasts, Birds, Plants, are now ready to offend us. . . . The Heavens threaten us with their Comets, Stars, Planets. . . . The greatest enemy to man, is man himself. . . . That which crucifies us most, is our own folly, want of government . . . by which means we metamorphize ourselves, and degenerate into beasts . . . transform ourselves, overthrow our constitutions, provoke God to anger, and heap upon us this of *Melancholy*, and all manner of incurable diseases, as a just and deserved punishment of our sins. (1621, fols. A1–4)

Instead of the dominant man Hamlet had been in the sun of his father's masculine court, or the sun he expected to be following his father's death, Hamlet finds himself merely "in the sun" of a stepfather who (in his mind) destroyed his world by stealing its phallic resources. Thus, cast down from his previous mountain into an archaic female position, unable to do anything but "batten" [grow fat] on his own personal moor, and unaccustomed to the melancholy/melancholia created by such a sudden and wholly undesired access to his formerly repressed feelings of powerlessness, rage, and marginality, Hamlet, no longer the man he once was, admits "I have of late, but wherefore I know not, lost all my mirth, forgone all custom of exercise" (2.2.287–88). "Denmark's a prison" (2.2.239). The cosmos, bereft of its customary substance, is nothing but garbage: a "weary, stale, flat and unprofitable . . . sterile promontory" [i.e., a nonphallic, penilized lump] (1.2.133–34; 2.2.290). The heavens, once the location and source of life itself, have become "a foul and pestilent congregation [mass] of vapors" (2.2.293). Life is nothing but "outrageous fortune," "a sea of troubles," "Th'oppressor's wrong," "fardels" [burdens] to bear, "ills" (3.1.58 ff). And women, once chaste wives inside (or whores outside) the pales and forts of masculine space, are now seen to be indiscriminate mixtures, hiding their fickle, pernicious natures under misleading "paint" and treacherous disguises. The point is not that Hamlet, depressed, loses interest in the world around him; rather, the point is that this world, now rotten, is no longer the source of the powers and possibilities it once possessed. And in the wake of such a catastrophic loss, Hamlet has become a melancholic thing "of nothing."

Needless to say, Hamlet's melancholic reaction to decenteredness was not at all uncommon in early modern England. What we see in the mirror *Hamlet* holds up to Elizabethan society is that sociopolitical forces were dispossessing, disillusioning, and enraging large numbers of young gentlemen who had assumed that centrality was a natural and inevitable given (just as affirmative action legislation has decentered and enraged numerous white males and some females, who likewise regard their superiority and cultural centrality as natural and inevitable givens).

In the wake of such widespread destabilizing displacements, numerous doctors and theologians addressed themselves to the problem of how to understand and treat an increase of male melancholy that was becoming a virtual epidemic. Their knowledge concerning melancholy, however, though frequently insightful, was in the main confusingly encyclopedic and for the most part utterly inadequate, if not self-contradictory. Nevertheless, the knowledge these writers had on this subject, though blind to the actual causes of melancholy, is explicable if one begins with physics.

PHYSICS

The fundamental premise of early modern physics, like classical physics before it, was that "all natural bodies have their composition of the mixture of the elements, fire, air, water, earth" (Walkington 1607, 75). Jacob Bronowski and Bruce Mazlish's *The Western Intellectual Tradition* (1960) offers a modern version:

All things in nature were thought [prior to the scientific revolution] . . . to be compounded from a number of fundamental elements. The number which Aristotle had accepted, and which became general, was four . . . air and fire, water and earth. The elements were held to follow what we should want to call laws; but it would be wrong to think of their pattern of movement as if it had, or was meant to have, the exact sequence which we now seek in a natural law. The elements did not so much obey a law as express and follow their own ideal natures. The elements of water and of earth moved downward when they could, because they were striving to reach their own natural centers. The elements of air and of fire moved upward, again in order to reach their natural centers. . . . The striving of the elements to reach their true centers kept the world going. A piece of soil, for example, although it was not wholly earth, was mainly so; and therefore it strove to return to the earth. Each element had as it were a will of its own, and this will drove it to seek to fulfill its own essence. These strivings . . . kept nature going, not as a machine but as a hierarchy: a hierarchy in which each element was looking for its own fulfillment of itself. If ever that universal fulfillment were reached, nature would achieve completion; the universe would stand still and, in standing still, become God's perfect handiwork, no longer restless but fixed for ever. (109–10)

Given the terms of this physics, it was not accidental that man saw himself as being originally composed of rising fire and air, whereas women were nothing but falling earth and water, despite the fact that as a result of original sin these differently gendered materials were seen as being temporarily and indiscriminately mixed together. Despite this calamity, the eventual purgation of all archaic residues of female water and earth from man would (men thought) complete man's male deity's handiwork, and return man and his universe to their original unfallen perfection.

PHYSIOLOGY

As it had in the classical past, this elemental physics provided early moderns with a foundation for a humoral physiology. Just as four physical elements constituted everything in the universe (or macrocosm), so four physiological humors constituted the human body (or microcosm):

1. *blood*, hot and moist like air;
2. *phlegm*, cold and moist like water;
3. *yellow bile* (or yellow choler), hot and dry like fire; and
4. *black bile* (or black choler), cold and dry like earth.

La Primaudaye (1594) puts it well:

> We understand by a Humor, a liquid and running body into which the food is converted in the liver, to this end that bodies might be nourished and preserved by them. And as there are four elements ... so there are four sorts of humors answerable to their natures, being all mingled together with the blood. ... Now, concerning the first of them, we are to know that the proper nature of blood is to be hot and moist: wherein it answers to the nature of air. It is temperate, sweet, and fatty, as also the best and chief part of nourishment. ... Next, that thin skim which is seen on the top of it [i.e., on the top of the blood], resembling the flower of wine, is that humor that is called yellow choler, or the choleric humor which is hot and dry, of a bitter taste, and answering to the nature of fire. ... Moreover, those small streams of water, which we see mingled in the blood, proceed of the phlegmatic humor that is cold and moist, like to water of whose nature it holds. ... Lastly, the black humor and most earthy, which looks like the very bottom of a deep, red, and thick wine, or like the lees in a vessel full of wine or oil, is the melancholic humor, or as some term it, black choler, being cold and dry like to the earth, with which it hath some agreement. (II:lxiv, 523–24)

PSYCHOLOGY

Physiology in turn supplied the basis for early modern psychology in the sense that the properties and proportions of a person's physiological humors determined his/her psychological temperament, complexion, or temperature (a person's character or personality). In humoral terms, it is possible to think of one's body as a quartet of musical instruments performing in three strikingly different fashions.

1. If your four humors are in balance, you are a happy, productive, vital, spontaneous person, though, for most early modern theorists, such "an excellent and golden temperature . . . must only be understood and seen with the internal eyes of reason, seeing it has not [had] a real existence" since the fall of man (Walkington 1607, 151).

2. To the degree that one of your four humors plays somewhat louder or at a different tempo than the other three, you have what the age called a natural complexion or "temperature": that is, you were *sanguine* (optimistic to silly), *choleric* (angry to violent), *phlegmatic* (dull to slothful), or *melancholic* (gloomy to depressed) to the degree that your blood, yellow choler, phlegm, or black bile predominated (*melancholy* is borrowed from Greek, *melan*, black, *choli*, bile). La Primaudaye provides a useful introduction to this psychology:

> Hereof it is, that when there is excess of the phlegmatic humour in men, their natures are commonly slothful, they shun labor, and give themselves to bodily pleasures, they love dainties, and delicate meats and drinks, they are tender and effeminate, and clean contrary to stout and valiant men. And if there be excess of the choleric humor, their natures are easily provoked and stirred up to wrath: but their anger is as fire of thorns, that being kindled and making a great noise, is by and by quenched again. Their gestures also are more quick and vehement, and their hastiness is commonly foolish and turbulent: they babble much, and are like to vessels full of holes, unable to hold in and keep any secret matter: they are fierce in assailing, but inconstant in sustaining the assault, in some sort resembling the nature of dogs, which bark and bite if they can, and afterward fly away. And if there be excess of the melancholic humor, the natures of such are sad, still, hard to please, suspicious, conceited, obstinate, some more and some less. (II:lxviii, 535)

Note the implicit gendering of phlegm and black bile as female, which is another way of saying that for a man to be melancholic or phlegmatic is to be in the female position—that is, to have an excess of water and earth and, as a result, a deficiency of phallic blood and choler, air and fire.

3. To the degree, however, that one or more of your humors are "adust" (have been burnt) due to excessive heat, you would suffer one of the unnatural forms of these humors, or what modern medical discourse would term mental illnesses. La Primaudaye adds to the passage cited above, "if the choleric and melancholic humors be corrupt and mingled together, . . . their natures become monstrous, proud, full of envy, fraud, subtleties, venomous and poisonfull, hateful and diabolical," a condition commented on at greater length in a passage by Timothy Bright from *A Treatise of Melancholy*:

> Besides the former kinds, there are sorts of unnatural melancholia . . . of another nature far disagreeing from the other. . . . They rise of [from] the natural humors . . . by excessive distemper of heat, burned as it were into ashes in comparison of humor, by which the humor of like nature being mixed, turns in into a sharp lye. . . . This sort raises the greatest tempest of perturbations and most of all destroys the brain with all his faculties, and disposition of action, and makes both it, and the heart cheer more uncomfortably: and if it rise of the natural melancholy, beyond all likelihood of truth, [it will] frame monstrous terrors of fear and heaviness without cause. (1586, 110–11)

BLACK BILE, MELANCHOLY, MELANCHOLIA: CAUSE, SYMPTOMS, EFFECTS

As we have seen, when black bile predominates over the other humors in the body, natural melancholy results. However, should one's sludge-like black bile become corrupted by excessive heat, turn into noxious fumes, rise into the brain, and infect one's mental faculties (imagination, reason, memory), then *melancholia* results, a disease that is chronic and degenerative. In *The Whole Treatise* (1606), William Perkins illustrates the difference:

> Touching that which comes by Melancholy, sundry things are to be considered. . . . 1. First of all, if it be asked what Melancholy is? I answer, it is a kind of earthy and black blood, specially in the spleen, corrupted and distempered. . . . 2. The second is, what are the effects and operations of Melancholia? *Ans.* . . . There is no humor,

yea nothing in man's body, that has so strange effects as this humor has being once distempered. . . . Now the effects thereof . . . are of two sorts. The first is in the brain and head. For this humor being corrupted, it sends up noisome fumes as clouds or mists which do corrupt the imagination, and makes the instrument of reason unfit for understanding and sense. Hence follows the first effect, strange imaginations, conceits and opinions framed in the mind. . . . [And] because it corrupts the instrument [i.e., the mind], and the instrument being corrupted, the faculty cannot bring forth good actions. (I:2, 193)

For these reasons, it was not accidental that black bile diseases were greatly feared, not to mention the subject of much of the black ink that was expended in treatises on humoral conditions and illnesses, particularly with respect to the issue of *causation*, since effective techniques of medical intervention and prevention required this sort of practical knowledge.

For the religious, original sin was, as Burton indicates, the principal cause of melancholy; nevertheless, this sin was regarded as creating a potential for melancholy, since even though everyone is tainted with such sin only a few became moody, depressed, and suicidal. Regional causes also figured large in discussions: to be born in Scorpio or have Saturn dominant in one's horoscope, to be aged or a native of dryer, cooler, northern regions like Scandinavia or Scotland made one particularly susceptible to excesses of black bile; however, these were likewise seen more as contributing factors than as causes. Therefore, in need of practical ways to prevent and cure melancholic conditions, early modern doctors and ministers turned desperately (and futilely) to a number of specific causes. Knowing from their classical sources that black bile is dry and cold, they concluded that anything which "deprives the body of its natural heat and moisture," such as foods known to dry and chill the body, could cause melancholy (Babb 1951, 103). Similarly, to spend hours studying—for some, to read even a single book—could bring on depression, since studies "have great force to procure melancholia: if they be vehement, and of difficult matters, and high mysteries" (Bright 1586, 243). Indeed, this view of the danger of reading underwrites Hamlet's book scene with Polonius (2.2.169 ff), since for a man who is melancholic, if not mad, to have a book in his hands is to offer Hamlet's years of study at Wittenberg as a probable cause for his condition. Hamlet's madness is no more out of place in a library than in England where, as a gravedigger puts it, "the men are as mad as he" (5.1.142–43).

Though understanding melancholy was important, of far greater importance was knowing what caused *melancholia*. So numerous theorists asked, What allows a dram of black bile to so 'o' releaven' a person that in time it brings this person's noble substance to disrepair and scandal, if not despair, madness and death? In surveying their answers to this question (ones not dissimilar to Hamlet's), these writers were positioned in such a way that they could not identify melancholia's actual causes, but could only isolate peripheral, imaginary, or secondary causes. (Note that black bile itself is a wholly imaginary substance, just as the alleged motion of the sun around the earth is a wholly imaginary motion. Note, too, that black bile and the sun's alleged movements were concepts absolutely necessary to early modern dominant/residual power structures; thus, neither of these concepts was fully replaced until these structures themselves were replaced.)

Causes of Melancholia

What, then, caused black bile not just to play louder than the other humoral instruments, but, as it were, to lose tune and tempo so completely as to ruin the ensemble? What caused black bile to turn into noxious fumes that rotted the faculties of one's brain? In answering such questions, theorists correctly understood that *melancholia* was caused in part by traumatic loss: "Sorrow," Burton writes, is *"the mother and daughter of melancholy, her epitome, symptom, and chief cause"* (*Partition* I: 298). (Note, again, the degree to which male theorists like Burton felt the need to feminize this process.)

Among the kinds of loss early modern theorists catalogued were *object* losses (loss of a father, lover, friend, etc.), *attribute* losses (loss of one's social position, wealth, youth, physical strength, appearance or capabilities, or the proper functioning of one's mental faculties), and what may be called *subjunctive* losses (the failure of an expectation or wish with respect to a desired social position, erotic object, or ability). Of these sorts of losses, two particularly exercised early modern commentators: (1) loss of a specific erotic object, and (2) loss of a specific position within a social system, which is why these terms are the ones those onstage turn to to account for Hamlet's melancholy—Polonius confident that it is the result of Hamlet's thwarted love for Ophelia, Gertrude certain that it is "no other but the main / His fathers death, and our o'erhasty marriage" (2.2.56–57), and Hamlet and Claudius just as certain that it is Hamlet's frustrated ambition.

Effects of Loss I: Love Melancholia

Consider Hamlet's entrance into Ophelia's closet with "his stockings fouled, / Ungartered, and down-gyved to his ankle" (2.1.80–81; as gyves were fetters or shackles, down-gyved would mean that Hamlet's stockings, fallen around his ankles, acted like fetters). André du Laurens helps clarify why an early modern audience would *not* have thought Polonius mad to think Hamlet love mad, particularly since *love melancholia* had been commonplace in English culture at least as far back as Chaucer's *Troylus and Criseyde*: "Because he wanted to die, he neither ate or drank, for his melancholy" (V.1216).

Love therefore having abused the eyes . . . does suddenly imprint a burning desire to obtain the thing, which is or seems worthy to be beloved . . . but fearing herself too weak to encounter with reason, the principal part of the mind, she [i.e., love] posts in haste to the heart, to surprise and win the same: whereof when she is once sure . . . she afterward assays [tests] and sets upon reason, and all the other principal powers of the mind so fiercely, as that she subdues them, and makes them her vassals and slaves. Then is all spoiled, the man is quite undone and cast away. (1599, 118)

In reading this passage note the parallels male writers posit between passion and melancholy: both catastrophically destroy an initial state of male perfection, and both, alleged to be female in nature, come from down under or outside man's self—that is, from the female regions. Neither originates in man's mind nor is part of his essential psychic equipment. Both *penetrate* rational man from without, causing his noble, phallic self to be transformed (in the worst case scenario) into a strumpet's fool, a mere penile nothing, a worm: "then is all spoiled, the man is quite undone and cast away."

Effects of Loss II: Malcontentedness

At the end of the sixteenth century, a large number of young gentlemen no longer able to secure or maintain noble, not to mention heroic places in masculine structures of power, finding themselves superfluous, and hearing their sense of thwarted ambition, disappointment, alienation, and neglected superiority anticipated onstage by Hamlet's "I eat the air promise-crammed," "I lack advancement," and "while the grass grows, the proverb is something musty" (3.2.85–86, 314–15), became melancholic *malcontents*. Their excessive discontents, cares, crosses, miseries bubbled up, like Hamlet's, as satirical railing against, if not as active efforts to destroy the power structures that denied them entrance and centrality, as well as against the women whom they regarded as the cause of their failures. In fact, these malcontent types came to be as common on the streets of London (due in large part to the popularity of *Hamlet*) as in the drama of the first decades of the seventeenth century, with the result that the markers of malcontentedness quickly became conventional: "surly preoccupation . . . and unsociability . . . ; negligent disorder in dress; sense of superiority; tendency to rail enviously at an unappreciative world; inclination toward treachery and sedition," not to mention the characteristic attire and attitude of those, like Hamlet in his "inky cloak," who wore nothing but black, and stood "with folded arms, hat pulled low, and eyes morosely fixed" (Babb 1951, 83, 119).

Effects of Loss III: Other Symptoms of Melancholia

In addition to constructing Hamlet as love-mad and malcontented, the tropes catalogued in contemporary treatises on melancholy and melancholia also shaped Hamlet's behavior in numerous other respects. In fact, were we to unravel the implications of Claudius's line, "O'er which his melancholy sits on brood" (3.1.164), we would see that Claudius rather contemptuously regards Hamlet as a hen sitting over enough of the conventional markers of melancholy/melancholia to make his character a virtual anthology of its symptoms.

1. Hamlet's disinclination to be "in the sun" occurs in many treatises. In André du Laurens, *A Discovrse of the Preservation of the Sight* (1599), for example: "Melancholic men are . . . enemies

to the Sun, and shun the light, because their spirits and humors are altogether contrary to the light" (96).

2. Hamlet's sense that melancholy endows him with superior abilities originates from a text, *Problemata XXX*, attributed to Aristotle, that posits black bile as the source of genius: "Why is it that all those who have become eminent in philosophy or politics or poetry or the arts are melancholic, and some to such an extent that they are infected by diseases caused by black bile? . . . But many are affected by the diseases of madness or frenzy, which accounts for the Sibyls, soothsayers, and all inspired persons, when their condition is due not to disease but to a natural mixture" (953a10–14, translated by W. S. Hett).

3. Elements of Hamlet's antic disposition are also recognizable symptoms of black bile disorders. According to Timothy Bright, the melancholic often gives himself over to "unbridled laughter, rising not from any comfort of the heart, or gladness of spirit, but from a disposition in such sort altered, as by error of conceit, that gesture is in a counterfeit manner bestowed upon that disagreeing passion, whose nature is rather to extinguish itself with tears, then assuaged by the sweet breath of cheerfulness" [i.e., the melancholic laughs in uncontrolled fashion in order to mask the disagreeable passions and tears of his condition under an illusion of happiness] (1586, Chapter 18, 111; see also Bright's remarks on Sardonian laughter below).

4. Bright and others also regard procrastination an attribute of melancholy: "[the melancholic is] *doubtful before, and long in deliberation:* suspicious, painful in study, and circumspect, given to fearful and terrible dreams . . . because these domestic fears, or that internal obscurity, causes an opinion of danger in outward affairs where there is no cause of doubt" (Bright 1586, 124, 131).

5. Unstable plots and intrigues of the sort Hamlet pursues are, Thomas Walkington's *The Optick Glasse of Hvmors* (1607) tells us, likewise characteristic of melancholics: "oftentimes the melancholic man by his contemplative faculty, by his assiduity of sad and serious meditation is a brocher [instigator] of dangerous Machiavellisme, an inventor of stratagems, quirks, and policies, which are never put in practice" (129).

6. More important, virtually every theorist saw hallucinations and delusions as the most spectacular and disturbing effects of

melancholic diseases. Two passages cited below document the fact that melancholics were commonly seen as fabricating ghosts and apparitions that they regarded as real. Despite predating *Hamlet*, the excerpts read as though they are describing the process by which Hamlet produces his father's ghost.

(a) "True it is, that many men do falsely persuade themselves that they see or hear ghosts: for that which they imagine they see or hear, proceeds either of melancholia, madness, weakness of the senses, fear, or of some other perturbation" (Lavater 1572, 9–10).

(b) "The perturbations of melancholy are for the most part fearful . . . and sometimes merry in appearance, through a kind of Sardonian, and false laughter. . . . Those which are sad and pensive rise of that melancholic humor. . . . This for the most part is settled in the spleen, and with his vapors annoys the heart and, passing up to the brain, counterfeits terrible objects to the fantasy, and polluting both the substance and spirits of the brain, causes it without external occasion to forge monstrous fictions . . . which the judgment, taking as they are presented by the disordered instrument, deliver over to the heart, which has no judgment of discretion in itself, but giving credit to the mistaken report of the brain, breaks out into that inordinate passion against reason. . . . For where that natural and internal light is darkened, there fancies arise vain, false, and void of ground: even as in the external sensible darkness, a false illusion will appear unto our imagination, which the light being brought in is discerned to be an abuse of fancy. . . . This causes not only fantastical apparitions wrought by apprehension only of common sense, but fantasy, another part of internal sense, compounds and forges disguised shapes, which give great terror unto the heart. . . . Neither only is common sense and fantasy thus overtaken with delusion, but memory also receives a wound . . . which disables it both to keep in memory, and to record those things, whereof it took some custody before this passion . . . [was] defaced" (Bright 1586, Chapter xvii: "*How melancholy procureth feare, sadnes, dispaire, and such other passions*").

7. And, finally, Hamlet's contemplation of suicide was proverbial for the melancholic: "This black melancholy humor . . . will make the spirit & mind darkish, whereby it grows to be blockish, & the heart loses all his cheerfulness . . . which causes a man to hate & to be weary of all things, even of the light & of a man's self

so that he shall take pleasure in nothing but in his melancholy . . . refusing all joy & consolation. To conclude, some grow so far as to hate themselves, & so fall to despair, yea many kill & destroy themselves" (La Primaudaye 1586, 467).

STUDY QUESTIONS

1. Keeping in mind the passage from Burton's *Anatomy of Melancholy* cited at the beginning of this chapter, speculate as to what kind of man Hamlet was before his father died.

2. When does Hamlet's melancholy turn into *melancholia*? Why does this happen?

3. To what extent are malcontentedness and love-melancholy regular features of our culture's books and films? What gets men over these sorts of melancholy?

4. Explain why black bile, a wholly imaginary substance, was as necessary to dominant/residual structures of power as the equally imaginary belief that the sun circled the earth.

5. Why is it difficult for men in patriarchal cultures to avoid being melancholic, so much so in fact, that, as Robert Burton recognized, it is virtually impossible to be a patriarchal man and not be depressed: "from these Melancholy Dispositions, no man living is free, no Stoic, none so wise, none so happy, so patient, so generous, so godly, so divine, that can vindicate himself, so well composed, but more or less, sometime or other, he feels the smart of it" (1621 Folio A4).

6. Why was it necessary for the patriarchal authors of these early modern treatises on melancholy to cite a female cause for this disease?

7. Why did these theorists consider earth and water female, air and fire male? What are some of the far-reaching effects of this kind of gender labeling?

8. What would be the effect, from the perspective of these treatises, of letting women (or anything regarded as being female) into heaven?

QUESTIONS AND TOPICS FOR WRITTEN AND ORAL DISCUSSION

1. What is problematic about humoral psychology and why are these dominant/residual analyses of melancholic conditions hopelessly inadequate?

2. We tend to think, by analogy to our raw sensations of pain and pleasure, that our emotions are caused by external circumstances. Given this dominant way of thinking, it is difficult to rethink emotions as learned strategies that we use to accomplish a variety of tasks. Using rage, for example, discuss the general tasks we engineer such an emo-

tion to perform. Then ask if the same tasks could be accomplished with different tools? Is rage more economical, a better or worse way of accomplishing such tasks than these alternatives, if there are such? And why do we need to believe (or, at least, why have we been taught to believe) that emotions are phenomena that happen to us rather than technological strategies we use?

3. Discuss the conditions in which Hamlet is allowed to enjoy passionate sexual pleasure. What are the advantages and disadvantages of such an arrangement from an emergent perspective?

4. On the basis of what you have read, explain why patriarchal men have nothing but contempt for psychoanalysis, feminism, and other emergent analytical discourses.

SUGGESTED READINGS AND WORKS CITED

Aristotle. *Problems*. [322 B.C.]. Translated by W. S. Hett. Cambridge, MA: Harvard University Press, 1983.

Babb, Lawrence. *The Elizabethan Malady: A Study of Melancholia in English Literature from 1580 to 1642*. East Lansing: Michigan State College Press, 1951.

Bright, Timothy. *Treatise of Melancholy, Containing the Cavses thereof, & reasons of the strange effects it worketh in our minds and bodies*. London: Thomas Vautrollier, 1586.

Bronowski, J. and Bruce Mazlish. *The Western Intellectual Tradition*. New York: Harper and Row, 1960.

Burton, Robert. *The Anatomy of Melancholy, What it is. With all the Kindes, Cavses, Symptomes, Pronostickes, and Seuerall Cvres of it*. Oxford: Iohn Lichfield, 1621.

Chaucer, Geoffrey. *The Works of Geoffrey Chaucer*. Edited by F. N. Robinson. 2nd ed. Boston: Houghton Mifflin, 1961.

Foucault, Michel. *Madness and Civilization: A History of Insanity in the Age of Reason*. New York: Vintage, 1967.

Freud, Sigmund. "Mourning and Melancholia" [1917]. In *A Standard Edition of the Complete Psychological Works*. London: The Hogarth Press, 1957. Vol. 14, 243–258.

Irigaray, Luce. *Speculum of the Other Woman*. Translated by Gillian C. Gill. Ithaca: Cornell University Press, 1985.

Jackson, Stanley W. *Melancholia and Depression*. New Haven: Yale University Press, 1989.

Kristeva, Julia. *Black Sun: Depression and Melancholia*. Translated by Leon S. Roudiez. New York: Columbia University Press, 1989.

La Primaudaye, Pierre. *The French Academie*. Translated by Thomas Bowes. London: G. Bishop, 1594.

Laurentius, Andreas [André du Laurens]. *A Discovrse of the Preservation of the Sight: of Melancholike Diseases; of rheumes, and of Old age*. Translated by Richard Surphlet. London: Felix Kingston, 1599.

Lavater, Ludwig [Lewes]. *Of ghostes and spirites, walking at nyght, And of straunge noyses, crackes, and sundrie forewarnings*. Translated by R. Harrison. London: H. Benneyman, 1572.

MacDonald, Michael. *Mystical Bedlam*. Cambridge: Cambridge University Press, 1981.

Perkins, William. *The Whole Treatise of the Cases of Conscience, Distinguished into Three Bookes*. London: Iohn Legat, 1606.

Walkington, Thomas. *The Optick Glasse of Hvmors, Or the touchstone of a golden temperature . . . Wherein the foure complections Sanguine, Cholericke, Phligmaticke, Melancholicke are succintly painted forth*. London: J. Windet, 1607.

5

Enter Ghost . . . Exit Ghost

> But what if *two* people claim to see a ghost?
> —Terry Castle, "Contagious Folly"

There is no ghost in the legendary source for *Hamlet*. Apparently one was first added to this material by the author of the no longer extant Ur-*Hamlet*, a play produced in or before 1589 that featured a "ghost which cried . . . miserably at the Theatre, like an oyster-wife, *Hamlet, revenge*" (Jenkins 1982, 83). Why was a ghost needed in this earlier "Hamlet" play, not to mention in *Hamlet*? What problems could a ghost solve that no other theatrical device would solve as well? In Chapter 3, we discussed this question in terms of Hamlet's needs and desires. It is necessary now to see how this question can be answered for the culture at large and, as importantly, for popular public theatres. Two concerns claim our attention: how and why early modern English culture gradually derealized ghosts and spirits. Why it did so was because ghosts functioned, in the main, to prevent significant change; how it did so was to make ghosts more and more negative until they could be staged in theatres as embodiments of social formations emergent elements of English culture could no longer tolerate.

To organize this complex material—and introduce the numerous documents excerpted below—it is helpful to list the kinds of

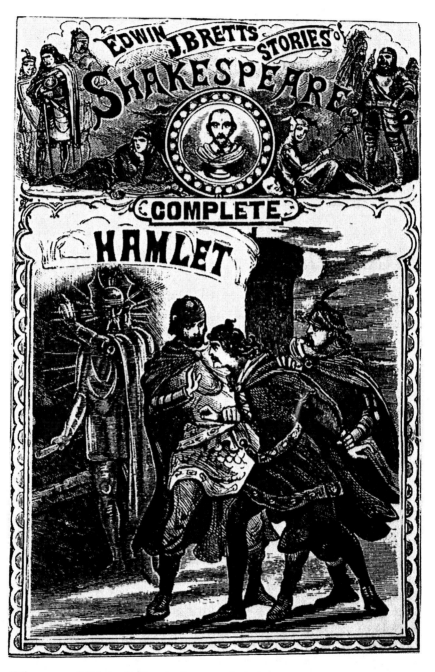

Title page of Edwin J. Brett's *Stories of Shakespeare* (nineteenth century). Courtesy of the Davidson Library, University of California, Santa Barbara.

ghosts constructed and used by early modern (1) Catholics, (2) Protestants, (3) skeptics, and (4) theatres. The objective is not to answer the long-debated questions: "Is the ghost in *Hamlet* real or not?" or "Is it Catholic, pagan, or Protestant?"—questions that reduce Hamlet's ghost to one or another impossible and pointless unity. Rather, to borrow an insight from Mary Douglas, a famous anthropologist, the objective is to see that a ghost "is never a unique, isolated event. . . . For the only way in which [ghosts] make sense is in reference to a total structure of thought. . . ." (1966, 36, 42).

A crucial thing to do when trying to understand early modern apparitions is not to collapse six of their kinds into one; moreover, it is the last of these six, stage ghosts, that gets the most overlooked but is, for our purposes, finally the most important. For early modern Catholics, five kinds of apparitions operated in the everyday world on virtually a daily basis: (1) angels from heaven, (2) ghosts of the dead temporarily returned from purgatory, (3) demons from hell disguised as ghosts of dead persons, (4) ghost-hallucinations in the minds of the mad, and (5) ghost-frauds perpetuated by criminals. Protestants reduced this Catholic array to the last three, deciding in the first place that God no longer needed to use angels to send messages from heaven since he communicated with his true believers directly through the medium of the Holy Ghost, and, in the second, that since purgatory does not exist, neither do purgatorial ghosts. Skeptics further reduced this array to the last two on the ground that, as hell also does not exist, neither do demonic apparitions. For skeptics convinced, in Francis Bacon's terms, that ghosts are "idols imposed by words . . . names of things which do not exist" (1620, 69), ghosts became nothing but hallucinations or frauds. In other words, "preternatural phenomena were demonized" by Protestant doctrine, and then, in the minds of the skeptics, "the demons were deleted, leaving only the natural causes" with the result that a ghost became "a new kind of fact" that signified nothing more than what it tells us about the contents of some person's head (Datson 1991, 250). The point of these reductions is clear: the more a culture desires to maintain a status quo, the more likely it is to construct ghosts as real, whereas the more it wants to embrace significant change the more it will de-realize ghostly remnants of its past and the social formations these ghosts helped construct.

STAGE GHOSTS

Up to this point we have been discussing ghosts as everyday people thought of them. If we turn now to the theatres, it is clear that these venues borrowed the ghosts of everyday life, imitating all five categories on their stages. However, in addition to functioning for characters on stage as ghosts did in everyday life—narrating events in the past, enforcing church authority, demanding revenge, saying goodbye to a loved one, among other things— stage ghosts also performed functions (modelled on the use of stage ghosts in the classical plays of Aeschylus, Sophocles and Seneca) specific to playwrights and theatre audiences. Of several, one is particularly crucial for *Hamlet*, namely the use of a stage ghost, patterned after the ghost of Achilles mentioned in Euripides and Seneca, to epitomize a social formation, Hamlet's father's world, that insists on lifting its head in Denmark's present as a way of refusing to die. In contrast then to the ghost Hamlet constructs to serve his purposes, Shakespeare's play uses Hamlet's ghost, as Hamlet also does, to embody the patriarchal past undermining Gertrude's new Denmark. But where Hamlet assigns positive value to this ghostly embodiment of Denmark's past, Shakespeare's *Hamlet* negates it.

GROUP SIGHTINGS

"But what if *two* people claim to see a ghost?" What if *eleven* sightings of the ghost are experienced by *four* different people in *Hamlet*? The paradoxical answer that follows is that a person may see a ghost, but that a person never sees one solely by him/herself, since anyone who sees a ghost is always already part of a culture or subculture that sees/needs/constructs ghosts and teaches their members to do likewise. So, for four people to see the same ghost means that four people share the same cultural codes, need the same problem (or a similar one) solved, and conspire, however unwittingly, to solve it with a tried and true technology: *Enter ghost!* From an emergent perspective, then, it is no more difficult to explain group hallucinations than individual ones. In fact, group hallucinations are the best evidence that ghosts are structural elements of specific cultures. In other words, every ghost sighting is always already a group sighting, a group hallucination (whether the group is physically present or not). More to the point, patriarchal cultures of the past not only encouraged but required collective sightings: all early modern Catholics must see ghosts, all Protestants must deny purgatorial ghosts. This is why the number of persons viewing a ghost is irrelevant in terms of evidence: for those who need ghosts (who believe in them), one witness is as good as a thousand, just as for those who do not, a thousand witnesses are no more convincing than one.

But how is it that *two* soldiers see the ghost of Hamlet's father *before* Horatio or Hamlet do? Four scenarios follow.

1. A small group of disillusioned soldiers suffering stress and anxieties after the death of their leader and needing what Hamlet needs—an image of their past heroic leader—read Hamlet's mind and give him what he desires, the spirit of "the king [his] father" (1.2.191).

2. Having tried other ways of getting Hamlet to act in phallic fashion like his father, and convinced they have to turn Hamlet into a warlord so as not to have to depend (in their minds) on an effeminized Claudius to deal with Fortinbras, a splinter group in the army conspires to put Hamlet in a situation where it can say, "We saw 'a figure like your father, / Armed at point exactly, cap a pe' " [from head to foot] (1.2.199–200).

3. Having read Machiavelli and needing a ghost for the reasons cited in Chapter 3, Hamlet tells Marcellus, his most loyal soldier: You saw a ghost the last two nights, didn't you, soldier? And you will see it again tonight, and you will convince the sharer of your watch that he saw it too (you'll know the best man to employ), and the two of you will bend Horatio to your view, and then the three of you will come and tell me about the ghost you saw, won't you, soldier?

4. *All* of these scenarios happen unconsciously and simultaneously without anyone in this military subculture needing to say anything to anyone else, since in a culture where a situation arises in which a ghost needs to appear, it appears, the stage having been set for its entrance long before it hears itself repeating the lines it is needed to say!

It would not have been a problem for skeptical and/or emergent thinkers in early modern England to hear Hamlet's father's ghost speak. Reginald Scot was not the only Elizabethan who was convinced that ghostspeak was ventriloquized speech (*ventriloquism* is from *venter*, the belly, and *loqui*, has spoken). Consider his remarks on how it was that the ghost of Samuel conjured up by the Witch of Endor was able to speak to Saul: "this [witch] being *Ventriloqua*; that is, speaking, as it were, from the bottom of her belly, did cast herself into a trance, and so abused Saul, answering to Saul in Samuel's name, in her counterfeit hollow voice" (1584, chap. 13).

RESIDUAL CATHOLIC GHOSTS

SAINT THOMAS AQUINAS (1225–1274)

Of those who formulated Catholic ghost doctrine, Aquinas was the most influential. Relying on earlier Church fathers, Aquinas defended the ability of saint-souls to visit the living, affirmed the existence of purgatory and the return of ordinary ghost-souls, and acknowledged that demons from hell tested the living. The text excerpted below, though attributed throughout early modernity to Aquinas, was in fact written by his disciple, Reginald of Piperno.

FROM REGINALD OF PIPERNO, *SUPPLEMENTUM* TO AQUINAS'S
SUMMA THEOLOGICA, QUESTION LXIX
(c. 1274; English trans., New York: Benziger Brothers, Inc., 1948),
2832

There are two ways of understanding a person to leave hell or heaven. First, that he goes from there simply, so that heaven and hell be no longer his place. . . . Secondly, they may be understood to go forth for a time: and here we must distinguish what befits them according to the order of nature, and what according to the order of Divine providence. . . . According to the natural course, the separated souls consigned to their respective abodes are utterly cut off from communication with the living. . . . Nevertheless, according to the disposition of Divine providence separated souls sometimes come forth from their abode and appear to men, as Augustine . . . relates of the martyr Felix who appeared visibly to the people of Nola when they were besieged by the barbarians. It is also credible that this may occur sometimes to the damned, and that for man's instruction and intimidation they be permitted to appear to the living; or again in order to seek our suffrages, as to those who are detained in purgatory.

MEDIEVAL GHOSTS

Among the thousands of incidents involving ghosts recorded in the Catholic middle ages, the following text is particularly relevant to *Hamlet*. It seems that bored members of night watches so frequently "amused themselves by summoning up ghosts during the hours of darkness" that "regulations for medieval gilds sometimes included a clause banning" such behavior (Keith Thomas 1971, 588).

FROM *ORDINANCES OF THE GILD OF THE PALMERS*
(Ludlow, 1284; translation by Toulmin Smith, *English Gilds*,
London: Early English Text Society, 1870), 194

If any man wishes, as is common, to keep night-watches with the dead, this will be allowed, on the condition that he neither calls up ghosts, nor makes any mockeries of the body or its good name, nor does any other scandal of the kind; lest, by such scandals, the discipline of the church may be brought into contempt. . . .

DEMONIC GHOSTS

The following passage suggests that the Catholics in Shakespeare's audience would have little difficulty in thinking Hamlet's ghost a demon, and would have concluded that Hamlet is not following correct procedure for coping with such a creature.

FROM NOEL TAILLEPIED, *A TREATISE OF GHOSTS, BEING THE
PSICHOLOGIE, OR TREATISE UPON APPARITIONS AND SPIRITS, OF
DISEMBODIED SOULS, PHANTOM FIGURES, STRANGE PRODIGIES,
AND OF OTHER MIRACLES AND MARVELS*
(1588; English trans. Montague Summer, London: The Fortune
Press, 1971), 95, 99, 168–69

A ghost will naturally, if it is possible, appear to the person whom he has most loved while on earth, since this person will be readiest to fulfill any wish then communicated by the departed. But if it be an evil Spirit, yes, truly he has a thousand subtle fetches and foul tricks, and will again and again deceive. . . . This evil Spirit goes about seeking whom he may devour, and should he chance to find a man already of a melancholic and Saturnian humor, who on account of some great loss, or haply because he deems his honor tarnished, the demon here has a fine field to his hand, and he will tempt the poor wretch to depths of misery and depression. . . . Now these Spirits appear in very many forms and shapes. . . . Sometimes they even appear under the likeness of some individual who can at once be recognized, a man either still living, or it may be long since dead. . . . If we see some figure or appearance, we must not at once conclude that this is a disembodied Spirit manifesting itself to us, but let us rather, as did the boy Samuel, ask and inquire two or three times. Neither let us be overmuch startled and alarmed by sudden shrieks and clamor or loud yells, for if evil Spirits appear they cannot do us any further harm than God permits. If they are good Spirits they will entreat us well. If it is a mere phantasm without volition or intelligence, a mere shadow, how foolish to be afraid of it! It is quite true that we are naturally affrighted and our hair will rise and prickle on our heads, nevertheless even if it be a spirit of evil and malignant aspect do not fear any the more, but boldly say: *If thou art of God, speak; if thou art not of God, be gone.* . . . While it is necessary not to give way to any panicky fear, a man seeing a ghost should not be over-confident in himself and presumptuously daring. Some men in dealing a blow at a phantom have felt as though they encountered a soft feathery substance. On such occasions no sword of tempered steel however trusty will avail, we must fight with spiritual weapons.

FRAUDULENT GHOSTS

In the following passage la Primaudaye, an orthodox Catholic who believed in angels and purgatorial ghost-souls, makes an argument for assigning "natural causes" to ghost sightings conjured up by the deranged, or fradulently constructed out of thin air by cranks and malicious sorts.

FROM PIERRE LA PRIMAUDAYE, *THE FRENCH ACADEMIE*
(3rd ed.; Eng. trans. Thomas Bases, London: G. Bishop, 1594),
167–68

True it is, and cannot be denied, that many are thought to be possessed with Devils, when indeed they are nothing so. For there are some counterfeit cranks, as many have been taken with the manner, who upon some occasion have by mere knavery feigned themselves such. And some also there are that be but melancholy mad, and carried away by some disease of the brain: but because their melancholy and fury is very violent and strange, ignorant people suppose they are possessed with some spirit. Notwithstanding we may not doubt, but that evil spirits desirous to hurt men both in their goods, bodies, and souls, use all the means and occasions they can possibly invent and find out, to execute their malice when it pleases God to give them leave.

DOMINANT PROTESTANT GHOSTS

BIBLICAL PRECEDENTS FOR A NEW IDEOLOGY

Subversive Catholics were publishing translations of scriptures in vernacular tongues long before Protestantism divorced itself from Rome or England declared itself as a Protestant nation. Among the things these "protestants" discovered by paying close attention to the text they regarded as the word of their deity was that the Bible forbade human intercourse with spirits on two grounds: first, because apparitions, whatever their source, are evil; and second, because the Protestant deity communicates with his believers through the Bible. As Ludwig Lavater wrote in *De Spectris*: "God does not send us souls hither to inform us. The common and ordinary way whereby it pleases God to deal with us, is his word" (1570, 126).

FROM *THE GENEVA BIBLE, DEUTERONOMIE*
(Geneva: R. Hall, 1560)

XVII: 10 Let none be found among you that makes his son or his daughter . . . go through the fire, or that uses witchcraft, or a regarder of times, or a marker of the flying of souls, or a sorcerer,
   11 Or a charmer, or that counsels with spirits, or a soothsayer, or that asks counsel at the dead.
   12 For all that do such things are abomination unto the Lord, and because of these abominations the Lord thy God doth cast them out before thee.

FROM *THE GENEVA BIBLE, IOHN*
(Geneva: R. Hall, 1560)

IIII: 1 Dearly beloved, believe not every spirit, but try the spirits whether they are of God: for many false Prophets are gone out into the world.

CONSTRUCTING A PROTESTANT IDEOLOGY

When Protestants secured sufficient power to protect themselves from Catholic reprisals, they disseminated their views concerning ghosts and apparitions primarily by attacking Catholic doctrine. The ideological agenda they had to prove in the face of contrary Catholic ideology was that angels no longer descend from heaven (though they could if they wanted to), that the only true ghost is the inner holy ghost, and that so-called walking spirits from purgatory (which, of course, does not itself exist) are demons, melancholic hallucinations, or outright frauds committed by unscrupulous priests or equally unscrupulous criminals. The first major writer to take on this task was Ludwig (or Lewes) Lavater, a Swiss reformer. Lavater's book, *De Spectris* (1570), was a bestseller throughout Protestant areas of Europe, particularly England where it went through numerous editions after R. Harrison translated it under the title *Of ghostes and spirites, walking at nyght* (1572). The passage cited below is from a section of Lavater's book which proves that the ghost of Samuel conjured up by the Witch of Endor was not the spirit of Samuel, but a devil. To succeed at his mission Lavater felt that he had to "cut and tear" the doctrine of purgatory and its walking spirits in so many pieces that Catholics "shall never be able to cobble and clout them up again."

FROM LUDWIG [LEWES] LAVATER, *OF GHOSTES AND SPIRITES, WALKING AT NYGHT, AND OF STRAUNGE NOYSES, CRACKES, AND SUNDRIE FOREWARNINGS*
(1570; Eng. trans. R. Harrison, London: H. Benneyman, 1572), 86, 127–28, 130–31

It is a notable history which we read in the second Book of Samuel concerning Saul, who, at what time the Philistines warred upon him, and that he was in very great danger of them, he came to a woman who was a witch, and desired her to raise Samuel from death, that he might know his counsel touching the success of the wars. She raised him up one, whom Saul took to be Samuel in deed, who also told him what event should come of the wars.

Now touching the examples by them commonly alleged, which do think that the souls of the dead do return again unto the living upon the earth: I will first entreat of Samuel's apparition, of which matter now a days there is great contention and reasoning. And (as I trust) I shall prove by strong arguments, that very Samuel himself did not appear in soul and body, neither that his body was raised up by the sorcerers, which perchance then was rotten and consumed unto dust in the earth, neither that his soul was called up, but rather some devilish spirit. . . . For that as we have a little before said, the law of God has severely by a great threatening forbidden [us] to learn ought of the dead, and would not have us to search for the truth of them, nor that any man should use divination by spirits, and such other devilish Arts. Secondly, if very Samuel in deed appeared, that must of necessity have come to pass, either by the will of God, or by the work of art Magic. But God's will was not that Samuel should return. For he hath condemned Necromancy, and would not have us to ask counsel at the dead. . . . And that those things were done by the force and operation of Art Magic, we can not affirm. For the wicked spirit has no rule or power over the souls of the faithful to bring them out of their places.

Fifthly, if he had been the true Samuel, he would no doubt have exhorted Saul to repentance, and willed him to wait for aid from God. . . . For though the Prophets do often chide and threaten men, yet do they again revive and solace them. Now because this Samuel doth beat no other thing into his head, but that God was displeased with him, and had already forsaken him, we may not believe that he was the true, but a mere counterfeit Samuel.

PROTESTANT STRATEGY IN SCOTLAND

Published in Edinburgh six years before its author succeeded to throne of England as James I, and two or three years before *Hamlet* was first produced, James VI's *The Thirde Book of Daemonologie* exercised his abilities as a Protestant philosopher-king against magic, witchcraft, and ghosts. All three, James argues, are the Devil's work, and though his arguments are not particularly telling, James's status as king of Scotland made his text authoritative for dominant members of Scottish and, in time, English society. James's ghost-debunking strategy is cleverly simple. To rid Scotland of spirits and apparitions (and Catholics), James decrees that all ghosts and spirits are Satanic, and that the Christian deity only permits demonic spirits to harass the wicked. Thus, to admit that you have seen an apparition is to admit that you are a sinner. In the dialogue that follows, *Philomathes* asks the questions; *Epistemon* (Greek for "the knowledgeable one") gives James's answers.

FROM JAMES VI OF SCOTLAND, *THE THIRDE BOOKE OF
DAEMONOLOGIE*
(Edinburgh, 1597; London: William Cotton, 1603)

EPI. I must forewarn you of one thing before I enter in this purpose: that is, that . . . I divide [demons] in diverse kinds, you must notwithstanding thereof note my phrase of speaking in that: For doubtlessly they are in effect, but all one kind of spirits, who for abusing the more of mankind, takes on these sundry shapes, and uses diverse forms of outward actions. . . . When [a ghost] troubles certain houses that are dwelt in, it is a sure token either of gross ignorance, or of some gross and slanderous sins among the inhabitants thereof: which God by that extraordinary rod punishes.

PHI. But by what way or passage can these Spirits enter in these houses, seeing [that] they allege that they will enter, Door and Window being steiked [bolted]?

EPI. They will choose the passage for their entrance, according to the form that they are in at that time. For if they have assumed a dead body whereinto they lodge themselves, they can easily enough open without dinne [noise] any door or window, and enter in there at. And if they enter as a spirit only, any place where the air may come in at is large enough an entry for them . . .

PHI. But where these spirits haunt and trouble any house, what is the best way to banish them?

EPI. By two means only may the remedy of such things be procured: The one is ardent prayer to God. . . . The other is the purging of themselves by amendment of life from such sins as have procured that extraordinary plague.

SKEPTICISM

GHOSTS AND FRENCH LAW

In the third book of his treatise on specters, le Loyer includes an account of a legal case that helped settle the question of whether ghosts could be admitted as evidence in French law courts. As its length (and the fact that it is in French) makes it impossible to reproduce here, a synopsis by R. Finucane is reprinted along with two interpolated passages from the original as translated by May Yardley. As Finucane notes, "This complex case is an interesting example of skepticism operating . . . within the institutions of a Catholic country" (1988, 99). If renters could invent ghosts to outwit landlords, couldn't Hamlet invent one to outwit a mother and a king?

FROM PIERRE LE LOYER, *IIII LIVRES DES SPECTRES OU
APPARITIONS*
(Paris, 1586; Synopsis by R. Finucane, Buffalo: Prometheus Books,
1988, 98–99; Trans. May Yardley, Oxford: Oxford University Press,
1929, 236–37)

A second legal wrangle . . . concerned a haunted house. We shall call the litigants A, who rented the house—a residence in the suburbs of Tours—and B, the owner. A short time after A moved in, the racket of ghosts was heard . . . which so disturbed the A family that they vacated and sued B for damages. It was argued that the presence of spirits, presumably known to owner B, made any such lease invalid from the start; the place should never have been offered to A. The seneschal of Tours listened, appointed judges, and in July 1575 a decision was rendered in favour of A, the ex-tenant. The owner appealed, hiring M. René Chopin to represent him. Tenant A was represented by M. Nau. The printed version of the legal arguments, which Loyer says is provided by M. Chopin himself, runs to nearly twenty pages. The gist of it is this: Chopin, arguing against the ghost theory, says the lower court was wrong to break a contract established by the statutes and customs of France just for some stupid claim about spirits. In fact the judges had made an evil example of themselves by encouraging others "à la superstition & à la folle croiance des Esprits qui reviennent," the superstitious, foolish belief in ghosts, in short. Even if, Chopin argues, "everyone says" that the dead return, does it follow that a judge too must go along with common opinion and rumours, rather than the accepted laws of the land? Never. In these courts such an appeal to visions and apparitions of ghosts is a novelty ("chose nouvelle") which will lead the less-well-educated into error (Finucane, 98).

This inferior judge, by his sentence admitting that spirits can return, would [Chopin argues] bring it about that the most assured of men and the least superstitious will be tainted with this same superstition. But indeed (you say), all the world buzzes with it, all the world is of the opinion that Spirits return. And is it to be allowed that a Judge should pay regard to the rumours of the people and not to the laws (Yardley, 236)?

Chopin concludes in the time-honoured fashion by firing a barrage of classical and ecclesiastical references, not failing to note St Augustine's scepticism about the return of the dead. Answering, M. Nau—in effect replying on behalf of the ghosts—says that the holy Fathers of the Church state that spirits of the dead can return. Also, judges should not ignore public opinion at all times, certainly not in this case (Finucane, 99).

For that which is commonly thought of the return of Spirits, is in no wise founded on a vain persuasion, on an intimation, or on special feelings, but on a certain foundation and immemorial tradition (Yardley, 237).

Nau then launches himself upon his own sea of classical and patristic references, rebutting Chopin's interpretations, citing materials from Norwegian writers, from contemporary examples of haunted, deserted houses, from cases about similar broken leases discussed in the courts of Granada, from lawyers who agree with him. In vain. In March 1576, the higher court reversed the earlier decision, directing that the contract was valid and the tenant bound by it, clattering ghosts or not (Finucane, 99).

EMERGENT THEATRE GHOSTS

THE GHOST OF ACHILLES

The passages cited below provide three accounts of the classical stage ghost that most powerfully shaped the ghost in *Hamlet*. The ghost of Achilles, angry that his Greek companions, after sacking Troy, are planning to return home without honoring his grave with human sacrifice, rises from the underworld and, addressing his son Pyrrhus, demands the sacrifice of Priam and Hecuba's daughter, Polyxena, a demand that epitomizes a cult of brutal violence and human sacrifice that many of Achilles' auditors, both Greek and Trojan, view with horror. Thus, the ghost of Achilles is one of the first of many stage ghosts who symbolize an archaic way of life that, though coming to an end (in much the same way that Hamlet's father's way of life is coming to an end), refuses to die peacefully or without blood on its grave. Reading through these three texts—the first from Euripides' *Hecabe*, the second from Seneca's *Troades* (itself a later adaptation of *Hecabe*), and the third from Jasper Heywood's *Troas* (an early modern translation of Seneca's *Troades* under that play's alternate title)—the lines given to Achilles' ghost grow from two in Euripides to ninety in Heywood, clearly a sign that a paternal ghost had to work harder to get his revenge demand obeyed in early modern England, or that this period had reason to amplify the horror of his request. In either case, the Achilles' ghost is the best classical example of a ghost whom, as a theatre audience, we are asked to view negatively, and whose archaic way of life we are encouraged to reject categorically.

EURIPIDES (484–407 B.C.)

The action of *Hecabe* takes place immediately after Troy is sacked by the Greeks. Most of the Trojans are dead, including Priam, who has been slaughtered in the temple of the gods by Achilles' son, Pyrrhus. Hecabe (or Hecuba as *Hamlet* renamed her) and a few other surviving Trojan women, now spoils of war, have been divided up among the victors. The Greeks, about to board their vessels and dip oars for home, stand amazed when dead

Achilles appears "above his tomb, and [holds] them back, demanding" that Polyxena "be sacrificed . . . as a gift of honor for his tomb" (2.43–44). In the scene cited below, we hear the Chorus, a Trojan woman prisoner, first remind Hecabe of the appearance and lethal demand of this terrifying apparition, and then we hear her detail the Greeks' response. Following this speech, were the rest of the play reprinted here, we would watch Hecabe's reaction to what she (and we) can only regard as an atrocious act of murder. Of particular value is that Euripides' play parallels features found in *Hamlet*: not just the ghost of a heroic father arrayed in his splendid armor asking his son to honor him with blood, but, as important, a conflict (internalized by Hamlet) between the Greek warriors who desire to obey Achilles' demand and those who desire not to obey it. Also important is the fact that the dilemma faced by these Greek warriors (and by Hamlet), like the genre that finds Hamlet's and his predecessors' solution to this dilemma tragic, had such an extremely lengthy theatrical history. One of Euripides' objectives, and a measure of his courage in staging Achilles' ghost's demand in front of an Athenian audience, many of whom cherished Achilles as their culture's greatest hero, was precisely to resignify, as a tragic crime, the sacrificial act these Achilles-identified Greeks regarded as a necessity. Clearly, Shakespeare's objective and courage in similarly staging and resignifying Hamlet's ghost's similar demand was to do for early modern audiences what Euripides had done for ancient ones. Both playwrights aimed brilliant plays against an allegedly heroic way of life still dangerously alive outside their theatres.

FROM EURIPIDES, *HECABE*
(425 B.C.; Eng. trans. Philip Velacott, Harmondsworth, UK: Penguin, 1963)

CHORUS: Hecabe, I have slipped away quickly to find you,
    From Agamemnon's tent, where we have been
    Since we were driven from Troy by the Achaeans [Greeks]
    As their spoils of war,
    Drawn for, and allotted to him as slaves.
    My news will not lighten your suffering;
    To carry such words is a grievous burden,
    And for you they are agony to bear.

The Achaeans, they say, in full assembly
Resolved to sacrifice your daughter to Achilles.

You remember when he appeared
Standing in golden armor above his tomb
And checked the sea-going vessels
When sails were already taut on the rigging
With this cry: "Where are you going, you Greeks,
Abandoning my grave without a gift?"

Then in the council of Greek spearmen
Two factions, like wave meeting wave,
Clashed in fierce dispute;
These cried "Sacrifice!" and those cried "No!"
The one who took your part was Agamemnon,
Faithful to his love for the frenzied prophetess [Cassandra];
But the two Athenians, the sons of Theseus,
Though making two different proposals,
Were united in this opinion,
That Achilles' tomb should be crowned with living blood.
It was wrong, they said, to give more consideration
To Cassandra's bed than to Achilles' spear.

And the argument pulled equally both ways,
Till that cunning, honey-tongued quibbler,
That pleaser of the mob, Odysseus, urged them
Not to dishonor the bravest of all the Greeks
For the sake of a slave's throat.
"Shall the dead souls," he cried,
"Who stand in the presence of Persephone
Say that the Greeks forget their debts to Greeks?
That we came away from the plains of Troy
Neglecting those who died there for our country?"

Very soon Odysseus will be coming
To drag your child from your embrace,
Pull hand from hand and take her.
So come, kneel at the altar,
Fall as a suppliant at Agamemnon's knees,
Cry aloud to the gods of heaven
And to the gods below the earth.
It may be, prayers can save you
From losing your daughter so cruelly; if not,
You must see her fall bleeding before a tomb,

While from her maiden throat
Over her gold necklace the dark flow gleams. (2.108–53)

LUCIUS ANNAEUS SENECA (A.D. c.1–A.D. 65)

Four centuries later, Seneca used Euripides' *Hecabe* as the basis of *Troades*. In the famous lines reprinted below, we first hear Talthybius, Herald of the Greek army, recount the appearance of Achilles' ghost. Then we listen as Achilles' son Pyrrhus and Agamemnon, leader of the Greeks, debate the legitimacy of its demand for human blood sacrifice. The objective in selectively reproducing the first half of the second act of this play is to provide access to a classical context that many in Shakespeare's audience would have relied on to help them understand *Hamlet*. Particularly telling is Agamemnon's hostile estimate of a son who is "driven by his father's spirit," as well as his contempt for the "foul murder" Pyrrhus desires to commit under the name of sacrifice. Also telling is Agamemnon's confession that he acted cruelly and dishonorably in razing Troy to the ground. Agamemnon speaks, then, for those like Seneca, who did not want sons sacrificing the living to appease the demands of raging, bloodthirsty fathers, however heroic or famous these fathers may have been.

FROM SENECA, *TROADES*

(A.D. 65; Eng. trans. E. F. Watling, Harmondsworth, UK: Penguin, 1966)

TALTHYBIUS: I shudder to tell; I shake with fear. . . .
    The first rays of the Sky God had but grazed
    The mountain tops, light chasing dark away,
    When from earth's hidden depths a roar was heard,
    And a convulsion tore her inside out.
        . . . A rift appeared,
    Caves yawned, hell gaped, earth parted and revealed
    A way from worlds below to worlds above.
    His tomb was burst asunder and there stood
    The living ghost of the Thessalian leader [Achilles]. . . .
    And now in every quarter of the coast
    His angry voice was heard: "Go, cowards, go!
    Steal off, leaving unpaid the debt you owe

To my departed spirit; go, hoist sail
And launch your thankless fleet upon my sea!
     . . . Polyxena
Was promised me; let her be sacrificed
Over my ashes; by the hand of Pyrrhus;
And let my tomb be watered with her blood."
And with those awful words he took his leave
Of this world's light, and went back to the dead.
As he descended, earth was joined again
And its deep caverns closed. . . .

       • • •

PYRRHUS [*to Agamemnon*]: So, when you spread your sails in eager haste
   To cross the sea for home, you had forgotten—
   You had forgotten Achilles, it appears.
   You had no thought for him whose single hand
   Had so struck Troy. . . .
   My father conquered Troy; you have but spoiled it.
    . . . . Achilles / Deserves all you can pay. . . .

AGAMEMNON: Young men cannot restrain their violence;
   It is their common fault. The zeal of youth
   Inspires them generally; Pyrrhus here
   Is driven by his father's spirit too. . . .
   Do you think fit to soil the honoured shade
   Of an illustrious leader with foul murder?
   Ere you do that, you would do well to learn
   What acts are fitting for a conqueror,
   What penalties for the conquered. . . .
   I own that I have been guilty, I have been headstrong
   In exercise of power, I have been proud. . . .
   I own I wanted to see Phrygia conquered,
   Conquered and punished; but reduced to ruin,
   Razed to the ground—I would have spared her that. . . .
   If anything of what we did that night
   Could have been called inhuman or unseemly,
   It was the work of anger, and of darkness—
   Itself a spur to cruelty—the work
   Of the triumphant sword, whose appetite,
   Once it has tasted blood, outruns all reason.
   If anything of ruined Troy can live,
   Then let it live; vengeance enough, and more,

Has been exacted. A princess to die,
A sacrificial victim, to imbrue
The ashes of the dead—a brutal murder . . .
—never! No! That I will not allow.   (2.170–282)

EMERGENT ENGLISH REVENGE TRAGEDY

In 1559 Jasper Heywood translated Seneca's *Troades* into early
modern English under its alternate title, *Troas* (the former title
means "the Trojan story"; the latter, "the Trojan Women"). He
also took the liberty of making Achilles' ghost a character who
appears onstage and speaks lines that, as we saw above, had previously been reported. To make this change (one anticipating
Hamlet), Heywood expanded the lines Seneca gave Talthybius into
a ninety-line speech for Achilles (of these ninety, nineteen are offered below). Heywood's stated reason for his innovation is that
his Seneca original "seemed unto me, in some places unper-
fected." So "with addition of mine own pen," Heywood supplied
"the want of some things." Among these is "the speech of Achilles'
spirit, rising from hell to require the sacrifice of Polyxena." As theatre, Heywood's ghost lacks dramatic economy since it digresses
at every possible juncture, and dramatic effect since Achilles prefers to orate to his offstage audience than talk to his fellow onstage
Greeks. As poetry, Heywood's lines could perhaps be worse. However, easy as it is to ignore or ridicule Heywood's rather dogged
ineptitude, he was the first to put the word *revenge* in Achilles'
mouth, the first to make Senecan revenge tragedy available to non-
university trained (i.e., non-Latin fluent) English readers, the first
English playwright to put a negative revenge ghost onstage, and
thus the first Elizabethan playwright to discredit onstage the demands of dead fathers whose "spirits" place barbaric demands on
their sons. Given the fact then, that Heywood's work initiated the
powerful emergent English revenge tragedy tradition that led to
Hamlet, it is perhaps permissable to honor his prefatory request:
"Take gentle reader this in good worth, with all his [its] faults.
Favor my first beginnings, and amend rather with good will, such
things as herein are amiss, then to deprave or discommend my
labor and pains" (2.150–59). Moreover, since Polyxena in Heywood's play is a stand-in for Elizabeth I, a twenty-six-year-old
queen in the first year of her reign, and since Heywood is defend-

ing her against the efforts of England's Catholic past to sacrifice her to appease the ghosts of those killed by her father, Henry VIII, Heywood's play is also one of the first theatrical defenses of Elizabeth's new social order. It is as well an instance of theatre used as a powerful political instrument, though here it is used, not to recreate the past as a necessity, but to delegitimize it as an atrocity.

FROM JASPER HEYWOOD'S *TROAS*, A TRANSLATION OF
SENECA'S *TROADES*
(London, 1559)
[*The sprite of Achilles added to the tragedie by the translatour*]

Forsaking now the places tenebrous [dark or gloomy],
And deep dens of the infernal region. . . .
Lo, here am I returned all alone,
The same Achilles whose fierce and heavy hand
Of all the world, no wight [person] might yet withstand. . . .
Hell could not hide Achilles from the light,
Vengeance and blood doth Orcus's [a name of the pagan god of
    hell] pit require,
To quench the furies of Achilles' ire [anger]. . . .
Now mischief, murder, wrath of hell draws near
and dire Phlegethon flood does blood require
Achilles' death shall be revenged here
With slaughter such as Stygian lakes desires. . . .
Polyxena shall sacrificed be,
Upon my tomb, their ireful wrath to please,
and with her blood, you shall assuage the seas. . . .
Your ships may not return to Greece again
Till on my tomb Polyxena be slain. . . .
I will that Pyrrhus render her to me,
and in such solemn sort bereave her life. . . .   (2.1)

STUDY QUESTIONS

1. Discuss the following claim: a person or culture believes in ghosts to prevent significant change, defend against an unknowable future, and make unnecessary the production of any new knowledge.

2. Why do critical assertions that Hamlet's ghost is pagan, Catholic, or Protestant tell us more about the persons making such assertions than about his ghost?

3. Why are the cultural categories, pagan, Catholic, and Protestant, inadequate labels for a Senecan stage ghost?

4. If in Hamlet's mind, Hamlet Sr. is, metaphorically speaking, the sun god Hyperion, then why does his ghost disappear when the sun rises?

5. In what ways is Hamlet's ghost an "old mole" that underlies Hamlet's actions as much as it lies under the stage of the Globe theatre during productions?

6. In what ways are Hamlet's ghost and the ghost of Achilles similar? In what ways do they differ?

QUESTIONS FOR ORAL AND WRITTEN DISCUSSION

1. Could the plot of *Hamlet* do without a ghost? Could the ghost's functions be performed by other less spectacular means?

2. Work out the similarities and differences between creating a poem, a novel, or new knowledge, on the one hand, and a ghost on the other.

3. In 1709, Nicholas Rowe (the first critical editor of Shakespeare) seems to have initiated the story that Shakespeare himself played the part of the ghost during Shakespeare's lifetime. What would be the point of creating such a myth? Speculate on the functions such a myth would serve.

4. How inevitable is it that some sort of ghost will exist in everyone's universe? What form do ghosts of this difficult-to-spot type take? What functions would they perform for those unaware of their existence?

SUGGESTED READINGS AND WORKS CITED

Bacon, Francis. *Novum Organum* [1620]. In *The Works of Francis Bacon.* Translated by James Spedding, R. L. Ellis, and D. D. Heath. London: Routledge, 1857–59.

Datson, Lorraine. "Marvellous Facts and Miraculous Evidence in Early Modern Europe." *Critical Inquiry* 18 (1991): 93–124.

Douglas, Mary. *Purity and Danger: An Analysis of the Concepts of Pollution and Taboo*. London and New York: Routledge, 1966.

Finucane, R. C. *Appearances of the Dead: A Cultural History of Ghosts*. Buffalo: Prometheus Books, 1988.

Jenkins, Harold, ed. *Hamlet*. Arden edition. London: Routledge, 1982.

Lavater, Ludwig [Lewes]. *Of ghostes and spirites, walking at nyght, And of straunge noyses, crackes, and sundrie forewarnings*. 1570. Translated by R. Harrison. London: H. Benneyman, 1572.

Prosser, Eleanor. "Appendix A: The Relevance of Religious Tests to the Stage Ghost, 1560–1610." *Hamlet & Revenge*. Palo Alto, CA: Stanford University Press, 1971.

Scot, Reginald. *The Discouerie of Witchcraft*. London: W. Brome, 1584.

Thomas, Keith. *Religion and the Decline of Magic: Studies in Popular Beliefs in Sixteenth and Seventeenth Century England*. London: Weidenfeld and Nicolson, 1971.

Yardley, May. "The Catholic Position in the Ghost Controversy of the Sixteenth Century with Special Reference to Pierre le Loyer's *IIII Livres des spectres ou apparitions* (1586)." In Lewes [Ludwig] Lavater, *Of ghostes and spirites walking by nyght*, edited by J. Dover Wilson and May Yardley. Oxford: Oxford University Press, 1929.

6

Revenge (,) the Crime

> . . . to cowards and men of no vertue, the timely death of the
> father hath euer brought hinderaunce: so to noble mindes: it
> is occasion whereby to shew themselues as they be.
> —Girolamo Cardano, *Cardanus Comforte* (1576)

Disoriented by loss, drowning in melancholia, unwilling to kill
himself, and unable to be patient, Hamlet evokes a ghost whose
imperative is blood vengeance because, in a patriarchal culture
where female patience is unthinkable, melancholia leads inevitably
to revenge if the only other available option is suicide (suicide
turns the aggression tied up in melancholia against the self; revenge turns it against someone else; patience invests in elsewhere—in a deity's or a state's justice). Thus, as revenge is one of
Hamlet's and his audiences' principal options, it is necessary to
consider the complex and contested issues raised by his, as well
as Pyrrhus's, Laertes's, and Fortinbras's recourse to private blood
revenge as a solution for loss and melancholy. Among others, two
issues complicate such an undertaking. Like melancholy and
ghosts, revenge is a phenomenon that takes on different functions
and values in different social formations. And because it is some-

thing that we have always done, always will do, and, in one form or another, must do, revenge is an immediate and inescapable aspect of our daily lives.

To understand the dominant values blood revenge has had over at least the last 40,000 years of the history of modern man, we may divide these millennia into four parts.

1. For roughly ninety percent of this time span, blood revenge was absolute necessary for hunter-gatherers, horticulturalists, and pastoralists organized in microcollectivities (i.e., families, kin-groups, clans, tribes), since if such groups did not take justice into their own hands, justice would not exist.

2. For approximately the next seven-and-a-half percent (c. 3,000 years), particularly for agriculturists, blood revenge, still justice and still a necessity, became a sacred duty once microcollectivities became structured as patriarchal societies.

3. Then, for two-and-a-half percent of this span in England (A.D. 1056 to the present, though this happened earlier elsewhere), a macrocollective emerged in the form of a national church/state, and blood revenge, unnecessitated, outlawed, and renamed *private* blood revenge, became a form of homicide as the responsibility for enforcing justice (vengeance) passed from the family/kin/clan to a monarchical church/state. In cases where the church/state could not, or did not, enforce justice, it became, officially speaking, the prerogative solely of the Christian deity and its agents: "Recompense to no man evil for evil . . . avenge not yourselves, but give place unto wrath: for it is written, Vengeance is mine; I will repay, saith the Lord" (*Rom.* 12: 17,19). The signal effect of this shift was that a 40,000 year-old imperative, "Revenge the Crime," was punctuated as an apposition, "Revenge, the Crime," and those who, from time immemorial, had relied on revenge to effect justice, were counseled, when injured, to wait patiently until the state or its deity exacted retribution (a shift anticipated and influenced by classical and Hebraic antecedents as well as Christian monarchies on the continent). Of course, for many in cases where deity, church, and/or state acted too slowly, justice was regarded as reverting back to the family or kin of the injured or deceased, thus creating a situation

of conflict between those who could be patient and those who could not.

4. For roughly the last four or five hundred years of these last thousand, an entirely new way of theorizing revenge emerged in England in conflict with both church/state doctrine and its transgressive alternative, wild justice. In this new thinking, *Hamlet* and the secular-urban forces shaping it were major players; indeed, much of *Hamlet*'s fame comes from its role in effecting the fourth of these sociocultural paradigm shifts.

To illustrate these four understandings of revenge, an engraving and portions of six texts are reproduced below. Section one highlights the archaic "Revenge the Crime" code that lingered on in early modern England. The second section documents a quasi-legal position in the masculine no-man's-land between old and new. The third turns to texts championing the new "Revenge, the Crime" code of the English church/state, and the fourth offers the earl of Essex as an instance of the problems created by the inadequacies of the Elizabethan church/state's code of patience. This fourth option is described more fully in the conclusion to this book.

THE "REVENGE THE CRIME" CODE AS IT OPERATED IN ARCHAIC FAMILIES AND CLANS

REVENGE AS JUSTICE

The central character of Apuleius's *The Golden Ass* is a young man whose transformation into an ass allows him to overhear tales like that of Charite, Tlepolemus, and Thrasyllus. In this story, two men are in love with the same woman, but since only one can win her, the other, suffering defeat, murders her husband and thereby becomes the object of her revenge. One reason to reproduce an abbreviated version of this story is to highlight conditions in which aggression and revenge are seen as necessities. Another is that several aspects of this story closely parallel Hamlet's behavior. At the point of loss, Charite desires to kill herself. Revenge is then prompted by the ghost of her husband whose account of his murder is taken by Charite (and the narrator of the tale) as legitimate evidence of foul play. (In George Pettie's 1576 version of this plot, there is no ghost; instead, the wife simply knows who killed her husband.) To accomplish her revenge, Charite puts on an antic disposition. Also relevant is the text's understanding that revenge is the only way to bring Thrasyllus to justice, and that we are to admire and celebrate Charite's revenge as an act of justice.

FROM LUCIUS APULEIUS, *THE GOLDEN ASS BEING THE METAMORPHOSES*
(c. A.D. 150; Eng. trans. William Adlington, 1566, rev. S. Gaselee, London: William Heinemann, 1915)

Book VIII: 1–14

There was a young gentleman dwelling in the next city, born of good parentage . . . but very much addicted to whore-hunting and continual revelling. . . . His name was Thrasyllus. . . . When Charite had come to an age ripe for marriage, he was among the chiefest of her suitors, but although he were a man more comely than the residue that wooed her, yet because he was of evil fame he had the repulse and was put off by Charite. And so our master's daughter married with Tlepolemus; howbeit this young man [Thrasyllus] secretly cherished his downfallen love, and moved somewhat at her refusal, he busily searched some means to work his damnable intent.

On a day Tlepolemus went to the chase with Thrasyllus to hunt for wild beasts. . . . When they were come to a great thicket on a hill they compassed round the goats, which had been spied out by trackers; and by and by warning was given to let loose the dogs to rout up the beasts from their lairs. . . . When on a sudden the signal was given they [the dogs] rushed in with such a cry that all the forest rang again with the noise; but behold there leaped out an horrible and dangerous wild boar, such as no one had seen before, thick with muscles and brawn foaming at the mouth, grinding his teeth, looking direfully with fiery eyes, and rushing like lightning as he charged with his furious jaws. The dogs that first set upon him he tare and rent with his tusks, and then he ran quite through the nets that had checked his first charges and escaped away.

Then Thrasyllus, having found opportunity to work his treason, said to Tlepolemus: "What, stand we here amazed like some timid woman? Let us mount upon our horses and pursue him. . . . Take you a hunting javelin, and I will take a spear"; and by and by they leaped upon their horses and followed the beast earnestly. But [the boar] returned against them burning with the fire of his wild nature, and gnashing his teeth, pried with his eyes on whom he might first assail with his tusks: and Tlepolemus struck the beast first on the back with his javelin. But Thrasyllus attacked not the beast, but came behind and cut the hamstrings of the hinder legs of Tlepolemus's horse, in such sort that he fell down in much blood to the ground and threw despite his will his master: then suddenly the boar came upon Tlepolemus, and furiously tare and rent first his garments and then him with his teeth as he would rise. Howbeit, his good friend Thrasyllus did not repent of his wicked deed to see him thus wounded, but when [Tlepolemus] was gored and essayed [attempted] to protect his fresh wounds from the heavy blows [of the boar], and desired [Thrasyllus's] friendly help, [Thrasyllus] thrust Tlepolemus through the right thigh with his spear. . . . [When the servants caught up with their masters,] Thrasyllus cloaked the matter with a sorrowful countenance, he feigned a dolorous face, he often embraced the body he himself slew, he played all the parts of a mourning person, saving there fell no tears from his eyes.

When [Charite and the townspeople] met the slain body of Tlepolemus, she threw herself upon him, weeping and lamenting grievously for his death, in such sort that she would have presently ended her life upon the corpse of her slain husband, whom she so entirely loved, had it not been that her parents and friends did comfort her, and hardly pulled her away. Then the body was taken up, and in funeral pomp brought to the city, and buried.

In the mean season Thrasyllus feigned much sorrow for the death of Tlepolemus, crying and beating his breast beyond all measure, but in his heart he was well pleased and joyful. . . . And to counterfeit very truth by words of kindness, he would come to Charite and say: "O what a loss have I had, by the death of my friend, my fellow, my companion, my brother Tlepolemus" (adding the name in a melancholy voice). . . . Howbeit, Charite, after the burial of her husband, sought the means to follow him [i.e., Tlepolemus], and tried every way [to kill herself], but especially that which is most gentle and easy, nor requireth any weapon, but is most like to quiet sleep: for she purposed to finish her life with starvation and neglecting herself, she buried herself deep in the darkness and had done with the light for good and all.

In the mean season Thrasyllus, not being able to refrain any longer, doubted not to demand her in marriage, and so very rashly detected the secrets and unspeakable deceits of his heart. But Charite detested and abhorred his demand, and as she had been stricken with some clap of thunder, she presently fell down to the ground all amazed with a cloud. Howbeit in the end, when her spirits were revived and that she returned to herself crying and shrieking like some beast, remembering all that had passed with the wicked Thrasyllus, she demanded respite to deliberate and to take advice on the matter.

In the mean season of delay the shape of Tlepolemus that was slain so miserably appeared to Charite as she chastely slept, with a pale and bloody face, saying: "O my sweet wife even if the memory of me in thy heart groweth dim, or the remembrance faileth of my pitiful death, in so much that our bond of love hath been severed, marry happily with any other person, so that you marry not with the traitor Thrasyllus; have no conference with him, eat not with him, lie not with him; avoid the bloody hand of mine enemy. . . . For those wounds, the blood whereof thy tears did wash away, were not all the wounds of the teeth of the boar, but the spear of wicked Thrasyllus parted me from thee." Thus spoke Tlepolemus unto his loving wife, and declared the whole residue of the damnable fact. Charite wetted her cheeks with her welling tears: and now aroused as by some new anguish, she began to cry aloud as if she renewed her dolour, to tear her garments, and to beat her comely arms with her furious hands: howbeit she revealed the vision which she saw to no manner of person, but dissembling that she knew the truth of the mischief, devised silently with herself how she might be revenged on the wicked murderer, and finish her own life, to end and knit up all sorrow.

Again came Thrasyllus the detestable demander of the pleasure that
should betray him, and wearied the closed ears of Charite with talk of
marriage in so much that she was enforced to seem conquered by him,
and to speak to him in this manner: "My friend Thrasyllus, this one thing
must thou grant to my earnest prayers, that we should take our pleasure
in such sort and so secret, that no servant of the house may perceive it
until the whole year be complete and finished." Then Thrasyllus, trusting
the false promises of the woman, consented gladly to her secret embraces, and was joyful in his heart and looked for night, when as he might
have his purpose, preferring his inordinate pleasure above all things in
the world. "But come you quietly about midnight," said Charite, "covered up and disguised without all company. And do but hiss at my chamber door, and await; my nurse shall attend sitting before the barrier for
thy coming. Then shall she let thee in, and bring thee without any light,
that might betray us, to my sleeping-room."

This counsel of fatal marriage pleased Thrasyllus marvellously; who,
suspecting no harm, and in a turmoil of expectation when at last the sun
gave way to the night, he disguised himself and went straight, full of
hope, to her chamber, where he found the nurse attending for him with
feigned diligence. She fed him with flattering talk, brought silently cups
and a flagon, and gave him drink mingled and doled with sleepy drugs,
excusing the absence of her mistress Charite by reason that she attended
on her father being sick, until such time that with sweet talk and operation of the wine, he fell in a sound sleep. Now when he lay prostrate
on the ground ready to all attack, Charite (being called for) came in, and
with manly courage and bold force stood over this sleeping murderer,
saying: "Sleep careless, dream that thou art in the hands of the merciful,
for I will not hurt thee with thy sword or with any other weapon; God
forbid that I should make thee equal to my husband by a like death. But
thy eyes shall fail thee still living, and thou shalt see no more save when
thou dreamest. . . . I will make libation with the blood of thine eyes upon
the grave of my husband, I will pacify his holy shade with these eyes of
thine."

When she had prophesied in these words, she took a great needle from
her head and pricked out both his eyes: which done, leaving him blind
and waking in great pain (though he knew not whence it came) from his
drunkenness and sleep, she by and by caught the naked sword which her
husband Tlepolemus was accustomed to wear, and ran throughout all
the city like a mad woman towards the sepulchre of her husband. . . .
Then we with all the citizens left our houses and ran incontinently [im-
mediately] after her, exhorting each other to take the sword out of her
furious hands; but she, clasping about the tomb of Tlepolemus, kept us
off with her naked weapon, and when she perceived that every one of

us wept and lamented, she spake in this sort: "I pray you, my friends, let there be no unasked tears for me nor laments unworthy of my courage, for I am revenged of the death of my husband, I have punished deservedly the wicked breaker of our marriage; now it is time to seek out with this sword the way to my sweet Tlepolemus." And therewithal, after she had made relation of the whole matter which was declared unto her by the vision of her husband which she saw, and told by what means she deceived Thrasyllus, thrusting the sword under her right breast and wallowing in her own blood, she babbled some uncertain words and at length with manly courage yielded up the ghost.

REVENGE AS FILIAL OBLIGATION

At the end of his 1582 French translation of the Danish legend that served as the source for Shakespeare's *Hamlet* (discussed in Chapter 7), Belleforest goes out of his way to praise the exceptionally violent revenge Hamblet takes on his uncle, Fengon, for killing his father and marrying his mother, Geruth. The passage reproduced below is taken from a 1508 English translation of Belleforest. The objective of both of these translations was to open a door to a pagan, archaic past where revenge was permissible, and thus to support those who desired to take justice into their own hands. In fact, if we put ourselves in the position of early modern readers of these texts, it is clear that this text is encouraging us to identify with Hamblet's vengeance, and understand that what he does is not only praiseworthy but politically necessary. The point of mapping *Hamlet*'s many differences with respect to Belleforest is to see that Shakespeare not only complicates his hero's situation (in the original there is no question of Fengon's guilt, for example), but also that Shakespeare rewrites as a tragedy an action that Belleforest and the legend he translates into French celebrate as a comedy. In short, of the many texts *Hamlet* radically opposes, the one it opposes the most is its legendary source. The excerpt cited below begins just after Hamblet, having torched Fengon's hall and incinerating everyone inside, gives his uncle Fengon, "such a blow upon the chin of the neck, that he cut his head clean from his shoulders." (The first four chapters of this story are included in Chapter 7).

FROM *THE HYSTORIE OF HAMBLET*
(London: Richard Bradocke, 1608)

Chap. V.

[Hamblet was a] man (to say the truth) hardy, courageous, and worthy of eternal commendation, who arming himself with a crafty, dissembling, and strange show of being distract out of his wits, under that pretense deceived the wise, politick, and crafty, thereby not only preserving his life from the treasons and wicked practices of the tyrant, but (which is more) by an new and unexpected kind of punishment revenged his father's death many years after the act committed: in such sort that directing his courses with such prudence, and effecting his purposes with so great boldness and constancy, he left a judgment to be decided among men of wisdom, which was more commendable in him, his constancy or magnanimity, or his wisdom in ordering his affairs according to the premeditated determination he had conceived.

If vengeance ever seemed to have any show of justice, it is then, when piety and affection constrains us to remember our fathers unjustly murdered, as the things whereby we are dispensed withal, and which seek the means not to leave treason and murder unpunished: seeing David a holy and just king, and of nature simple, courteous, and debonair, yet when he died he charged his son Salomon (that succeeded him in his throne) not to suffer certain men that had done him injury to escape unpunished. Not that this holy king (as then ready to die, and to give account before God of all his actions) was careful or desirous of revenge, but to leave this example unto us, that where the prince of country is interested, the desire of revenge cannot by any means (how small so ever) bear the title of condemnation, but is rather commendable and worthy of praise.

Hamblet, having in this manner revenged himself, does not presently declare his action to the people, but to the contrary [was] determined to work by policy, so to give them intelligence what he had done, and the reason that drew him thereunto: so that being accompanied with such of his father's friends that then were rising, he stayed to see what the people would do when they should hear of that sudden and fearful action. The next morning the towns bordering there about, desiring to know from whence the flames of fire proceeded the night before they had seen, came thither, and perceiving the king's palace burnt to ashes, and many bodies (most part consumed) lying among the ruins of the house, all of them were much abashed, nothing being left of the palace but the foundation. But they were much more amazed to behold the body of the king all bloody, and his head cut off lying hard by him; whereat some began to threaten revenge, yet not knowing against whom; others beholding so lamentable a spectacle, armed themselves, the rest rejoicing, yet not daring to make any show thereof; some detesting the cruelty, others lamenting the death of their Prince, but the greatest part calling Horvendile's [Hamblet's father] murder to remembrance, acknowledging a just judgment from above, that had thrown down the pride of the tyrant. And in this sort, the diversities of opinions among that multitude of people being many, yet every man ignorant of what would be the issue of that tragedy, none stirred from thence, neither yet attempted to move any tumult, every man fearing his own skin, and distrusting his neighbor, esteeming each other to be consenting to the massacre. Hamblet then seeing the people to be so quiet, and most part of them not using any words, all searching only and simply the cause of this ruin and destruction, not minding to lose any time, but aiding himself with the commodity thereof, entered among the multitude of people, and standing in the middle spoke unto them as follows. . . . [In his extremely long oration Hamblet places himself at the mercy of the community, constituted as a kind of legal assembly: "you yourselves shall be judges," he says. He then reveals himself as the agent of Fengon's death: "It is I" who am "the minister and executor" of "this piece of work." He then recounts his misery and humiliation as a counterfeited mad man, defends his massacre as just vengeance against a parricidal tyrant rather than the murder of a king, claims to "have washed the spots that defiled the reputation of the queen," and calls upon his auditors to destroy Fengon's body so completely that no trace of it will taint Denmark. "It is fit," Hamblet argues, "that the land refuse to give him a place for the eternal rest of his bones," and, in closing, claims that he is "lawful successor in the kingdom."]

This oration of the young prince so moved the hearts of the Danes, and won the affections of the nobility, that some wept for pity, others for joy, to see the wisdom and gallant spirit of Hamblet; and having made an end of their sorrow, all with one consent proclaimed him king of Jute and Chersonnese, at this present the proper country of Denmark. And having celebrated his coronation, and received the homages and fidelities of his subjects, he went into England to fetch his wife, and rejoiced with his father in law touching his good fortune.

HISTORICAL PARALLEL BETWEEN MARY, QUEEN OF SCOTS AND *HAMLET*

To savor a sensational act of blood revenge in life instead of in legend, Elizabethans could turn to events that took place in Scotland some thirty years before *Hamlet* was written. In 1565, in an effort to strengthen her already powerful claim to the English throne, a widowed twenty-three-year-old Catholic, Mary, Queen of Scots married her English Catholic cousin, Henry Stuart, Lord Darnley. At first Mary was deeply infatuated with her husband, but in time came to dislike him and rejected his demands for greater power. Angry at her refusal and jealous of David Rizzio, an Italian musician who was Mary's friend and advisor, Darnley instigated or, perhaps, joined a plot to destroy his rival. As a result, Darnley, the earl of Morton, and a group of nobles broke into Mary's apartment and murdered Rizzio. Mary seduced Darnley back to her side, and then escaped to Dunbar to be joined by the earl of Bothwell and other loyal nobles. In June 1566, Mary bore her son, James (later James VI of Scotland who became James I of England). At this time she also fell in love with Bothwell. Darnley was making himself ever more unpopular, and her closest counselors encouraged Mary to separate herself from him. At night on February 9, 1567, the house in which Darnley was staying was blown up, and Darnley was found strangled in a garden nearby. Bothwell was suspected of the murder, but was acquitted at trial. On April 24, Bothwell intercepted Mary on her way to Edinburgh, carrying her off to Dunbar Castle. Bothwell then secured a divorce from his wife, and on May 15 he and Mary were married. In the wake of this remarriage, Mary lost the support of the people and her lords, first by her failure to punish the man believed to be her husband's murderer, and then by marrying him. Forced to surrender, and then imprisoned in Lochleven, Mary abdicated. Defeated at Langside a year later, she fled to northern England where a trial before an English tribunal cleared her of complicity in Darnley's murder. For sixteen years she was a prisoner of the English government and was beheaded on February 8, 1587 by Elizabeth's government. That Mary was generally accused of abetting the murder of her husband, and of hastily remarrying his suspected assassin would have made it difficult for her not to have stood, in *Hamlet*'s audiences' minds, as a possible historical analogue for Gertrude. And with this one parallel in place, others would have followed. That James's stepfather, Bothwell, was thought to have killed James's natural father, Darnley, would have made James a historical prototype for Hamlet, a connection strengthened by the fact that James married a Danish princess and spent part of a lengthy matrimonial embassy in Den-

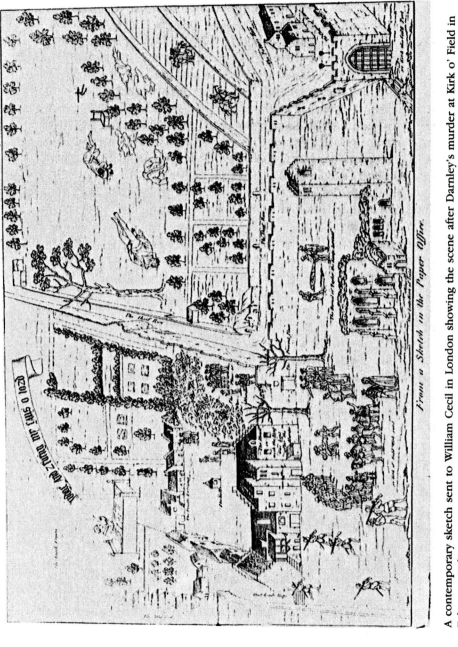

A contemporary sketch sent to William Cecil in London showing the scene after Darnley's murder at Kirk o' Field in February 1567.

mark at Elsinore. The James–Hamlet connection would have been additionally strengthened by the fact that numerous "Revenge the Crime" imperatives, like that argued by the reproduced sketch, were laid on James by various parties to this affair. This sketch shows the half-naked bodies of Darnley and his servant lying dead in a garden (*top right*), the demolished building (*center left*), and Darnley's infant son in his bed with an enscrolled legend attached to his hands, "Judge and Avenge my cause, O Lord" (*top left*). Moreover, in time, James took revenge, assuming no doubt that as king he was his Lord's proper minister and scourge. In Alvin Kernan terms, "Death pursued with extraordinary thoroughness all those lords, like Morton, who had been involved in one way or another in the murder of Darnley and in the subsequent deposition of Mary. . . . James's hand was not always visible in these deaths, but the revenge was spectacularly gory and complete. . . . Perhaps James was still playing the role of avenger of the death of his father when he did nothing to prevent the execution of the mother who was complicit in that death" (1995, 41–42). By revenging his father's death, James maintained the ancient feud culture of the past, not to mention inadvertently creating a parallel for *Hamlet* which, like its legendary Hamblet source, Shakespeare's play repudiates as tragic.

BETWEEN OLD AND NEW UNDERSTANDINGS
OF REVENGE

REVENGE: LEGAL AND ILLEGAL

The advice Queen Elizabeth's Garter king of arms, Sir William Segar, gave Elizabethan gentlemen in a popular book on dueling opposes revenge, yet contradictorily defends a gentleman's right to engage in private battle. Rejecting the dominant view that all injuries unpunished or unpunishable by the church/state should be left to the Christian deity's discretion, Segar champions the view that in these cases justice reverts to private hands if it takes the form of open combat between armed opponents of equal rank and training. At a later point, however, this principle considerably deteriorates when Segar legitimizes, after having initially rejected, more dubious forms of blood revenge: "for revenge of cowardly and bestial offenses, it is allowable to use any advantage or subtilty, according to the Italian proverb, which is, that one advantage requires another, and one treason may be with another acquitted." Possessed either of a divided mind, or, more likely, by a need to quasi-legalize a range of acts he knows to be illegal, Segar opportunistically exploits the ambiguous meanings of revenge to voice a contradiction basic to his age.

FROM SIR WILLIAM SEGAR, *THE BOOK OF HONOR AND ARMES*
(London: Richard Iohnes, 1590)

To the Reader.

The cause of all Quarrel is Injury and reproach, but the matter is Justice and Honor. For love whereof, we shun no care of mind, loss of wealth, nor adventure of life. . . . For who so is persuaded to have truth and reason on his side, does not only constantly believe that so it is, but also being thereof denied, holds himself injured, and consequently burdened. True it is, that the Christian law wills men to be of so perfect patience, as not only to endure injurious words, but also quietly to suffer every force and violence. Notwithstanding, for so much as none (or very few men) have attained such perfection, the laws of all Nations, for avoiding further inconveniences, and the manifestation of truth, have permitted that such questions as could not be civly proved by confession, witness, or other circumstances, should receive judgment by fight and Combat, supposing that GOD (who only knoweth the secret thoughts of all men) would give victory to him that justly adventured his life for truth, honor, and justice.

Seeing then that all humane laws have permitted the trial of Arms, and that every injurious action not repulsed is by common consent of all martial minds held a thing dishonorable, infamous, and reproachful; it cannot be but [that] at some times and occasions such questions and quarrels shall arise as necessarily must receive trial by the Sword. . . . By these reasons it appears that the trial by Arms is not only natural, but also necessary and allowable.

And albeit I am not ignorant that public Combats are in this age either rarely or never granted; yet for that (as is before said) no providence can prevent the questions and quarrels that daily happen among Gentlemen and others professing Arms, it shall not be amiss, but rather behoveful that all men should be fully informed what injury is, and how to repulse it, when to fight, when to rest satisfied, what is Honor and good reputation, how it is gained, and by what means the same is kept and preserved. . . . This book does not incite men to unadvised fight, or needless revenge (as some simple wit may surmise) but informs the true means how to shun all offenses: or being offended, shows the order of revenge and repulse, according unto Christian knowledge and due respect of Honor.

"REVENGE, THE CRIME" IN EARLY MODERN CHRISTIAN MONARCHICAL ENGLAND

THE CODE OF PATIENCE

The number of dominant attacks on private revenge published in early modern England is too great to compress into the space available. A workable alternative is to excerpt one very brief passage before turning to a longer piece. Each of these texts is certain that if private revenge is allowed to flourish, it would destroy the Tudor church/state's ability to function as a commonwealth of law, and would cause England to revert back to a past no different from the blood feud cultures visible on its Scottish and Welsh borders. (In any given year in James VI's reign, for example, there were upward of fifty major blood feuds going on simultaneously in Scotland [Keith Brown 1989].) The fear is that a spark of revenge could quickly ignite a destructive conflagration, and patience is seen as the sole means a society has of extinguishing such sparks before they burst into flame. A code of patience that may seem both excessively overstressed and fragile from a modern point of view might best be thought of as the only fire extinguisher available in the extremely flammable timber houses of the sixteenth century—that is, as the difference between life and disaster.

FROM STEPHEN HAWES, *PASTIME OF PLEASURE*
(London: W. de Worde, 1509)

Who is oppressed with a little wrong,
Revenging it he may it soon increase;
For better it is for to suffer among
An injury, as for to keep the peace,
Than to begin which he shall never cease.
Wars once begun, it is hard to know
Who shall abide and who shall overthrow.

THE CODE OF PATIENCE ELABORATED

A *Fig for Fortune* is a poorly written 1,770 line allegorical poem, the clichéd plot of which occasionally drags us up significance's hill, but far more often lets us suffer stretches of bad rhymes, obtuse allusions, and tedious doctrine. However, as bad as it is, this poem is extremely useful in (1) helping identify the options (suicide, revenge, patience) Elizabethans faced when overwhelmed by loss and melancholy and, (2) identifying as well the too limited and too ideal individual whom dominant culture sought to create as a way of solving the divisive legacy of aggression and revenge it had inherited from its past. Copley's poem, anticipating many of Hamlet's structural features (crowing cock, break of day, fleeing ghost), begins with its hero Elizian, lost, like Hamlet, in self-pitying melancholy after adversity ruins his hopes of worldly glory. This diseased condition is allegorically figured by the fact that Elizian rides a black horse named Melancholy. Adrift and wandering, Elizian meets the ghost of Cato, an ancient Roman for whom suicide was preferable to loss of glory. Cato advises Elizian to adopt the same solution and then vanishes in a stinking sulphurous cloud (the first 33 stanzas of the poem). After contemplating and rejecting Cato's advice, Elizian meets Revenge, whose solution is to get even (stanzas 34–71). But just when Elizian is about to rise to this challenge, day breaks, Revenge flees, Elizian's horse Melancholy goes beserk and, after dashing hither and yon, comes to a stop in front of a white horse, Good Desire, that takes Elizian to a place where Catechrysius, an ancient sage, heals him by prescribing an enormous dose of religious doctrine on the evils of suicide and revenge (stanzas 40–119). And this is merely the beginning of a monologue that goes on for 172 more stanzas. Reproduced below is an abridged rendition (less than one-tenth) of the first 119 stanzas of this poem. In short, this poem is probably the absolute opposite to *Hamlet* in terms of both the quality of its verse and its ending, since Elizian, unlike Hamlet, takes the path of patience which guarantees that he ends up in the arms of religion (not to mention safely ensconsed in the genre known as divine comedy) where he no longer needs to give—and does not give—"a fig for fortune." Elizian gets to this utterly predictable and typical finale by submitting to the age's official medicine for melancholy—that is, he maintains perfect patience while waiting for his deity to make good on its promise of vengeance—a solution for loss and melancholy that proved viable only for those in Elizabethan England who could be as saintly, and as divorced from everyday life, as Elizian is. (Stanza breaks and refrain indentations have been ignored.)

FROM ANTHONY COPLEY, *A FIG FOR FORTUNE*
(London: Richard Iohnes, 1596)

> . . . exiled from Joy,
> I ranged to seek out a propitious place
> Where I might sit and descant of annoy[ance]. . . .
> At last, even in the confines of the night
> I did discern aloof [a distance away] a sparkling light.
> Then set I spurs unto my Melancholy,
> A jade whereon I had ridden many a mile,
> Which less than in the twinkling of an eye,
> Brought me unto . . . *Cato's* Ghost . . . [who says:]
> "Be not injaild [kept captive] to base Adversity,
> Rather flip out your life at glory's window,
> One stab will send you to eternity,
> And rid you quite and clean of all your woe . . .
> There is no hell like to declined glory. . . ."
> With that I drew out my emboldened blade,
> Resolved to massacre my loathed life:
> When (lo) the Ghost from out my sight did fade . . .
> But such a Sulfur stench he left behind him
> That I in dread thereof shook every limb.
> And therwithall my sword fell to the ground
> And I misdoubted some illusion. . . .
> So then remounted on my Sable jade,
> I ranged ore craggy cliffs and dessert dales. . . .
> Thrice drew I out my dagger for to stab me
> And then so oft I mused why *Cato* stunk so,
> Me thought there should no such disglory be
> In sacred Ghosts, freed from the filth of woe. . . .
> Then on I rode, and riding through a dale . . .
> A sudden fatal blast did me assail
> And drove me to a second damned doom . . .
> Where I might hear a voice that roared out

"Revenge, revenge, your dolorous disgrace":
And then eftsoons [soon] all in a Sulfur-flame
Appeared unto my sight . . . [a figure, who said:]
"I am Revenge, the doom of injuries:
The Miser's refuge . . . pith of Tragedies
The sum of policy in all distress:
Wrath's thunder-bolt, and triumph over those
That in their jollity work other's woes. . . .
To be faire Fortune's ever Carpet-darling
Is female glory: But Revenged disgrace
That's truly Masculine, and rich triumphing. . . .
What manhood is it still to feed on Chickens. . . .
Give me the man that with undaunted spirit
Dares give occasion of a Tragedy. . . .
'Tis human fate, sometime to slip and fall,
But to grovel in dirt is beastly base:
To rise again, oh that is jovial,
Or else revenge to death the down-disgrace. . . .
Lo, I [Revenge] . . . will be at hand with poison, and with daggers
To execute each plotted tragedy. . . .
What greater glory can betide the valley
Than force the Mountain-top a down to fall?
Rise from your ruins . . . To act the stately tragic personage . . .
Breathing Revenge's bright and sacred flames. . . ."
So said, she . . . stared, and trembled, and began to pout
And suddenly she vanished out of sight
Because now in the East it dawned daylight. . . .
Now Chanteclere the vigil of the night
Crew broad daylight . . . So on I hastened at my jade's behest. . . .
When (lo) anon with a religious pace
A snow-white Jennet towards me advanced:
His name was *Good Desire* . . . [and took me] . . . unto
    Devotion. . . .
There kneeled a revered [Sage, *Catechrysius*,] all in tears . . .
His heart was wholly fixed on Christ his Passion. . . .
Standing behind him, he was in a trance, . . .
I [to myself] argued [my] case: . . .
Cato and Revenge were black, and both to blame
Th'one in sulfur stench, th'other in light's abhorr[ence],
And Melancholy was the Jade of shame
That darkling brought me to that double door;
A better horse [i.e., *Good Desire*] has brought me hither
For both the place is bright, and 'tis fair weather.

Long have I ranged to find a place of ease
Where I may pass away my pensive plaints,
And happily if this be now that place of peace
Here rest I ever in my woe's attaintes. . . .
While thus with infant-zeal I did applaud
The in-come grace of God into my heart
In full detest of sore-affected fraud. . . .
Lo, now this penal [penalty judging] Sage began [to speak:]
"Rejoice (quoth he) at this eternal truth,
The man is blest that for God's justice sake
Sustains with patience reproach and ruth [sorrow]. . . ."
With that my heart exulted in my breast. . . .
I told him of my dreary journement
On moody Melancholy; and how I sped
With *Cato*, and *Revenge's* babblement,
And how, along the Desert as I fled
I met with *Good Desire*, a goodly Steed,
That brought me thither in my ghostly need.
I would have told him more. . . .
But he eftsoones prevented me, and said: . . .
"Not to despair and die as *Cato* told you,
For that is base. . . .
As vain it is to think Revenge's deed
Can counter-doom your bale [woe] to blessedness. . . .
. . . Revenge . . . is a haggard ill,
A Luciferial rank uncharity . . .
Unreason's rage; spawn of Impiety,
Breath of Despair, Prime-brat of Envy's brood. . . .
Revenge's arm reared up against the Foe
Aims to defeat God of his interest
Who clausually [specifically] reserved that work of woe
Unto his own judicial behest . . ."

PROBLEMS WITH DOMINANT EARLY
MODERN VIEWS OF REVENGE AND PATIENCE

HAMLET AND THE EARL OF ESSEX: AN ON- AND
OFFSTAGE COMPARISON

For those watching a performance of *Hamlet* at the Globe between 1599 and 1601, it would have been difficult not to remark
the similarities between the Hamlet they saw on stage and the earl
they saw playing an equally large and troubled role in Elizabeth's
court—the handsome earl of Essex, Robert Devereux, who had
been Elizabeth's favorite courtier, soldier, and (in a sense) scholar,
at least since 1586. Both the thirty-year-old character and the thirty-
two- to thirty-four-year-old earl, regarded as first among peers,
were restless, dissatisfied, melancholic malcontents unwilling to be
patient, unable to find an action heroic enough for their self-image,
and certain that their ambitions were being thwarted by inferi-
or men. In Ophelia's and no doubt in Gertrude's eyes, Hamlet
was "The courtier's, soldier's, scholar's, eye, tongue, sword, /
Th'expectancy and rose of the fair state, / The glass of fashion, and
the mold of form, / Th'observ'd of all observers" before he was
"quite, quite down" (3.1.150–53), just as, in the eyes of numerous
Elizabethans and certainly in the eyes of Elizabeth, Essex was the
same expectancy, rose, glass, and mold before he, too, was "quite,
quite down." Hamlet draws a sword in Gertrude's closet; Essex,
boxed on the ear by the queen, clasped his sword in Elizabeth's
presence. Hamlet uses a play, *The Murder of Gonzago*, from the
repertoire of a group of traveling players as part of a failed effort
to put down a king; Essex, the week before his treasonous uprising
in 1601, commissioned a production of Shakespeare's *Richard II*
as part of a failed attempt to put down a queen. In an antic Hamlet,
Ophelia sees "a noble mind . . . o'erthrown" (3.1.149); in Essex's
last speeches to Elizabeth, Sir John Harrington (one of Elizabeth's
courtiers and, for a time, Essex's friend) heard language that "becomes no man who has *mens sana in corpore sano*" [a sound
mind in a sound body]. Hamlet kills Polonius, and Claudius issues
a royal proclamation to be given to the English king; Essex rises

in rebellion, and Elizabeth issues a proclamation to be distributed throughout the English nation. Hamlet, given to ambushes of wit and exhibitions of temper, fights a duel with his "mighty opposite," Claudius, that eventually turns lethal; Essex, famous for outbursts of wit and temper, also was fighting a duel with his mighty opposite, Elizabeth, that did turn lethal. Hamlet gives his dying voice to Fortinbras, a Northerner who crossed Denmark's border with an army; Essex, since 1598, "had been in correspondence with James [king of Scotland] . . . the effect of which was that James should prepare an army, should march at the head of it to the borders and there fulminate a demand to the English government of an open declaration to the right of the succession" [to the English throne upon the death of Queen Elizabeth] (John Bruce, Introduction to *James's Letters*, cited by Lillian Winstanley 1921, 162). In short, no "great one" watched by Shakespeare's audience during Elizabeth's reign had moved from deferential patience to rebellious revenge as spectacularly as Essex did in the period just prior to his execution for treason on February 25, 1601. So, whereas the sensational Darnley murder (discussed at the beginning of this chapter) provided audiences with a historical parallel for the *Hamlet* plot in the recent past, Essex provided them with an even more sensational parallel in the immediate present. The point, however, is *not* that Hamlet and Essex should have learned to be patient or that they should have killed their monarch and taken power; rather, the point is that failing to create new options, both Hamlet and Essex wasted their lives trying to navigate the Bermuda Triangle created by the inadequate options—suicide, patience, and revenge—offered by their age.

FROM SIR JOHN HARRINGTON, "BREEFE NOTES AND
REMBRAUNCES," *NUGAE ANTIQUAE*
(c. 1600–1601; London: J. Wright, 1804)

It rests with me in opinion, that ambition thwarted in its career, does speedily lead on to madness; herein I am strengthened by what I learn in my lord of Essex, who shifts from sorrow and repentance to rage and rebellion so suddenly, as well proves him devoid of good reason or right mind. In my last discourse [conversation], he uttered strange words bordering on such strange designs, that made me hasten forth and leave his presence. . . . His speeches of the Queen become no man who has *mens sana in corpore sano*. . . . The Queen well knows how to humble the haughty spirit; the haughty spirit knows not how to yield, and the man's soul seems tossed to and fro, like the waves of a troubled sea.

STUDY QUESTIONS

1. Under what conditions, if any, does one have the right to take justice into one's own hands?
2. If suicide, revenge, and patience are not viable solutions to loss and melancholy, what is?
3. Are minor forms of revenge like malicious slanders, vindictive abuse, fist fights, and petty theft necessary to a happy, healthy life? Are these things we cannot do without if we are to be powerful in a competitive modern world?
4. Why do people who believe in private revenge scorn institutions like the United Nations?
5. Why can't Hamlet be the patient young man his mother and stepfather want him to be?

TOPICS FOR WRITTEN AND ORAL DISCUSSION

1. It is possible to give up private aggression and revenge in all situations? Put yourself in a south-central Los Angeles gang, or on one or the other side of the conflicts presently taking place in Northern Ireland, the Middle East, or the former Yugoslavia, and ask yourself, as Hamlet must be asking himself: Is the world my mother is constructing a good deal, or merely the unacceptable loss of those blood bonds, that violence, those vital blood urges that I and so many before me have found irreplaceably valuable? What would it take to end private blood revenge in these areas where private blood revenge is still a condition of everyday life?
2. Discuss the point of having several revenge plots in *Hamlet* other than Hamlet's. Why include Fortinbras's, Pyrrhus's, and Laertes' attempts to get even for the loss of their fathers?
3. How difficult was it for early modern cultures to go against the approximately 39,000 years during which it was necessary for persons to exact blood revenge? Speculate on the strategies these cultures used to erase such a deeply inscribed, powerful, and virtually "natural" former necessity? What are the conditions under which a society can successfully prohibit private blood revenge? What conditions have to be met before citizens will give up this ancient "right"?
4. Read up on the earl of Essex and then speculate on what would be necessary, culturally speaking, for such a gifted young man's life not to end with an execution.

5. After reading *Hamlet* and Euripides's *Orestes* (c. 410 B.C.), or a prose
version of the myth the latter takes over from Aeschylus and Sophocles, compare the lives and revenge activities of these two legendary
cult figures.

SUGGESTED READINGS AND WORKS CITED

Bowers, Fredson. *Elizabethan Revenge Tragedy*. Princeton: Princeton
University Press, 1940.

Brown, Keith M. *Bloodfeud in Scotland, 1573–1625*. Edinburgh: J. Don-
ald, 1989.

Daly, Martin, and Margo Wilson. *Homicide*. New York: Aldine de Gruyer,
1988.

Kernan, Alvin. *Shakespeare, the King's Playwright*. New Haven: Yale University Press, 1995.

Jacoby, Susan. *Wild Justice: The Evolution of Revenge*. New York: Harper
and Row, 1983.

Prosser, Eleanor. *Hamlet & Revenge*, 2d. ed. Palo Alto: Stanford University
Press, 1967.

Smith, Lacey Baldwin. *Elizabeth Tudor: Portrait of a Queen*. Boston: Little, Brown, 1975.

Somerset, Anne. *Elizabeth I*. New York: St. Martin's Griffin, 1991.

Winstanley, Lillian. *Hamlet and the Scottish Succession*. Cambridge: Cambridge University Press, 1921.

A drawing of Amblet, Rørigs Dattersøn (King Rørig's daughter's son) from a manuscript dated 1597. Reprinted with permission from the Royal Library, Stockholm, Sweden.

7

Antic Dispositions: The Hero as Fool

To conceal beneath error the secret enterprise of truth
—Michel Foucault

Elizabethan audiences watching *Hamlet* had three perspectives from which to view and evaluate Hamlet's antic disposition: a biblical text and two pagan ones. Each of these texts yokes vengeance/revenge by someone *not* in an official position of power to different understandings of what it means for a hero to put on an antic disposition. The oldest and most available of these texts is the biblical account of David's attempt to feign madness while Saul was king of Israel (after 972 B.C.), a text from the *First Boke of Samuél* that finds such behavior ill-advised. Of the two pagan texts, the southern European one records events in the life of Lucius Junius Brutus (509 B.C.), while the northern European one (from before the ninth century A.D.) retells the Scandinavian legend of Amløthi, or Amleth. These European accounts, both vastly longer than the David story, take positive views of this strategy; however, they lead to different conclusions: the Brutus version uses an antic disposition to *end* kingship in ancient Rome, the Amløthi one uses it to *restore* kingship in pagan Denmark. Reading these texts, we will be in a position to understand why this strategy has commanded and divided people's attention since the beginning of recorded histories.

DAVID (after 972 B.C.)

Saul, the first king of the ancient Hebrews, sought several times to destroy David, his protégé and rival. On one occasion, finding himself in danger, and unwilling to strike back, David fled. In danger from Achish with whom he sought shelter, David feigned madness. This strategy failing, he hid in a cave. In other words, putting on an antic disposition not only does not work for David, but, with respect to the larger scheme of things, it cannot work because it does not square with the way David's deity operates. If Israel's God did not have things under control, and if David did not have a family, then an antic disposition might have been a viable solution for his problems; but, as divine control is not in question, and as David's "brethren and all his father's house" are on hand to help him, hiding his true self behind a pretense of madness is proscribed.

FROM *THE GENEVA BIBLE, THE FIRST BOKE OF SAMUÉL*
(Geneva: R. Hall, 1560)

XXI: 10 And David arose and fled the same day from the presence of Saul, and went to Achish the King of Gath.

11 And the servants of Achish said unto him, "Is not this David the King of the land? Did they not sing unto him in dances, saying, Saul has slain his thousand, & David his ten thousand"?

12 And David considered these words, and was sore afraid of Achish the King of Gath.

13 And he changed his behavior before them and feigned himself mad in their hands, and serabled [scraped and scratched with his hands] on the doors of the gate, and let his spetle fall down upon his beard.

14 Then said Achish unto his servants, "Lo, you see the man is beside himself, wherefore have you brought him to me?"

15 "Have I need of mad men, that you have brought this fellow to play the mad man in my presence? Shall he come into my house?"

XXII: 1 David therefore departed thence, and saved himself in the cave of Adullam: and when his brethren and all his father's house heard it, they went down thither to him.

LUCIUS JUNIUS BRUTUS (509 B.C.)

Since the account from Livy cited below assumes some knowledge of the story of Lucius Brutus, it is helpful to let John Lempriere's famous 1839 *Classical Dictionary* provide an introductory summary.

> Lucius's father and elder brother were murdered by Tarquinius Superbus, and Lucius, unable to revenge their death, and dreading the power of the tyrant, pretended to be insane. This artifice saved his life; he was called *Brutus* for his stupidity, which he, however, soon after shewed to be feigned. When Lucretia killed herself in consequence of [being brutally raped by] Tarquin's son, Sextus, Brutus snatched the dagger from the wound, and swore upon the reeking blade, immortal hatred to the royal family. His example animated the Romans. The Tarquins were proscribed by a decree of the senate, and royal authority was vested in the hands of consuls chosen from patrician families.

(In 1594, while writing *The Rape of Lucrece*, Shakespeare used a Latin version of Livy.)

FROM *THE ROMAN HISTORY WRITTEN IN LATINE BY TITUS LIVIUS*
[LIVY], II, LVI–LIX
(A.D. 17; English trans. John Freinshemius and John Dujatius,
London: A. Churchill, 1686)

While Tarquinius was thus employed, a terrible portent appeared to him, and that was, a snake crawling out of a wooden pillar, which putting him into a fright, made him run into the palace, but did not astonish him so much with sudden fear, as it filled his breast with anxious thoughts. Therefore to *Delphos*, to the most famous oracle upon the face of the whole earth, he sent his two sons, *Titus* and *Aruns*, who had for their companion, *Lucius Junius Brutus*, son to Tarquinia, the king's sister, a young man of quite different temper, from what he seemed. He [Brutus] having heard that the chief men of the city were murdered by his uncle, and that his brother was one, resolved to give the king no occasion of fear from any designs of his, nor any reason to covet his fortune, but to be safe, by being contemned, since there was little security in law and justice. He therefore industriously feigned himself a fool, and permitting the king to dispose of his person and estate as he thought fit, he did not refuse even the surname of *Brutus* [foolish or sottish], to the end, that under the covert of that surname, his latent soul which, once, was like to be the deliverer of the *Roman* people, might in due time show it self. He therefore, at that time, being taken to *Delphi*, along with the *Tarquinii*, for a laughing-stock, more than a companion; ('tis said) he carried a golden staff, enclosed [inside a staff] of the corneil-wood, which was hollowed for that purpose, as a present to *Apollo*, which was an emblem of his own ingenuity. Where, when they came, having executed their father's commands, the young men were very desirous to know, *To which of them the* Roman *kingdom should fall*: whereupon (they say) there came a voice out of the bottom of the cave, saying, *He among you three shall have the chief dominion at Rome, who gives his mother the first kiss.* The *Tarquinii*, to the end that *Sextus*, who was left at *Rome*, might not know the answer, and so be deprived of the empire, commanded it to be kept with all secrecy imaginable; and drew lots among themselves, which of them, when they came to *Rome*, should first kiss his mother. But *Brutus* imagining that the oracle had some other meaning, pretended to fall down by chance, and kissed the earth; for that, he considered, was the common mother of all men living. Then they came back to *Rome*, where there were great preparations making against the Rutuli [a hostile tribe].

The *Rutuli* . . . tried first to take *Ardea*, by a sudden onset, but that not succeeding, attacked the enemies by siege and counter-works. In that campaign . . . they [the Romans] had liberty enough of passing to and fro, but the officers more than the common soldiers. The king's sons and kinsmen did often spend their time in feasting and treating one another, and as they were drinking with *Sextus Tarquinius*, where *Collatinus Tarquinius*, the son of *Egerius*, then also supped, there happened a discourse concerning their wives, upon which, each man most wonderfully praised his own, and thence a quarrel arising, *Collatinus* said, *It was in vain to talk, since it might easily be known, and in a sort time, how much his* Lucretia *excelled the rest; wherefore, if you have an vigor in you, let us mount our horses, and go see with our own eyes, what kind of women our wives are; and that shall be the test, which occurs to each man upon his sudden arrival.* They were all heated with wine and therefore cried, *Come on, 'tis agreed*; and so galloped to *Rome*: whither when they came, about the edge of night, they went forward thence to *Collatia*; where they found *Lucretia*, not like the rest of the king's daughters-in-law, whom they saw spending their time with their equals in banqueting and luxury, but sitting late at night in the middle of her house amongst her maids a spinning. Whereupon, *Lucretia* was most commended, who received her husband and the *Tarquinii* very kindly, and her husband who was the victor in that controversy, very courteously invited the royal youths to supper: at which time, *Sextus Tarquinius* was seized with a lustful desire to ravish Lucretia, being incited both by her beauty and known chastity; and when they had ended their juvenile pastimes for that night, they returned to the camp.

Some few days after, *Sextus Tarquinius*, without the knowledge of *Collatinus*, took one companion only with him, and came to *Collatia*; where being received very kindly by them who knew nothing of his design, when, after supper, he was conducted into his lodging chamber, being inflamed with love, as soon as he thought all things secure enough, and every body fast asleep, he came, with his sword drawn, to *Lucretia's* bedside, and laying his left hand upon her breast, *Lucretia* (said he) *hold your tongue, I am Sextus Tarquinius, and I have my sword in my hand; if you speak one word you shall die.* The woman being frightened out of her sleep, and seeing death so nigh, without any hopes of relief, *Tarquinius* began to tell her how he loved her, to entreat her, and to mix menaces with his entreaties, and endeavored to persuade her by all manner of means. But when he saw her obstinate, and that she could not be prevailed upon, even by the fear of death, he added disgrace to fear, and told her, *He would stab a slave, and lay him naked by her when she was dead, so that a report should be raised, how she was killed in the very act of such sordid adultery.* By which terror, when his prevailing lust had overcome her obstinate chastity, and *Tarquin* having conquered the honor of a woman, was gone to *Rome*, Lucretia being very sad upon such a dismal occasion, sent the same messenger to *Rome* to her Father [Lucretius], and to *Ardea* to her husband, to desire them, that they would come thither each of them with a trusty friend, and that with speed too, for a grievous accident had befallen her.

[They came, the one accompanied with Junius Brutus, the other with Publius Valerius; and found] *Lucretia* sitting very pensive in her chamber. . . . Her husband asked her, *Art thou not well, my Dear? No,* (said she) *How can a Woman be well that has lost her chastity? There are yet the signs of another man, Collatinus, in thy bed: but my body only is violated, and my mind guiltless, of which my death shall be a witness: but give me your hands and your promises, that the adulterer shall not escape unpunished. Sextus Tarquinius is the man, who like an enemy, instead of a guest, the last night came armed to my bed, and thence forced pleasures, which, if you are men, will prove as fatal to him as me.* They all, one after another, gave her their word; comforting her grieved heart, and turning the guilt from her who was compelled, upon him who was the author of the crime; and telling her, *That her mind, not her body could only commit the offense, and where there was no consent, there could be no fault. Do you* (said she) *consider what he deserves; though I absolve my self from the crime, I will not be free from punishment; nor shall any unchaste woman live to say, Lucretia was her example.* With that, she took a knife which she had got under her garment, and stuck it into her heart, and falling forwards upon her wound, dropped down dead; at which her husband and her father set up a loud cry.

Brutus, while they were full of grief, drew forth the bloody knife out of Lucretia's wound, and said, *I swear, by this Blood, which was so chaste before the king stained it, and you, the gods, I take to witness it, that I will cut off L. Tarquinius Superbus, his wicked wife and all his children, with sword, fire, or any other violent means that I can; nor will I suffer either them, or any other, from this time forward, to be king of Rome.* Then he delivered the knife to *Collatinus*, and after that, to *Lucretius* and *Valerius*, who wondered to see that *Brutus* his disposition should be so suddenly altered: wherefore they swore, as he had done before them; and being wholly turned from lamentation to fury, immediately followed *Brutus*, who incited them to go and extirpate kingly government. They carried the body of *Lucretia* out of the house into the marketplace; where they stirred up the people (as it usually happens) at the sight and indignity of such a strange action, and every one complained of the king's outrage and violence, nor did her father's lamentations only move them, but *Brutus* restraining their tears and vain complaints, persuaded them to do what became men and Romans, by taking up arms against the common enemy. Immediately . . . the rest went armed after *Brutus* to *Rome*, where when they arrived, they being in arms, put the people into dread. . . . Wherefore the people ran from all parts of the city into the marketplace . . . where [Brutus] made an oration. . . . ["wherewith the people were so moved that with one consent and a general acclamation the Tarquins were all exiled and the state government changed from kings to consuls."] [This last sentence is from "The Argument" to Shakespeare's *The Rape of Lucrece*.]

THE HYSTORIE OF HAMBLET (1608)

The following excerpt is from a 1608 English translation of Belleforest's 1582 French translation of the 1514 Latin edition of Saxo
Grammaticus's 1200 rendition of an Icelandic legend of Amløthi
that dates from before the end of the ninth century A.D. And
though this English translation postdates Shakespeare's *Hamlet* (at
one point, in fact, it quotes a line, "a rat," from *Hamlet*) it allows
us to measure, to a degree, the extent Shakespeare altered his
French source for *Hamlet*. Of particular interest are the three
"test" scenes that parallel Ophelia's nunnery scene, Gertrude's
closet scene, and Rosencrantz and Guildenstern's ship scene. What
follows is approximately one-sixth of this English translation. Principally omitted are Belleforest's extensive ethical and political di-
gressions. All but one of Belleforest's allusions to the Brutus and
David material cited above have also been omitted. (Elisions within
sentences have not been indicated.)

FROM *THE HYSTORIE OF HAMBLET*
(London: Richard Bradocke, 1608)

Chap. I.

King Rodericke divided the kingdom [of Denmark] into divers provinces
giving the government of Jute to two valiant and warlike lords Horvendile
and Fengon, sons to Gervendile. Now the greatest honor that men of
noble birth could at that time win was in exercising the art of piracy
upon the seas, wherein Horvendile obtained the highest place in his time:
whose great fame so moved the heart of Collere, king of Norway, that he
was much grieved to hear that Horvendile surmounted him in feats of
arms. This valiant and hardy king having challenged Horvendile to fight
with him body to body, the combat was by him accepted, with conditions
that he which should be vanquished should lose all the riches he had in
his ship, and that the vanquisher should cause the body of the vanquished to be honorably buried. And to conclude, Collere, king of Norway was in the end vanquished and slain by Horvendile, who presently
caused a tomb to be erected, and therein (with all honorable obsequies
fit for a prince) buried the body of King Collere. And having slain the

king's sister, returned home again laden with much treasure, sending the most part thereof to his sovereign, King Rodericke.

The king, allured by those presents, and esteeming himself happy to have so valiant a subject, sought by a great favor and courtesy to make him become bound unto him perpetually, giving him Geruth his daughter to his wife, of whom he knew Horvendile to be already much enamored. . . . And to be brief, of this marriage proceeded Hamblet, of whom I intend to speak, and for his cause have chosen to renew this present history.

Fengon, brother to this prince Horvendile, who only fretting and despighting [spiteful] in his heart at the great honor and reputation won by his brother in warlike affairs, but solicited and provoked by a foolish jealousy to see him honored with royal alliance, and desiring to be only governor determined (whatsoever happened) to kill him. Fengon, having secretly assembled certain men, and perceiving himself strong enough to execute his enterprise, Horvendile his brother being at a banquet with his friends, suddenly set upon him, where he slew him as traitorously, as cunningly he purged himself of so detestable a murder to his subjects, so that instead of pursuing him as a parricide and an incestuous person, all the courtiers admired and flattered him in his good fortune. . . . Which was the cause that Fengon, bolded and encouraged by such impunity, dared venture to couple himself in marriage with her whom he used as his concubine during good Horvendile's life, in that sort spotting his name with the two-fold impiety, as incestuous adultery and parricide murder: and that the unfortunate and wicked woman, that had received the honor to be the wife of one of the valiantest and wiseth princes in the north, debased herself in such vile sort, as to falsify her faith unto him, and which is worse, to marry him, that had bin the tyrannous murderer of her lawful husband; which made divers men think that she had been the causer of the murder, thereby to live in her adultery without control. . . . But let us leave her in this extremity of lasciviousness, and proceed to show you in what sort the young prince Hamblet behaved himself, to escape the tyranny of his uncle.

Chap. II.

Geruth having (as I said before) so much forgotten herself, the prince Hamblet perceiving himself to be in danger of his life, as being abandoned of his own mother, and forsaken of all men, and assuring himself that Fengon would not detract the time to send him the same way his father Horvendile was gone, to beguile the tyrant in his subtleties counterfeiting the mad man with such craft and subtle practices, that he made show as if he had utterly lost his wits: and under that veil he covered his pretense, and defended his life from the treasons and practices of the tyrant his uncle. And all though he had been at the school of the Roman Prince, who, because he counterfeited himself to be a fool, was called Brutus, yet he imitated his fashions, and his wisdom. For every day being in the queen's palace, (who as then was more careful to please her whoremaster, than ready to revenge the cruel death of her husband, or to restore her son to his inheritance), he rent and tore his clothes, wallowing and lying in the dirt and mire, his face all filthy and black, running through the streets like a man distraught, not speaking one word, but such as seemed to proceed of madness and mere frenzy.

Hamblet, in this sort counterfeiting the mad man, many times did diverse actions of great and deep consideration, and often made such and so fit answers, that a wise man would soon have judged from what spirit so fine an invention might proceed; for that standing by the fire and sharpening sticks like poniards [daggers] and pricks, one in smiling manner asked him wherefore he made those little staves so sharp at the points? I prepare (said he) piercing darts and sharp arrows to revenge my father's death. Fools, as I said before, esteemed those his words as nothing; but men of quick spirits, and such as had a deeper reach began to suspect somewhat, esteeming that under that kind of folly there lay hidden a great and rare subtlety, such as one day might be prejudicial to their prince, saying, that under color of such rudeness he shadowed a crafty policy, and by his devised simplicity, he concealed a sharp and pregnant spirit: for which cause they counseled the king to try and know, if it were possible, how to discover the intent and meaning of the young prince; and they could find no better nor more fit invention to entrap him, than to set some fair and beautiful woman in a secret place, that with flattering speeches and all the craftiest means she could use, should purposely seek to allure his mind to have his pleasure of her. . . . To this end certain courtiers were appointed to lead Hamblet into a solitary place within the woods, whether they brought the woman, inciting him to take their pleasures together, and to embrace one another. . . . And surely the poor prince at this assault had him in great danger, if a gentleman (that in Horvendile's time had been nourished with him) had not shown himself more affectioned to the bringing up he had received with Hamblet, than desirous to please the tyrant, and therefore by certain signs, he gave Hamblet intelligence in what danger he was like to fall, if by any means he seemed to like the wanton toys and vidious provocations of the gentlewoman sent thither by his uncle. . . . The prince in this sort having both deceived the courtiers, and the lady's expectation, that affirmed and swore that he never once offered to have his pleasure of the woman, although in subtlety he affirmed the contrary, everyman there upon assured themselves that without all doubt he was distraught of his senses, that his brains were as then wholly void of force, and incapable of reasonable apprehension, so that as then Fengon's practice took no effect: but for all that he left not off, still seeking by all means to find out Hamblet's subtlety, as in the next chapter you shall perceive.

Chap. III.

Among the friends of Fengon, there was one that above all the rest doubted of Hamblet's practices in counterfeiting the madman, who for that cause said, that it was impossible that so crafty a gallant as Hamblet, that counterfeited the fool, should be discovered with so common and unskillfull practices which might easily be perceived, and that to find out his politic pretense it were necessary to invent some subtle and crafty means, more attractive, whereby the gallant might not have the leisure to use his accustomed dissimulation; which to effect he said he knew a fit way to effect the king's desire. . . . His device was thus, that King Fengon should make as though he were to go some long voyage concerning affairs of great importance, and that in the meantime Hamblet should be shut up alone in a chamber with his mother, wherein some other should secretly be hidden behind the hangings, unknown either to him or his mother, there to stand and hear their speeches, assuring the king that if there were any point of wisdom and perfect sense in the gallant's spirit, that without all doubt he would easily discover it to his mother, and withal offered himself to be the man that should stand to harken and bear witness of Hamblet's speeches. . . . The invention pleased the king exceeding well, esteeming it as the only and sovereign remedy to heal the prince of his lunacy; and to that end making a long voyage, issued out of his palace, and road to hunt in the forest. Meantime the counselor entered secretly into the queen's chamber, and there hid himself behind the arras, not long before the queen and Hamblet came thither, who being crafty and politic, as soon as he was within the chamber, doubting some treason, and fearing if he should speak severely and wisely to his mother touching his secret practices he should be understood, and by that means intercepted, used his ordinary manner of dissimulation, and began to come like a cock beating with his arms upon the hangings of the chamber: whereby, feeling something stirring under them, he cried, "A rat, a rat!" and presently drawing his sword thrust it into the hangings, which done, pulled the counselor (half dead) out by the heels, made an end of killing him, and being slain, cut his body in pieces, which he caused to be boiled and then cast it into an open vault or privy, that so it might serve for food to the hogs. By which means having discovered the ambush, and given the inventor thereof his just reward, he came again to his mother, who in the mean time wept and tormented herself. . . . And while in this sort she sat tormenting herself, Hamblet entered into the chamber, who having once again searched every corner of the

same, distrusting his mother as well as the rest, and perceiving himself
to be alone, began in sober and discreet manner to speak unto her saying.
. . . [In the extremely long speech that follows, Hamblet berates Geruth,
asking her at one point if she has played] "the part of a queen, and
daughter to a king? to live like a brute beast, to follow the pleasure of
an abominable king that had murdered a far more honester and better
man then himself in massacring Horvendile, the honor and glory of the
Danes. . . . O, queen Geruth, it is the part of a bitch to couple with many,
and desire acquaintance of diverse mastiffs: it is licentiousness only that
has made you deface out of your mind the memory of the valor and
virtues of the good king your husband and my father; it is not the part
of a woman, much less of a princess, in whom all modesty, courtesy,
compassion, and love ought to abound, thus to leave her dear child to
fortune in the bloody and murderous hands of a villain and traitor. Brute
beasts do not so, for lions, tigers, ounces and leopards fight for the safety
and defense of their whelps, but you, to the contrary, expose and deliver
me to death, whereas you should defend me. . . . Be not offended, I pray
you, Madame, if transported with dolour and grief, I speak so boldly unto
you, and that I respect you less then duty requires; for you, having forgotten me, and wholly rejected the memory of the deceased king my
father, must not be abashed if I also surpassed the bounds and limits of
due consideration. Behold into what distress I am now fallen, and to
what mischief my fortune, and your over great lightness, and want of
wisdom have induced me, that I am constrained to play the mad man to
save my life. . . . The face of a mad man serves to cover my gallant countenance, and the gestures of a fool are fit for me, to the end that guiding
myself wisely therein, I may preserve my life for the Danes, and the memory of my late deceased father; for the desire of revenging his death is so
engraved in my heart, that if I die not shortly, I hope to take such and
so great vengeance, that these countries shall for ever speak thereof. . . .
To conclude, weep not (madame) to see my folly, but rather sigh and
lament your own offense."

Although the queen perceived herself nearly touched, and that Hamblet moved her to the quick, where she felt herself interested, nevertheless she forgot all disdain and wrath, which thereby she might as then
have had, hearing herself so sharply chidden and reproved, for the joy
she then conceived, to behold the gallant spirit of her son, and to think
what she might hope, and the easier expect of his so great policy and
wisdom. And so, overcome and vanquished with this honest passion, and
weeping most bitterly, having long time fixed her eyes upon Hamlet, as
being ravished into some great and deep contemplation, and as it were
wholly amazed, at the last embracing him in her arms (with the like love
that a virtuous mother may or can use to kiss and entertain her own

child), she spoke unto him in this manner. . . . [In the long speech that follows Geruth explains her behavior as the consequence of her power-lessness, and then tells Hamblet:] "I have often been a means to hinder and impeach the shortening of your life, which being taken away, I will no longer live here upon earth. For seeing that your senses are whole and sound, I am in hope to see an easy means invented for the revenging of your father's death. Nevertheless, mine own sweet son, if you have pity of yourself, or care of the memory of your father I pray you, carry your affairs wisely: be not hasty, nor over furious in your enterprises, neither yet advance yourself more than reason shall move you to effect your purpose that I may rejoice in your prosperity, and therewith content myself, seeing with what courage and boldness you shall take vengeance upon the murderer of thy father."

"Madame (said Hamblet) I will put my trust in you, and from hence-forth mean not to meddle further with your affairs, beseeching you that you will from hence forth no more esteem of the adulterer, mine enemy, whom I will surely kill, or cause to be put to death, in despite of all the devils in hell."

After this, Fengon (as if he had been out some long journey) came to the court again, and asked for him that had received the charge to play the intelligencer, to entrap Hamblet in his dissembled wisdom, was abashed to hear neither news nor tidings of him, and for that cause asked Hamblet what was become of him, naming the man. The prince that never used lying, and who in all the answers that ever he made (during his counterfeit madness) never strayed from the truth answered and said that the counselor he sought for was gone down through the privy, where being choked by the filthiness of the place, the hogs meeting him had filled their bellies.

Chap. IIII.

A man would have judged anything, rather than Hamblet had committed that murder, nevertheless Fengon could not content himself, but still his mind gave him that the fool would play him some trick of legerdemain, and willingly would have killed him, but he feared king Rodericke, his grandfather, and further dared not offend the queen, mother to the fool, whom she loved and much cherished, showing great grief and heaviness to see him so transported out of his wits. And in that conceit, seeking to be rid of him, determined to find the means to do it by the aid of a stranger, making the king of England minister of his massacring resolu-tion, choosing rather that his friend should defile his renown with so great a wickedness, than himself to fall into perpetual infamy by an exploit of so great cruelty, to whom he purposed to send him, and by letters to desire him to put him to death.

Hamblet, understanding that he should be sent into England, presently doubted the occasion of his voyage, and for that cause speaking to the queen, desired her not to make any show of sorrow or grief for his departure, but rather counterfeit a gladness, as being rid of his presence; whom, although she loved, yet she daily grieved to see him in so pitiful estate, deprived of all sense and reason: desiring her further, that she should hang the hall with tapestry, and make it fast with nails upon the walls, and keep the brands for him which he had sharpened at the points, then, when as he said he made arrows to revenge the death of his father: lastly, he counseled her, that the year after his departure being accomplished, she should celebrate his funerals; assuring her that at the same instant she should see him return with great contentment and pleasure unto her for that his voyage. Now, to bear him company were assigned two of Fengons faithful ministers, bearing letters engraved in wood, that contained Hamblet's death, in such sort as he had advertised the king of England. But the subtle Danish prince (being at sea) while his companions slept, having read the letters, and known his uncle's great treason, with the wicked and villainous mines of the two courtiers that led him to the slaughter, razed out the letters that concerned his death, and instead thereof graved others, with commission to the king of England to hang his two companions; and not content to turn the death they had devised against him upon their own necks, wrote further, that King Fengon willed him to give his daughter to Hamblet in marriage. And so arriving in England, the messengers presented themselves to the king, giving him Fengon's letters; who having read the contents, said nothing as then, but stayed convenient time to effect Fengon's desire, mean time using the Dane's familiarly, doing them that honor to sit at his table.

[Omitted are the several legendary adventures Hamblet undergoes in England.]

The [English] king admiring the young prince, and beholding in him some matter of greater respect then in the common sort of men, gave him his daughter in marriage, according to the counterfeit letters by him devised, and the next day caused the two servants of Fengon to be executed, to satisfy, as he thought, the king's desire. But Hamblet, although the sport pleased him well, made as though he had been much offended, threatening the king to be revenged, but the king, to appease him, gave him a great sum of gold, which Hamblet caused to be molten, and put into two staves, made hollow for the same purpose, to serve his turn therewith as need should require; for of all other the king's treasures he took nothing with him into Denmark but only those two staves, and as

soon as the year began to be at an end, having somewhat before obtained
license of the king his father in law to depart, set sail for Denmark.

Chap. V.

Hamblet in that sort sailing into Denmark, entered into the palace of his
uncle the same day that they were celebrating his funerals, and going
into the hall, procured no small astonishment and wonder to them all,
no man thinking other but that he had been dead. . . . Their amazement
at the last being turned into laughter, all that as then were assistant at
the funeral banquet of him whom they esteemed dead, mocked each at
other, for having been so simply deceived, and wondering at the prince,
that in his so long a voyage he had not recovered any of his senses, asked
what was become of them that had born him company into Great Britain?
to whom he made answer (showing them the two hollow staves, wherein
he had put his molten gold, that the king of England had given him),
and said, "Here they are both." Whereat many that already knew his
humors, presently conjectured that he had plaid some trick of legerdemain, and to deliver himself out of danger, had thrown them into the pit
prepared for him: so that fearing to follow after them and light upon
some evil adventure, they went presently out of the court. And it was
well for them that they did so, considering the tragedy acted by him the
same day; for when every man busied himself to make good cheer, and
Hamblet's arrival provoked them more to drink and carouse, the prince
himself at that time played the butler and a gentleman attending on the
tables, not suffering the pots nor goblets to be empty, whereby he gave
the noble men such store of liquor, that all of them being full laden with
wine and gorged with meat, were constrained to lay themselves down in
the same place where they had supped, so much their senses were dulled,
and overcome with the fire of over great drinking, which when Hamblet
perceiving, and finding so good opportunity to effect his purpose and be
revenged of his enemies, and by the means to abandon the actions, gestures, and apparel of a mad man, occasion so fitly finding his turn, and
as it were effecting itself, failed not to take hold thereof, and seeing those
drunken bodies filled with wine, lying like hogs upon the ground, some
sleeping, others vomiting the over great abundance of wine which without measure they had swallowed up, made the hangings about the hall
to fall down and cover them all over; which he nailed to the ground, and
at the ends thereof he stuck the brands, whereof I spoke before, by him
sharpened, which served for pricks binding and tying the hangings in
such sort, that what force soever they used to loose themselves, it was
impossible to get from under them: and presently he set fire in the four
corners of the hall, in such sort that all that were as then therein not one

escaped away, but were forced to purge their sins by fires, and dry up the great abundance of liquor by them received into their bodies, all of them dying in the inevitable and merciless flames of the hot and burning fire: which the prince perceiving, became wise, and knowing that his uncle, before the end of the banquet, had withdrawn himself into his chamber, which stood apart from the place where the fire burnt, went thither, and entering into the chamber, laid hand upon the sword of his father's murderer, leaving his own in the place, which while he was at the banquet some of the courtiers had nailed fast into the scabbard, and going to Fengon said: "I wonder, disloyal king, how you can sleep here at your ease, and all your palace is burnt, the fire thereof having burnt the greatest part of your courtiers and ministers of your cruelty and detestable tyrannies; and which is more, I cannot imagine how you should well assure yourself and your estate, as now to take your ease, seeing Hamblet so near you armed with the shafts by him prepared long since, and at this present is ready to revenge the traitorous injury by you done to his lord and father."

Fengon, as then knowing the truth of his nephew's subtle practice, and hearing him speak with strayed mind, and which is more, perceived a sword naked in his hand, which he already lifted up to deprive him of his life, leaped quickly out of the bed, taking hold of Hamblet's sword, that was nailed into the scabbard, which as he sought to pull out, Hamblet gave him such a blow upon the chin of the neck, that he cut his head clean from his shoulder. [See Chapter 6 for the conclusion of the story.]

STUDY QUESTIONS

1. In what situations do individuals put on various kinds of dispositions by feigning ignorance, innocence, or expertise? Why do they do so?

2. Why doesn't dissimulation help David? Why is a strategy regarded as invaluable by Livy and Saxo of no interest to the author of *Samuél*?

3. What, in Livy's account, is the point of Tarquin's dream about "a snake crawling out of a wooden pillar"? What do the snake and the wooden pillar symbolize?

4. Does Tarquinius Sextus put on a kind of antic disposition? Does Fengon? If so, in what ways do their dispositions differ (if they do) from Brutus's and Hamblet's?

5. Why doesn't Hamblet kill Fengon earlier? How does the text account for his delay?

6. In what ways does *The Hystorie of Hamblet* legitimize Hamblet's actions as legal vengeance instead of a massacre?

7. What is the point of the gold-filled wooden staves in the Brutus and Hamblet narratives?

8. What are the chief differences between *The Hystorie of Hamblet* and Shakespeare's play?

9. In what ways does Christianity complicate for Hamlet the issues Brutus and Hamblet face as pagans? (Note the ways *The Hystorie of Hamblet* intrudes Christian consciousness into the pagan tale it is translating.)

QUESTIONS AND TOPICS FOR WRITTEN AND ORAL DISCUSSION

1. What are the larger political issues involved with respect to, and what is the powerful relationship between an antic disposition and tyranny?

2. How do women function in Livy's account of the Brutus story? What linkings of rape and resistance to tyranny have taken place in recent history?

3. In what ways does *The Hystorie of Hamblet* represent women? Why does it represent them in these ways? Can a woman legitimately feign madness?

4. How are pleasure and sexual desire (male and/or female) represented in *The Hystorie of Hamblet*? That is, in what ways do sex and pleasure function in this text?

5. In taking over the materials of his source, Shakespeare often relocates them. For example, where in *Hamlet* does he put, and how does he alter the "dead spy going through a privy hole into the bellies of hogs" passage in *Hamblet*?

6. If feigning is inevitable for participation in human society, how then does one decide between the modes of feigning one must do without, and those one cannot do without?

7. Compare the closet scene in *Hamlet* (3.4) to the parallel scene in *The Hystorie of Hamblet*.

SUGGESTED READINGS

Bacon, Francis. "Of Simulation and Dissimulation." In *The Essayes or Covnsels, Civill and Morall*. London: R. Whitaker, 1625.

Hansen, William F. *Saxo Grammaticus & the Life of Hamlet, A Translation, History, and Commentary*. Lincoln and London: University of Nebraska Press, 1983.

Gollancz, Sir Israel. *The Sources of* Hamlet: *With an Essay on the Legend*. London: Oxford University Press, 1926.

Jenkins, Harold, ed. *Hamlet*. Arden edition. London and New York: Routledge, 1982, 85–96.

8 ⸻⸻⸻⸻⸻⸻⸻⸻⸻

Gertrude, Thy Name Is Woman

> It is getting around . . . that women diffuse themselves according to modalities scarcely compatible with the framework of the ruling symbolics. Which doesn't happen without causing some turbulence, we might even say some whirlwinds . . . spreading to infinity.
>
> —Luce Irirgary

Gertrude is the most unjustly treated character in *Hamlet*. An angry ghost slanders her. Hamlet "will speak daggers to her, but use none" (3.2.366). In the ghost and closet scenes, Gertrude, put on trial, is told she is what is rotten in Denmark. And at the end she is abandoned and killed. Identifying with these accusers and rubber stamping their accusations, numerous critics have written large outside the play the attack Hamlet and the ghost articulate within it with the effect that much of the critical literature on Gertrude is little more than a litany of abuse echoing and amplifying the indictments men level against her onstage. These judgments are extremely problematic, however, since virtually none of them are true. The Gertrude we find in the play (unless productions or criticism make her otherwise) is, with one exception, not guilty of any of these crimes. After hearing the defense argue Gertrude's case on the basis of the documentary materials included in the rest of this chapter, readers will, of course, construct their own rebuttals for or against Gertrude.

To begin, let us list the charges made by the prosecution. Gertrude is allegedly guilty of

1. committing adultery: "makes marriage vows / As false as dicers' oaths" (3.4.43–44);

2. being complicit in the murder of her husband and living with the assassin of her deceased husband: "As kill a king and marry with his brother" (3.4.28);

3. failing to observe proper mourning: "a beast that wants discourse of reason / Would have mourned longer" (1.2.150–51);

4. remarrying excessively fast: "The funeral baked meats / Did coldly furnish forth the marriage tables" (1.2.179–80), and "O most wicked speed" (1.2.156);

5. committing incest: "With such dexterity to incestuous sheets!" (1.2.157);

6. being compulsively sexual: "to live / In the rank sweat of an enseamed [greasy] bed / Stewed in corruption, honeying, and making love" (3.4.82–83);

7. exercising gross lack of judgment: "married with mine Uncle, / My father's brother, but no more like my father / Then I to Hercules" (1.2.151–53), "to decline / Upon [this] wretch . . . and prey on garbage" (1.5.50–51, 57);

8. neglecting her duty to her son: "I lack advancement" (3.2.311);

9. being fickle and false: "frailty, thy name is woman" (1.2.146), and "most seeming vertuous queen" (1.5.46).

In the face of these charges, then, what proof to the contrary? The first two charges are easily dismissed since there is no evidence in the text to support them. Though Hamlet's words frequently are taken as proof of adultery, neither the ghost nor Hamlet accuses Gertrude of sleeping with Claudius while Hamlet Sr. was alive, and no other evidence supports such a conclusion. Thus, this allegation is without merit, though left open are any number of other ways the prosecution may think Gertrude guilty of making her "marriage vows / As false as dicers' oaths." Moreover, in light of the way Gertrude responds in the closet scene (3.4), Hamlet relinquishes his belief that Gertrude is complicit in his father's death or knows she is living with the man who murdered her first husband. In short, the first two charges are hasty, unfounded fabrications based solely on the legendary source.

This leaves, in the main, three matters to deal with: Gertrude doesn't mourn long enough after the funeral and remarries too suddenly (charges 3 and 4); she commits incest by marrying her brother-in-law (charge 5); and she ignores the proper conduct expected of widows by continuing to be sexually active, and by neglecting her alleged duty to her son (charges 6, 7 and 8). Each is dealt with in a separate section below, followed by materials clarifying why Hamlet hustles his mother into the ancient category of *"wikked wyf"* (charge 9). In a final section, Jane Anger, an early modern author whose name is much to the point, takes over the defense of woman, if not specifically of Gertrude. Before turning to these arguments and these materials, several prefatory matters will lay a foundation for the defense.

First, Hamlet's rage. Rage so powerful that it makes him wish Gertrude were not his mother, so powerful that he momentarily desires to kill her—a violent repudiation of woman anticipated by the length he goes to in the earlier nunnery scene to expel Ophelia from his life (3.1). No doubt there are several causes for this rage. One is that (in his mind) his mother has destroyed his hopes of becoming king after his father's death, and this is painful for a man who has been waiting for a considerable number of the thirty years he has been alive for the day he would follow in his father's footsteps, put on the crown, and say, "this is I, / Hamlet the Dane" (5.1.241–42). But when his mother's remarriage lets Claudius "pop in" between his hopes and his election, he takes his disappointment out on her, the most available scapegoat on whom he can shift the blame. That is, Hamlet doesn't take it out on himself, his father, or the patriarchal system that hasn't worked for him.

But blasted hopes are not the only cause of Hamlet's rage. Consider the possibility that Hamlet hasn't been feeling or doing what he thinks *he* ought to have been feeling and doing with respect to his father's death. Despite a cloak of inky black, he doesn't seem to have reacted much in the past, and he isn't reacting now with anything like the passion with which Hecuba mourns Priam's death in the passage Hamlet asks a player to recite. So one wonders how

Hamlet—a rather scholarly thirty-year-old prince who has been standing in the wings watching his father play the hero/god role—felt about this father while he was alive. If he didn't mourn, and, despite a single appearance to the contrary, is not mourning, is it possible that, plagued by guilt and fear, he is projecting his own "not reacting sufficiently" onto his mother in order to protect his image of himself as an ideal son?

Or, considering that Hamlet can't go back to Wittenberg or isolate himself with Ophelia, is it not possible that he may be projecting a guilt-producing desire to get on with something that would allow him to enjoy a happy life onto a mother who has gotten on with her life? Instead of accepting desires and feelings that, from an emergent perspective, are normal for a person in his situation, Hamlet apparently feels such guilt for not living up to an expectation that he deeply mourn that he displaces his failure to do so onto his mother where he can flagellate, reform, and end this failure in the maternal other. It is, in part, this unconscious strategy, driven by his desire to satisfy the desire of the paternal other (the defense will argue), that transforms Hamlet's depression and guilt into a repetition of the father's imagined rage, and then focuses this imitated rage, not on *his* own wayward desires nor on *his* imagined betrayals of the father, but on *her* desires and *her* imagined betrayals. This scapegoating also allows Hamlet to exercise his jealously and envy—jealousy that his mother is in a happy, satisfying relationship, and that he isn't; envy of the happiness and pleasure she has that is forbidden him by his father's world—by transforming his jealousy and envy into moral superiority, and by reducing her happiness to rank and detestable crimes he can sadistically punish. Furthermore, this moral superiority and the sadism it necessitates gives Hamlet something heroic to do (he thinks) in the face of not being able to figure out how to deal with Claudius, or how to have a viable relationship with Ophelia. Having no kingdom to rule, and no lover to embrace, "scourge and minister" become two of the many hopeless roles with which he chooses to fill up the nothing that, at present, has become his life.

The defense will assume, then, that Hamlet's allegations against his mother are motivated, not by what she has done or is doing, but by the error and shame that haunts Hamlet in the figure of a ghost, feelings he can only free himself of by piping them off onto her with the hope that the punishment these crimes cannot help but call down from above will strike her rather than himself. Hamlet employs this conventional scapegoat process on a woman whose activities in the months following her husband's death are unexceptionable for a woman in her society and in her position in society. Gertrude's behavior then, is not a crime for anyone in the world of the play except Hamlet; moreover (as we will see below), her behavior would not have been seen as a crime by anyone in the audience except those who identify with Hamlet's and the ghost's misogyny.

Needless to say, this scapegoat explanation for why Hamlet is abusing Gertrude is a working assumption. To some readers it will no doubt seem flimsy speculation. But, on reflection, it is (the defense argues) considerably less speculative, and considerably less flimsy than the working assumptions, long taken for granted, on which the prosecution has built its case: the assumption that Hamlet is, and has been, really mourning his father's death (that long closed and then all too briefly opened doorway to Hamlet's being king); and the assumption as well that Hamlet never had plans or desires—certainly never the desire to be king in his father's place—which might now cause him to feel as though he is betraying his father. The prosecution, in other words, works on the unproved assumption that the Hamlet seen in this play is a perfect nothing-but-dutiful son of a perfect father who is incensed only by the crimes someone else commits, whereas the defense will assume that Hamlet is doing and has done a number of things that create the melancholy and guilt that fuels the rage that turns his violence against everyone around him, particularly Gertrude.

Equally speculative and unproved is the prosecution's corollary assumption that Gertrude is the pernicious beast Hamlet and the ghost say she is. To be sure, Gertrude is not perfect, but neither is she a villain, so to make her the latter to elevate Hamlet to the former is to turn Shakespeare's complex play, as the prosecution does, into cheap melodrama. Far preferable (the defense maintains) is to understand what Gertrude has done and why she has done it, and why her doing so turns Hamlet into a "scourge and minister" of vindictive violence.

One thing Gertrude has done that Hamlet loathes concerns her relationship to Hamlet Sr. prior to his death. The prosecution assumes that Hamlet's present representations of Gertrude and Hamlet Sr.'s relationship accurately represents a past reality in which Hamlet's father was nothing but a loving husband ("a radiant Angel") and Gertrude was nothing but in love with him until he died:

> so loving to my mother,
> That he [Hamlet Sr.] might not beteem [let] the winds of heaven
> Visit her face too roughly. . . . Why, she would hang on him
> As if increase of appetite had grown
> By what it fed on, and yet within a month—
> Let me not think on't.   (1.2.140–46)

As a rule of thumb, anyone working in Gertrude's defense ought to be suspicious whenever Hamlet starts remembering or thinking, since what these verbs tend to mean when he uses them is that he is sentimentalizing and/or forgetting—in other words, reconstructing the past to square with how it now has to be if there is to be any legitimacy to his accusations against, and rage at, his mother. If Hamlet is describing the past accurately—if Gertrude and Hamlet Sr. really were in love to the degree Hamlet says they were—then it truly would be inexplicable why she should stop mourning so soon, fall for Claudius, and ruin Hamlet's opportunity to become king, however inadvertently.

So let us abandon the prosecution's myth of past perfection and work instead on the defense assumption that things in the past were not at all the way Hamlet "remembers" them, though one explanation of why he thinks they were is that his culture gives him no language with which to represent reality other than the good/bad, perfection/abomination discourse he is using, and because one of the principal functions of such binary language in patriarchal culture is precisely to cover up—ignore, deny, misrepresent, mythicize—the actual tracks of history by substituting perfection in their place (e.g., Hamlet Sr. as "a radiant Angel"). Hamlet (as we have seen) needs to have the past perfect so he can set it against what he regards as his mother's all too imperfect present. Moreover, his sense of an absolute difference between Gertrude's Edenic before and her fallen after might well be the product of the fact that she *seemed* the perfect wife and mother in the past. To be sure, she might have had to seem so, might well have had to play some such role in the theatre of Hamlet Sr.'s life. Nevertheless, whatever the appearance, at some level things could not have been (the defense will assert) as perfect or as satisfying as Hamlet makes them out to have been, since present effects have discernible historical causes, not mythic ones.

Gertrude (the defense will argue) wanted something other than, or more than, or less than, what was available with Hamlet Sr., and when she had the opportunity, perhaps for the first time in her life, to get what she didn't have and perhaps never had, and, finding it in Hamlet Sr.'s brother and/or in the opportunity to continue being Denmark's queen, she went for it when the occasion of Hamlet Sr.'s death freed her to satisfy her desire even though this meant disappointing her son of his monarchical hopes and ambitions. Presumably, given that Hamlet charges her with bestial lust, this something she lacked was neither just satisfaction of her sexual desires nor just Claudius's sexual abilities, though both no doubt were part of it. Rather, this something she desired must have been something like what it is that Ophelia needs from Hamlet and what Hamlet does not want to give (or is perhaps incapable of giving): a greater degree of power, equality, reciprocity, attention, intimacy, passion—relational and affectional modalities of being Hamlet is no more comfortable with, and no more capable of giving to a woman, than his father seems to have been capable of. And so, unable to face these realities, Hamlet is driven to manufacture the desperately defensive constructions of an ideal Hamlet Sr. and a grotesque Claudius that he shoves, as "counterfeit presentments," in his mother's face, portraits that can only be read, from the perspective of the defense, as an attempt to cover up the extremely obvious fact that in Gertrude's eyes it is Claudius who was always closer to the ideal, and Hamlet Sr. who had verged on the grotesque.

What Hamlet and the ghost see then as a "falling off," must have been for Gertrude a wonderful release to a desired freedom, source of pleasure, satisfaction—in short, to a *life*. To be able at last to come down off the rocky, barren, but no doubt spectacular mountaintop of Hamlet Sr.'s emotional aridities where there is "food" only for her eyes, and feed her hands and ears, heart and mind, for the first time in the pastures of Claudius's interiorities is not to prey on garbage unless one is standing (or is required to stand, or requires oneself to stand) like Moses on the top of, finally, an inhuman battlement with an inhuman ghost. From the perspective of a moor, however, for Gertrude "to feed" is to have food for the first time in her life. To be sure, a moor may not be all that fertile and rich compared, say, to a lush valley; but in comparison to a mountaintop, for someone who has had to live her entire life on a mountaintop, a moor is a space no doubt of almost cornucopian abundance. In a culture where the mountaintop old Hamlet and old Norway constructed for themselves is the only masculine identity positively valued by sons like Hamlet and Fortinbras, a moor, however ugly in these sons' eyes, must have been a rare thing for a woman's eyes to see, and a rarer thing for a man to be, or pretend to be.

Hamlet's "Have you eyes?" [3.4.66] is, then, absolutely the wrong question to ask Gertrude, since she seems to have become extremely tired of having to live life with eyes alone. By his very repetition of "Have you eyes?" Hamlet defensively denies the extent to which he is afraid to recognize that his mother also has ears, heart, mind, liver, stomach, genitals, feelings, desires for power, not to mention hopes and ambitions as urgent (and a lot older) than his. So there Hamlet stands, all too afraid of what her answer might be to questions like: Have you ambitions? Have you desires? desperately trying to convince himself that women only have eyes and that all they want to do is look passively at ideal masculine figures. Hamlet is completely unable to understand anything real about his own mother, much less the desires he projects onto her as base appetite. Moreover, he is totally confused and in despair that the way he was taught things were between men and women (and believed things to have been between his father and mother) is proving to be a patriarchal fiction, and terrified, too, that, in reality, his mother probably feels much the same way about him that she felt about his father, not to mention shocked to realize that she didn't want (simply wasn't able) to sacrifice any more of her life for him, a repetition of his father, once that mountain was leveled. So given over to perplexity, enraged, and banging about this way and that, he lashes out vindictively against Gertrude, accusing her of crime after crime in the desperately futile hope that scourging her soul will restore the idealized fantasy world he had long taken for granted. One of the many tragic things about this situation is that Hamlet lacks any discourse or knowledge which could even begin to deal with the turbulence and whirlwinds caused in his psyche and in his world by this newly liberated woman, and thus of necessity is forced to rely on the only knowledge he has, those ancient patriarchal "sawes" [wise sayings] and "formes" [mental concepts] and "pressures [impressions] past" that boot up as a ghost on the table of Hamlet's memory to erase and replace the sawes, formes, and pressures presently inscribed there by the new dominant order, but which are of absolutely no help to Hamlet except to fuel the rage that drives him in time to commit one violently destructive act after another, of which abuse of his mother is neither the least violent, nor the least destructive.

On their mountaintop, however, the prosecution remains totally convinced that Hamlet, a paragon of love, justice, rectitude, and reason, knows all there is to know and all one needs to know, and has a totally adequate language to talk about love and women, power and women, men and women, because the knowledge and language Hamlet has is an ancient, deeply self-serving, misogynist language that pontificates through Hamlet with reassuringly ghostly authority that Gertrude is a perfectly straightforward, clear case of yet one more woman who, having everything, let down the man (the "radiant Angel") who gave her everything.

To conclude this introduction, several rules of thumb. First, never argue with the prosecution on their turf where their working assumptions, taken for granted, remain invisible. Before entering into arguments concerning a subject like Gertrude's culpability, make visible the long taken-for-granted, invisible, and deeply pa-triarchal assumptions of one's opponents. That is, with respect to the woman on trial, recognize that the prosecution and the defense are in opposition: the former occupying the residual position, the latter an emergent one. And, second, do not fall for the prosecu-torial fiction that nothing more than a woman's crimes are at stake in a judicial undertaking such as this one, since what in fact is at stake in this matter of Gertrude's alleged criminality is nothing less than the adequacy of the way patriarchal culture was constructed in early modern England, and the way it remains constructed in much of the present. In short, to prove Gertrude falsely accused, the defense must put patriarchal culture itself on trial, and to do this it must learn and use the tactics worked out by those persons radically excluded from and disempowered by their position in a patriarchal/misogynous social order who learned to put this system of power itself on trial, and who won significant victories against it. Thus, Gertrude cannot be defended unless the defense learns to use the discourses developed by emergent, nonhomosocial minorities precisely for the purpose of reimagining and then reconstructing the symbolic order that minoritized them. Of these emergent discourses (as we will see), one was developed in early modern England in part by Jane Anger. But before we get to that early articulation of a powerful feminist discourse reaching far back before Anger, we must first work our way through those patriarchal discourses (those "sawes . . . [and] pressures past") that tragically fill Hamlet's head, because one of the functions of this Shakespearean tragedy is to encourage its audience to see just how lethal these sacred patriarchal discourses can be when they are put into practice by bright young men like Hamlet who become dead set on pleasing their fathers, or, rather, the ghostly images they have of them—bright young men in whose minds woman alone is seen to create the aperture through which history and thus death enter the sacred realm, a misperception that proves women to be the chief bane of their desperately pure and doggedly endless repetition of a fantasized, ritualized, and always already dead patriarchal past.

So if Gertrude is not the cause and source of Denmark's problems, what is? The answer this play offers is that which accuses her of being this cause and source, namely, patriarchal society itself, and, quite literally, a dead king's out of joint and rotting bodies: the disastrously limited and limiting way these bodies (his immaterial royal body *and* his material physical body) constitute cultural space, the inhuman demands they make on wife, son, and brother, the damage they inflict on everyone else in Elsinore, the legacy of misrepresentations they will to their heirs, the tragic poverty of their utterly inadequate yet allegedly omniscient knowledge—the list goes on and on. In short, to blame Gertrude for the rottenness in Denmark is yet once again to project the limitations and problems inherent to patriarchal culture, if not also the mortal nature of life itself, onto a woman and, through her, onto all women, and thus to do what patriarchy has endlessly done since it nominated Eve as the cause of man's first disobedience and everything awful that has ever happened thereafter.

The documents that follow turn attention to the specific charges made by the prosecution and to the work of establishing a point-by-point defense. The materials used to construct this case are substantial, for which there are three justifications. Gertrude is the

most unjustly treated character in the play, and the most neglected; the closet scene at the center of this play (3.4) traditionally
receives short shrift; and, with very few exceptions, what has been
argued about Gertrude in this scene does a great deal to help us
*mis*understand the function of both Gertrude and this scene in
this play. To put it bluntly, Gertrude, the closet scene, and the
issues they raise have been largely ignored and/or misread because
a great deal of male criticism has spent its energy idealizing the
play's masculine issues and characters at Gertrude's expense. To
reverse this tradition is to redistribute space to Gertrude. The gain?
A better understanding of *Hamlet*.

FUNERALS AND MOURNING

In part, the prosecution labels Gertrude a pernicious woman because she does not mourn long enough after the death of her first husband. No evidence exists in the surviving records of Elizabethan culture, however, that would support such a charge. In fact, the early modern texts on this subject indicate that by following Hamlet Sr.'s "body / Like *Niobe* all tears" for "a little month," as Hamlet himself confirms (1.2.147–49), Gertrude observed proper Elizabethan protocol. Moreover, these texts suggest that virtually *no* member of an early modern theatre audience would have expected Gertrude to mourn longer than she did. To be sure, funeral practices tended to go on longer as the seventeenth century moved toward its midpoint, and claims often were made that ritualized mourning exceeded periods longer than a month. In actual fact, however, few of these events measure up to the claims made. Take, for instance, the fact that in the middle ages, "widowed [Catholic] queens were expected to stay for a year or more in darkened rooms hung with black" (Puckle 1926, 98). Are these queens engaged in this practice because they are in deep mourning? Or are they engaged in it because they have been locked away in dark rooms by a new regime as a way of keeping them out of the way as it takes over and establishes its power, something it would presumably find more difficult to do if a previous queen were actively present at court? In this context Hamlet's desire to see Gertrude mourn longer than a "little month" can be read as a desire to see her place herself in a confinement that would preclude her from retaining any power, and thus allow him to take over.

MOURNING ETIQUETTE IN ELIZABETHAN ENGLAND

Of those in early modern England who would have had the last word on matters of etiquette, none would have had authority as final as Elizabeth's heralds, officers of the court who "presided at chivalric ceremonies and royal proceedings . . . compiled rolls of arms," and sometimes, as in the case of Sir William Segar, Garter king of arms, chief herald of England, wrote books (Bornstein, 1975 vii). Thus, it is difficult to think that Segar's *Honor Military and Civill*, dedicated to Queen Elizabeth and recognized in its own time as the definitive work in its field, would not know the length of time a noble woman was expected to mourn after her husband's death. The "little month" of Gertrude's mourning that Hamlet finds so utterly short is, according to Segar, exactly the length of time that "has ever been" considered proper in England as well as in ancient Israel, Rome, and France.

FROM SIR WILLIAM SEGAR, *HONOR MILITARY AND CIVILL*
(London: Robert Barker, 1602)

Of Funerals.

The Romans likewise used many ceremonies in burying of the dead. . . . This custom was also observed among the Egyptians, as appears in the last of *Gene.* where *Joseph* commanded his Physicians, that they should embalm the body of his father *Jacob.* In performing of which Ceremony they spent forty days, and thirty in mourning. In like manner, the people of Israel mourned for *Moses* thirty days. *Deut. 34.* And *Valerius tit. de Seruata relig.* makes mention that after the battle and slaughter at Canna, the Senate of *Rome* commanded that every matron of *Rome* should mourn thirty days, and not longer. Other customs among other Nations have been used: for some were enjoined to end their mourning within forty days: some others within three, and some in seven. But in *France* and *England* the use of mourning has ever been thirty days, chiefly among persons of honor, as may be conceived of a sentence given in *Burgundy* by an Official there, who having cited before him a Lady called *Jacquelina de la Trimoille* daughter to the King's Lieutenant in *Burgundy*, upon certain promises matrimonial, she answered by Proctor, her appearance ought be excused, in respect the thirty days of her father's death were not expired: During which time she might not go out of her house, which Plea was allowed.

INCEST

Incest, the first crime to be charged against Gertrude by Hamlet in the closet scene, is no doubt the first because, since she is her "husband's brother's wife" (3.4.14), incest is the only crime alleged against Gertrude the prosecution can prove. By marrying Claudius, Gertrude violates biblical prohibition, and Tudor ecclesiastical law as recorded in an appendix to the second *Book of Common Prayer* (1559): "A woman may not marry with her . . . husband's brother." And, as critics frequently tell us, Elizabethans thought that "the marriage of brothers- and sisters-in-law had been branded shameful over hundreds of years of moral teaching since Old Testament times" (Frye 1984, 77). Indeed, many in Biblical and classical legends who broke this prohibition were seen as coming to a bad end, as did Tarquinius Superbus and Fengon, both killers of brothers and husbands of widowed sisters-in-law. In light of these precedents, a number of critics have concluded that Shakespeare expected his audience to view the Claudius–Gertrude marriage with "as much abhorrence as the Athenians felt for the union of Oedipus and his mother Jocasta in Sophocles" (Frye 1984, 80, citing J. Dover Wilson). So, it will be asked, what evidence can the defense use to support its counterclaim that virtually no Elizabethan theatregoer would have responded to Gertrude's marriage with abhorrence at all? Consider the following case of *affinity* incest (sexual relations between persons like Gertrude and Claudius who are related to each other only by marriage), as opposed to *consanguinity* incest (sexual relations between persons descended from the same ancestor and thus of the same blood, like Oedipus and his mother, Jocasta). This case of affinity incest, tried in the Durham Ecclesiastical Court before 1560, is a case of incest between a man and his uncle's widow, not a man and his brother's widow; however, Elizabethan law was the same for both.

Glosses for the following document have been provided by the author.

FROM DURHAM ECCLESIASTICAL COURT RECORDS

(c. 1560; cited in Lisa Jardine, " 'No Offense i' th' World': Unlawful
Marriage in *Hamlet*." In *Reading Shakespeare Historically*. London
and New York: Routledge, 1996)

EDWARD WARD *of Langton near Gainford, husbandman, aged 40 years.*

He said that there is divers writing [a number of official proclamations]
hanging upon the pillars of their church of Gainford, but what they are,
or to what effect, he cannot deposse [he does not understand]; saying
that he and other parishioners do give their duties to be taught [had
dutifully received instruction in] such matters as he is [being] examined
upon, and is not instruct [but was not told] of any such [law concerning
his case].

He said, that he was married with the said Agnes in Gainford church
by the curat Sr Nicholas, about 14 days next after Christmas last past, but
not contrary to the laws of God, as he and she thought. And for the
residue [remainder] of the article he thinks [it] now to be true, but not
then. Examined whether that he, this deponent [i.e., Edward], did know
at and before the time of the marriage, that she the said Agnes was, and
had been, his uncle Christopher Ward's wife, yes or no, he said that he
knew that to be true, for she had, and has yet, five children of his the
said Christopher's. Examined upon the danger of their souls, and evil
example, he said that both he and many honest men in that parish thinks
that it were a good deed that they two might still live together as they
do, and be no further troubled.

AGNES WARD, ALIAS SAMPTON, *aged 40 years.*

—all the Lordship and paroch [parish clergyman] of Gainford knew how
nigh [how closely related] hir first husband [Christopher Ward] and last
husband [Edward Ward] was of kin, and yet never found fault with their
marriage, neither when they were asked in the church 3 sundry Sundays
nor since—they have been likened [linked?] together more and two year,
and yet never man nor woman found fault—but rather thinks good
thereof, because she was his own uncle's wife.

How, then, can we defend Gertrude against the abhorrence felt by
Elizabethans? Clearly, we would not have needed to defend her in
Durham since, as is clear from this passage, "never man nor
woman found fault" with Edward's and Agnes's technically incestuous marriage. Even in a court responsible for upholding eccle-

siastical law, there was nothing like the abhorrence Athenians felt about Oedipus and Jocasta. Moreover, in the spiritual courts of Essexshire during the entire reign of Queen Elizabeth (1558–1603), only *four* cases of affinity incest between sisters and brothers-in-law or brothers and sisters-in-law were tried and recorded—that is, four out of the approximately 2,000–3,000 entries recorded over forty-five years—and these cases were tried *only* because a person claiming personal damage in some other respect had brought a complaint. Lisa Jardine makes the point: "Someone had to draw the marriage to the attention of the courts; that person had to be someone to whom the 'unlawfulness' of the marriage gave some (material) offence" (41). What this means is that it was highly unlikely that anyone would be brought before a court for affinity incest in and by itself. It also means that an untold number of affinity incest relationships were never charged at all: "the codes rarely led to legal action" (41–42). "In a pioneer local study, A. D. J. Macfarlane recently came to some important conclusions with regard to the attitude of the ordinary [Elizabethan] people to incest. Contrary to the general critical view, 'the element of horror so often described by anthropologists . . . appears to have been completely absent in Tudor and Stuart England'; and he adds that 'incestuous marriages met with little disapproval' " (Emmison 1973, 36–37). In light of this evidence it is clear that virtually all members of Elizabethan popular theatre audiences would have reacted to Gertrude and Claudius's marriage in the same way every character on stage reacts to it other than Hamlet: they would *not* have seen it as a crime; rather, they would have regarded it as a technical infraction of an out-of-date and rarely enforced ecclesiastical code, a molehill Hamlet makes into a mountain for reasons of his own.

The following biblical text is one basis for the early modern incest law cited above.

FROM *THE GENEVA BIBLE, THE THIRD BOKE OF MOSÉS, CALLED LEUITICUS*
(Geneva: R. Hall 1560)

XVIII: 6 None shall come near to any of the kindred of his flesh to uncover *her* shame: I am the Lord. [*marginal gloss*: That is, to lie with her, though it be under title of marriage.]

16 Thou shall not discover the shame of thy brother's wife: for it is thy brother's shame.

XX: 21 So the man that takes his brother's wife, commits filthiness, because he has uncovered his brother's shame: they shall be childless.

WIDOWHOOD

For Gertrude, it is also, of course, about sex. Had she predeceased Hamlet Sr., Hamlet would have expected his father to go on having a sex life. But when his father predeceases Gertrude, he is appalled that she desires to continue being sexually active as he makes clear in the closet scene: "You cannot call it love, for at your age / The heyday in the blood is tame, it's humble, / And waits upon the judgment" (3.4.67–68). To defend Gertrude against the charge that she isn't being a proper widow is a more complicated issue than those charges encountered above, since early modern culture was deeply divided on an issue where principles often tended to give way to contradictory practice.

On the male side, some patriarchal authorities wanted women remarried as quickly as possible to keep them under male authority. Others supported second marriages, particularly for young widows, on the grounds that it was better for such women to have sex within a marriage than to do so outside matrimony and burn. And other patriarchs opposed widows remarrying to keep lines of inheritance from getting tangled by second families. On the female side some widows did not want to marry again, having been burnt once, and seem to have been happy retiring from the social world. Others had to remarry to keep a former husband's business going, or to have sex without guilt. But many, like Gertrude, were seeking to find in a second marriage what they hadn't found in their often arranged first marriage. As a later writer, Daniel Rogers, put it, these widows wanted "jollity, and a braver and fuller life then formerly they were content with" (1642, 45).

To make matters more difficult, little textual evidence exists for the full span of this controversy, since what is in print comes almost exclusively from the conservative side. The religious text reproduced below, for example, articulates the case for the prosecution, and gives us access to the residual discourse operating in Hamlet's head. This text acknowledges that it is not illegal for a widow to remarry; but it is certain that after a certain age a good widow would not think of doing so because it is inconceivable that she would want to have an active sex life. And given that Gertrude is at least forty-five (Hamlet is thirty and she can't have given birth to him much before fifteen), she clearly falls into this "of a certain age" category. Materials supporting an emergent point of view and the case for Gertrude's defense are hard to come by outside of plays like *Hamlet*, so the task of responding to the prosecution's case will be more speculative. The following pieces of information will begin the process:

1. Though Gertrude's critics charge her with uncontrolled sexuality (that rank lust Hamlet obsesses about), what in fact seems to be most irritating to critics of this sort is that her sexuality is *self*-controlled—that *she* controls it; that she decides what she will do with it.

2. Though Hamlet finds Gertrude's remarriage detrimental to his interests, it is possible to argue that Gertrude remarried in part to safeguard certain of his interests.

3. Between 1547 and 1603 "45 per cent of *all* marriages by license in London were remarriages . . . and 44 per cent of aldermen's widows are known to have remarried" (Williams, 1995, 505).

4. Then as now, one reason why remarriages were " 'seldom so comfortable and peaceable as the first' was the attitude of the children of earlier unions, who could not put up with stepparents. The inward contempt, grumbling and undutiful behavior of most children towards stepparents brought much grief to natural parents and caused 'much discord and dissension' between natural and stepparents. Children's resentment towards stepparents, which sometimes broke into abuse or even physical violence, is amply documented in wills and the records of litigation." (Cawdrey 1600, 240–42).

SIXTEENTH CENTURY PROTESTANT DOMESTIC IDEOLOGY

A Canterbury preacher as well as a prolific writer of Christian educational materials for the home and family, Thomas Becon is one of the best representatives of those who codified Protestant domestic ideology in the sixteenth century. In his *Catechism* Becon uses the technology of paternal interrogation not so much to educate his son, Theodore, as to display this son's theological education—to show that Theodore has perfectly introjected the Law of the Father. Implicit in the performance of his son as the perfect product of paternal technology is the claim that (to use the language of *Hamlet*) "all trivial fond records" have been wiped from Theodore's mind, and that his Father's commandments "all alone [do] live / Within the book and volume of [his] brain / Unmixed with baser matter" (1.5.99 ff) In other words, Theodore's brain is the ideal Christian "book" to which Hamlet's brain, inscribed by the revenge law of the natural father, would be a negative instance, though on the subject of a mother's remarriage, Hamlet and Theodore would agree.

On the subject of widows remarrying, Becon's *Catechism*, like all religious advice tracts, is a heavy dose of doctrine, but its historical virtue is that it eventually gets to the practical problems confronting early modern widows. In addition then, to holding up a mirror to patriarchal law, it also holds one up to a number of the realities of early modern life, particularly those facing (1) young widows who, not wanting to submit themselves a second time to patriarchal dominance and unwilling to give up sexual pleasure, organize a satisfying sex life for themselves outside matrimony; and (2) older women who want to continue having an active sexual life after the death of their husbands even though they are past child-bearing. It is in pursuing this second line of attack that Becon strikes specifically, though indirectly, at the erotic activities of the nobility and thus anticipates the kind of attention Queen Elizabeth would demand from courtiers like the earl of Essex in the 1590s. On the subject of older rich widows who are fleeced and abandoned, Becon is almost as sympathetic as he is moralistic. Needless to say, Gertrude would not be at all interested in being the kind of good widow Becon's ideology prescribes.

FROM THOMAS BECON, "OF THE OFFICE OF WIDOWS,"
CATECHISM
(London: I. Day, 1564)

Father. What say you of widows and of their office?

Son. St. Paul describes two kinds of widows; the younger, and the elder. The office of the elder or ancient widow is to be occupied about matters of God and about businesses of the congregation, and wholly to give herself to the exercises of the spirit, as to frequent the temple in the time of prayer, to be present at the sermons, to visit the sick, to relieve the needy, to wash the feet of the saints, to be rich in good works, to continue in prayers and supplications both day and night, and to be holy both in body and mind. . . . As touching the younger widows, forasmuch as many of them are wanton against Christ, and follow Satan, breaking their first faith and promise, which they made to God at their baptism (which is to abstain from all uncleanness both of body and mind, and to lead a pure and honest life), and so cast themselves into the danger of everlasting damnation; it is convenient, by the doctrine of St. Paul, that they marry again, bring forth children, guide their house virtuously, and so live in the holy state of matrimony (1 *Tim.* 5).

Father. The counsel of the holy apostle is good and necessary. For what is more convenient and meet [proper] for such widows as are ancient, old, aged, and (as they use to say) past the world, than to apply their minds unto the exercises of spiritual and heavenly things, always meditating death, and their departure from this vale of misery . . . ? Again, what is more seemly for a young widow, which is apt to be a wife and to bring forth children, than to marry in the fear of God, and to take unto her an husband, by whom she may have children, and godly to bring them up, and to govern her household virtuously, and to do such other things as appertain unto an honest and godly wife? For how light, vain, trifling, unhonest, unhousewife-like, young widows have been in all ages, and are also at this present day, experience doth sufficiently declare.

Son. Old widows also in this our age are not free from fault. For many of them, which by the course of nature are not only past child-bearing, but also ready to go to their grave, do so dote and are so mad in these our days, that when they ought to leave the world, they begin to think anew of the world, and when they should only meditate and consider spiritual and heavenly things, they set their mind on fleshly pleasures; insomuch that some of them, being almost fourscore years old, have been known to marry with boys of eighteen years old: another sort, being so plagued with diseases that they were not almost able to stir in their beds, have notwithstanding given themselves to marriage, being far grown in age, yea, and that unto such husbands as, the riches once past, have little esteemed their wives; but, leaving them in all misery whom they found rich and wealthy, they have entangled themselves with strange love, utterly forsaking the company of their old and toothless wives.

Father. Fruits worthy such monstrous marriages; marriages in times past hated even of the very heathen and infidels. It is good for so many as have the gift of continency [self-restraint] to keep themselves free from marriage, that they may the more freely serve God; but specially for old women, which by the course of nature are past children-bearing: for their marriages are prodigious [abnormal and unnatural] marriages.

Son. You say truth.

PATRIARCHAL IDEOLOGY

This section and the next place Gertrude's trial in a larger debate concerning women that had long exercised Elizabethan culture, because to defend her against the remaining crimes with which she is charged—that she is a wicked wife—we need to know the sources of the venom in Hamlet's head, the discourses, the commonplaces, the patriarchal software, in short, the "sawes" and "formes" installed on his hard drive. Of this voluminous sexist literature, the two instances printed below will more than suffice to illustrate the age's already clichéd truths about women's frailty and fickleness. The first is a dominant tract; the second, a residual diatribe.

What these two documents have in common with hundreds of similar texts is an absolute refusal to permit a women to be a SUBJECT, meaning that women, since they lack subjectivity by definition, cannot be the grammatical subject of a long list of verbs and predicates. For instance, a woman *cannot* say (though, as we will see in the second excerpt, there were powerful exceptions): "I am a sovereign ruler," "I am independent," "I teach adults," "I am rational," "I have a higher education," "I speak in public," "I gaze at men just as men gaze at me," "I enjoy sex," "I disagree with the views of male authority figures," "I plead cases before a judge," "I know Latin and Greek," "I have no superiors," "I am as smart as any man." However, the texts cited below are equally certain that a woman is, and can only be, a *subject* in the sense of being subject to male rule, because she is "weak, frail, impatient, feeble, and foolish." In short, a vertical binary:

> strong, rational, educated, independent, public-sphere men on top
> (i.e., SUBJECTS)
>
> ---
>
> weak, frail, impatient, feeble, foolish, fickle women on the bottom
> (i.e., subjects)

Once this absolute disparity is hammered home, women are then given a choice. They can crawl their way up out of the pit of their uselessness by becoming silent, passive, obedient good wives, or, should they try to storm the top and take on the characteristics, rights, freedoms, power, and authority of men, they sink even lower and become whores, witches, hags, crones, and the like. For a woman to move up in this system in any way other than by being a good subject instantly makes her a criminal. This inevitability produces a four level universe:

1. god and angels

2. men

3. good women (good mothers in Catholic, and good wives in Protestant patriarchies)

4. bad women (shrews, whores, etc.)

Once on the bottom it is extremely difficult for a woman, practically speaking, to get back up to level three, although, theoretically speaking, it is not impossible. So Hamlet's disingenuous advice, after he has "cleft" Gertrude's "heart in twain," is to tell her to "throw away the worser part of it, / And live the purer with the other half" (3.4.148–49).

Needless to say, no woman in this system can ever be equal to a man, because no woman can ever get to the upper half; in fact some patriarchal architects went so far as to insist that there are no women in, and that no woman could ever get into, their heaven. As is also obvious, patriarchal cultures long went out of their way after imagining such a system to do whatever it took to actualize their blueprint in the real—to do what it took to manufacture women as weak and as feeble as possible, so they could represent the product they had designed and manufactured as *natural*. They wrote the script, built the theatre, cast the characters, and set the play called *patriarchy* in motion years before a woman like Gertrude found herself caught up in a role she no longer wants to act, with lines she no longer wants to speak, and a stage on which she no longer wants to be.

This program also, of course, creates a rating system in which a woman's *value* is determined solely by men. So, to know what Gertrude is worth is to ask whether the patriarchal men in her life judge her to be an item on the third or fourth shelf of their universe. Needless to say, the prosecution's view of where Gertrude stands is obvious. As Hamlet puts it, she is a "pernicious woman." Moreover, the documents excerpted below would agree, though they differ with respect to the measures a patriarchal man must take to reform such a woman, one counseling a degree of leniency, the other demanding whatever measures are necessary. Hamlet's method—to be a "scourge and minister" to such a woman— clearly reeks of the excesses of the latter. After reading these documents, you might ask if there is anything but this patriarchal software on Hamlet's hard drive?

ELIZABETHAN DISCOURSE ON MATRIMONY

Of the countless number of pages written in early modern England that are devoted to the apparently delicious patriarchal task of detailing the "natural" and "inevitable" limitations of woman, the following excerpt from the Elizabethan government's widely distributed and much quoted *Homily on Matrimony* will stand as a moderate dominant instance. It is also a particularly good context in which to set Hamlet's injunction to himself before entering his mother's closet—"be cruel, not unnatural, / . . . speak daggers to her, but use none" (3.2.365–66)—as well as his behavior once he's in.

FROM *AN HOMILY ON THE STATE OF MATRIMONY*
(London: R. Jugge, 1563)

For the woman is a weak creature, not endued with like strength and constancy of mind: therefore they be the sooner disquieted, and they be the more prone to all weak affections and dispositions of mind, more than men be; and lighter they be and more vain in their fantasies and opinions. These things must be considered of the man, that he be not too stiff; so that he ought to wink at some things, and must gently expound all things, and to forbear.

Howbeit, the common sort of men do judge that such moderation should not become a man: for they say that it is a token of a womanish cowardliness; and therefore they think that it is a man's part to fume in anger, to fight with fist and staff. Howbeit, howsoever they imagine, undoubtedly St Peter does better judge what should be seeming to a man, and what he should most reasonable perform. For he said reasoning should be used, and not fighting. Yea, he said more, that the woman ought to have a certain *honor* attributed to her; that is to say, she must be spared and borne with, the rather for that she is *the weaker vessel*, of a frail heart, inconstant, and with a word soon stirred to wrath.

ONE REACTIONARY PATRIARCH

Depending on one's point of view, the most (in)famous (mis)representation of women in the period was *The First Blast*. From John Knox's perspective, the patriarchal world he was accustomed to living in was changing radically, and his reaction was to vent outraged invective against the two monstrous women he regarded as causing and benefiting from such a change: Mary Tudor of England (1516–1558) and Mary, Queen of Scots (1542–1587). As a representative of man, Knox will not tolerate any loss of dominance over women, any loss of superiority to women, or any loss of man's exclusive enjoyment of privileges and rights long denied to women. In short, Knox will not stop being a man as this character is scripted by patriarchal culture, nor will he stop acting this man's part, speaking its lines, wearing its costumes, and the like, since, in his mind, man is in power or he is a cowardly slave; indeed, writing this angry and abusive tract is one of the ways in which Knox intends to stay on top. Though written to blast the allegedly monstrous rule of the two Marys, it was published just prior to Elizabeth's ascension to the throne in 1558, thereby inadvertently creating a third royal target for Knox's invective. Like Hamlet's, Knox's inspiration stems from a *locus classicus* of misogynist thinking, *Ecclesiasticus* 25: 26, 28: "Of the woman came the beginning of sin, and through her we all die. . . . If she walk not in thine obedience. . . . Cut her off then from thy flesh . . . and forsake her." Clearly a text more to Hamlet's liking than the *Homily* excerpted above.

FROM JOHN KNOX, *THE FIRST BLAST OF THE TRUMPET AGAINST THE MONSTROUS REGIMENT OF WOMEN*
(Geneva, 1558)

To promote a woman to bear rule, superiority, dominion or empire above any realm, nation, or city, is repugnant to nature, contumely to God, a thing most contrarious to his revealed will and approved ordinance, and, finally it is the subversion of good order, of all equity and justice. . . . And first, where that I affirm the empire of a woman to be a thing repugnant to nature, I mean not only that God by the order of his creation has spoiled woman of authority and dominion, but also that man has seen, proved and pronounced just causes why that it so should be. Man, I say, in many other cases blind, does in this behalf see very clearly. For the causes be so manifest, that they can not be hid. For who can deny but it is repugnant to nature, that the blind shall be appointed to lead and conduct such as do see? That the weak, the sick and impotent persons shall nourish and keep the whole and strong, and, finally, that the foolish, mad, and frenetic shall govern the discrete, and give counsel to such as be sober of mind? And such be all women, compared unto man in bearing of authority. For their sight in civil regiment is but blindness: their strength, weakness: their counsel, foolishness: and judgment frenzy, if it be rightly considered.

Nature I say, does paint them forth to be weak, frail, impatient, feeble and foolish: and experience has declared them to be inconstant, variable, cruel, and lacking the spirit of counsel and regiment. And these notable faults have men in all ages espied in that kind, for the which not only have they removed women from rule and authority, but also some have thought that men subject to the counsel or empire of their wives were unworthy of all public office. . . . What would [Aristotle] (I pray you) have said to that realm or nation where a woman sits crowned in parliament among the midst of men. Oh fearful and terrible are thy judgments (o Lord) which thus have abased man for his iniquity! I am assuredly persuaded that if any of those men [in the classical past], which illuminated only by the light of nature, did see and pronounce causes sufficient, why women ought not to bear rule nor authority, should this day live and see a woman sitting in judgment or riding from parliament in the midst of men, having the royal crown upon her head, the sword and scepter borne before her, in sign that the administration of justice was in her power; I am assuredly persuaded, I say, that such a sight should so astonish them that, they should judge the whole world to be transformed into Amazons, and that such a metamorphosis and change was made of all the men of that country . . . or at least, that albeit the outward form of men remained, yet should they judge that their hearts were changed from the wisdom, understanding, and courage of men, to the foolish fondness and cowardice of women. Yea they further should pronounce, that where women reign or be in authority, that there must needs vanity be preferred to virtue, ambition and pride to temperance and modesty, and, finally, that avarice, the mother of all mischief, must needs devour equity and justice. . . . To the further declaration of the imperfections of women, of their natural weakness, and inordinate appetites, I might adduce histories proving some women to have died for sudden joy, some for impatience to have murthered themselves, some to have burned with such inordinate lust, that for the quenching of the same, they have betrayed to strangers their country and city: and some to have been so desirous of dominion, that for the obtaining of the same, they have murdered the children of their own sons. Yea, and some have killed with cruelty their own husbands and children.

FEMINIST DEFENSE AND COUNTERATTACK

> . . . we know what we are, but know not what we may be.
> Ophelia (4.5.42–43)

Emergent software on the subject of women existed in early modern England that is not in Hamlet's head but could have been. For this reason, a defense of Gertrude is not something that modern readers do on their own. Nor is Knox's patriarchal discourse the only early modern discourse in which Gertrude would have been meaningful to Elizabethans; a number of early modern feminist and quasi-feminist texts existed that provide alternative discourses with which to understand Gertrude. Moreover, many in Shakespeare's audience, knowing these discourses, would have used them to reject Hamlet's and his ghost's accusations. What these audience members would have seen in Hamlet was not a bright young culture hero accurately mapping the terrain in which he lived, but a tragic figure caught up in a reactionary backlash that offered women nothing except dutiful silent submission or pain and death. What they would have seen in Gertrude was a courageous woman terminated by this reactionary patriarchal culture because she sought to imagine and sustain a life and maximize a mode of happiness prohibited by patriarchal law. Refusing to be a good woman any longer, and rejecting as well the name of whore, Gertrude briefly writes a comedy that proves impossible to stage in a rotting patriarchal Denmark because enraged son, false lover, and embittered ghost conspire to purge her and purify Denmark.

EARLY EMERGENT FEMINISM

The name Jane Anger, possibly a pseudonym, dramatically symbolizes the emotion fueling the argument of the text printed below. And though nothing is known about her life, Anger is the first published emergent English woman author to defend her sex. In England prior to Anger, defenses of women had been written by men or were put in the mouths of female characters in male-authored texts. Margery Kempe's defense of herself as a self-

IANE ANGER
her Protection
for VVomen.

To defend them againſt the
SCANDALOVS REPORTES OF
a late Surfeiting Louer, and all other like
Venerians that complaine ſo to bee
ouercloyed with womens
kindneſſe.

Written by Ia: A, Gent.

At London

Printed by Richard Iones, and Thomas
Orwin. 1589.

Title page of *Jane Anger her Protection for Women* (1589). This item is reproduced by permission of The Huntington Library, San Marino, California, RB 49047.

empowered Christian woman was written, for example, by a male cleric, Margery being illiterate. The most outspoken defender of female liberty prior to Anger probably was Chaucer's Wife of Bath, a character in *The Canterbury Tales*. On the continent, published debate was likewise almost exclusively a male-male controversy, and centered, except for texts like Agrippa's *Treatise* and Boccaccio's *Decameron*, on proving or disproving women's capacity to live up to ideal religious role models—that is, whether women could indeed be good women rather than dissimulators or whores. Like Gertrude, Anger clearly isn't interested in playing either of these patriarchal roles, recognizing that they cast women into cleft halves because patriarchal men need good women *and* bad ones to satisfy the antithetical ends of their desires. For this reason Anger is one of the first self-acknowledged feminists in the culture, though in her own time she clearly was not alone. Mannish women, or *"hic mulier*, or, the man-woman" as they were described by their enemies, were becoming an increasingly acknowledged feature of London society, as were the "roaring girls" modeled after Mol Cutpurse (1584–1659), who, like Mol, saw themselves celebrated onstage by, among other popular plays, Middleton and Dekker's *The Roaring Girl* (1611). In other words, *Jane Anger her Protection for Women* is part of an increasingly powerful early modern feminist activist movement.

The occasion for *her Protection* is the anonymous work Anger attacks throughout her text, *Book: his Surfeit in Love*, which, though no longer extant (if in fact it ever existed), seems to be a debauched lover's fatuous rant about how little he is getting in return for all he puts into sex and poetry ("surfeit" he means something like "a morbid condition of disgust caused by excessive indulgence in sexual debauchery and the poetry and flattery that led up to it"). It is against *Surfeit*'s various modes of sexual exploitation and the aggression hiding behind it that Anger desires to protect women. In short, Anger was made mad enough by the gender rubbish she found in *Surfeit in Love* to denounce patriarchal constructions of sexuality. With this text, Jane Anger publicly proclaims herself the subject of verbs and predicates in sentences like: "I teach," "I have a right to be angry with stupid men," "I am not available for male abuse, sexual or otherwise"—a list, longer in later feminist texts, that is already very long in Anger's.

FROM *JANE ANGER HER PROTECTION FOR WOMEN*
(London: Richard Iones, 1589)

To all Women in generall, and gentle Reader whatsoever

Fie on the falsehood of men, whose minds go oft a madding, and whose tongues can not so soon be wagging, but straight they fall a railing! Was there ever any so abused, so slandered, so railed upon, or so wickedly handled undeservedly, as are we women? Will the gods permit it, the goddesses stay their punishing judgments, and we ourselves not pursue their undoings for such devilish practices? . . . Shall surfeiters rail on our kindness, you stand still and say naught, and shall not Anger stretch the veins of her brains, the strings of her fingers, and the lists of her modesty, to answer their surfeitings? Yes truly. And herein I conjure all you to aid and assist me in defense of my willingness, which shall make me rest at your commands. Fare you well.

> Your friend,
> Ja. A.

A Protection for Women. &c.

The desire that every man has to show his true vein in writing is unspeakable, and their minds are so carried away with the manner, as no care at all is had of the matter: they run so into rhetoric, as often times they overrun the bounds of their own wits, and go they not whether. If they have stretched their invention so hard on a last, as it is at a stand, there remains but one help, which is, to write of us women. . . . And therefore that the god may see how thankfully they receive his liberality, they fall straight to dispraising and slandering our silly [innocent] sex. But judge what the cause should be of this their so great malice towards simple women. Doubtless the weakness of our wits, and our honest bashfulness, by reason whereof they suppose that there is not one amongst us who can, or dare reprove their slanders and false reproaches: their slanderous tongues are so short, and the time wherein they have lavished out their words freely, has been so long, that they know we cannot catch hold of them to pull them out, and they think we will not write to reprove their lying lips.

We are contrary to men, because they are contrary to that which is good: because they are spur blind, they cannot see into our natures, and we too well (though we had but half an eye) into their conditions, because they are so bad. . . . They are comforted by our means: they nourished by the meats we dress: their bodies freed from diseases by our cleanliness. . . . Without our care they lie in their beds as dogs in litter.

The smooth speeches of men are nothing unlike the vanishing clouds of the air, which glide by degrees from place to place, till they have filled themselves with rain, when, breaking, they spit forth terrible showers: so men gloze, till they have their answers, which are the end of their travel, and then they bid modesty adieu, and entertaining rage, fall a-railing on us which never hurt them. . . . It is a wonder to see how men can flatter themselves with their own conceits: For let us look, they will straight affirm that we love, and if then lust pricks them, they will swear that love stings us: which imagination only is sufficient to make them assay the scaling of half a dozen of us in one night, when they will not stick to swear that if they should be denied of their requests death must needs follow. Is it any marvel though they surfeit, when they are so greedy, but is it not pity that any of them should perish, which will be so soon killed with unkindness? Yes truly. Well, the onset given, if we retire for a vantage, they will straight affirm that they have got the victory. Nay, some of them are so carried away with conceit, that shameless they will blaze abroad among their companions, that they have obtained the love of a woman, unto whom they never spoke above once, if that: Are not these forward fellows, you must bear with them, because they dwell far from lying neighbors. They will say *Mentiri non est nostrum* [we are not liars], and yet you shall see true tales come from them, as wild geese fly under London bridge. Their fawning is but flattery: their faith falsehood: their fair words allurements to destruction: and their large promises tokens of death, or of evils worse than death. Their singing is a bait to catch us, and their playings, plagues to torment us: and therefore take heed of them, and take this as an axiom in logic and a maxim in the law: *Nulla fides hominibus* [there is no faith in men]. . . . I have set down unto you (which are of mine own sex) the subtle dealings of untrue meaning men: not that you should contemn all men, but to the end that you may take heed of the false hearts of all and still reprove the flattery which remains in all. . . .

CONCLUSION

> I am poysned.
>
> Gertrude (5.2.297)

Gertrude is charged with: (1) adultery, (2) complicity in murder, (3) insufficient mourning, (4) hasty remarriage, (5) incest, (6) sexuality, (7) lack of judgment, (8) neglect of duties, and (9) fickleness. From a residual perspective, she is guilty of all nine charges. From a dominant one, she is innocent of the first four, technically guilty of number 5, and, despite compelling evidence to the contrary, guilty in some men's minds of numbers 6, 7, and 8, and in most men's minds of number 9. From an emergent perspective (and this is what the defense has established), Gertrude, though technically guilty of number 5, is not guilty of any of these nine charges as argued by the prosecution. This emergent Gertrude, needless to say, has not been seen on a stage from 1660 to the present, having been "poysned" by dominant/residual prejudices long before she speaks her first, much less her final line.

STUDY QUESTIONS

1. In what ways, despite age and other differences, was the life of Diana, Princess of Wales like that of Gertrude's life? Was Diana viewed negatively and charged with crimes from conservative perspectives, yet defended from emergent ones?

2. Imagine a production in which Gertrude and Claudius, rather than subordinated to bit parts backgrounding Hamlet's virtuoso concerto, are given power and presence equal to Hamlet's. Then explain how this restoration would be accomplished in a production.

3. It was customary in older cultures to give a woman and a job to men who served and obeyed the patriarchs. What happens to this arrangement when, as in early modern London, women came into positions of power and were more able and more likely to say "No"? Why would some woman say "Yes" to such an arrangement?

4. In *Hamlet and Oedipus* (New York: Norton, 1949), Ernest Jones, following Freud's lead, identified Hamlet's relationship to Gertrude as nothing but incestuous. Is there any evidence in the play to support such an argument? What motives fueled such an argument? Why is this argument inadequate?

5. How is John Knox using the concept of *nature* to keep women in their place, and what is problematical about using this category to establish and maintain cultural gender differences?

6. How does Anger relate to her culture's ongoing debate about the value of theatre? Speculate on her views about roles, theatre, makeup, costumes, stages. What role is she herself acting?

7. What difficulties, if any, might a twentieth-century feminist have with Anger's feminism?

QUESTIONS AND TOPICS FOR WRITTEN AND ORAL DISCUSSION

1. Discuss ways in which John Knox's *First Blast* is massively self-contradictory, and ponder how Knox must be aware of at least some of these contradictions and yet at the same time totally unaware of them.

2. Write a feminist counter-blast to John Knox's *First Blast*.

3. How would Jane Anger respond to Hamlet's fulminations against Ophelia and Gertrude? Put Anger in Ophelia's place in the nunnery scene (3.1. 30–187) and/or in Gertrude's place in the closet scene (3.4)

and then rewrite these scenes with Anger's insights and power. In other words, let Hamlet try picking on a woman not as enclosed by patriarchal restraints as those he finds in Denmark.

4. In this chapter we have been defending Gertrude principally against residual abuse and have done so from an emergent position. Now, having defended her, how might someone in an emergent position critique her behavior? To be sure, as a woman she is in a subjected position in the dominant order, but as a queen she is also part of this dominant order. So what does and doesn't Gertrude do that might irritate someone like Anger?

5. What, according to Anger, is the cause of male lust? Is it *natural*, or is it a male disposition constructed by patriarchal cultures to serve specific objectives? What are these objectives?

SUGGESTED READING

Bornstein, Diane, ed. *The Book of Honor and Armes (1590) . . . by Sir William Segar*. Delmar, NY: Scholar's Facsimiles and Reprints, 1975.

Cawdrey [Cleaver], Robert. *A Godlie Forme of Householde Gouernment: for the Ordering of Private Families*. London: F. Kingston, 1600.

Dusinberre, Juliet. *Shakespeare and the Nature of Women*. London: Macmillan, 1975.

Emmison, F. G. *Elizabethan Life: Morals and the Court Mainly from Essex Archidiaconal Records*. Chelmsford: Essex County Council, 1973.

Frye, Roland Mushat. *The Renaissance "Hamlet."* Princeton: Princeton University Press, 1984.

Girard, Rene. *The Scapegoat*. Translated by Yvonne Freccero. London: The Athlone Press, 1986.

Heilbrun, Carolyn G. "The Character of Hamlet's Mother." In *Hamlet's Mother and Other Women*. New York: Columbia University Press, 1971.

Irigaray, Luce. *Speculum of the Other Woman*. Ithaca: Cornell University Press, 1985.

Kahn, Coppélia. *Man's Estate: Masculine Identity in Shakespeare*. Berkeley: University of California Press, 1981.

Kolodny, Annette. "Dancing Through the Minefield: Some Observations on the Theory, Practice, and Politics of Feminist Criticism." *Feminist Studies* 6 (1980), 1–25.

McCabe, Richard A. *Incest, Drama and Nature's Law: 1550–1700*. Cambridge: Cambridge University Press, 1993.

Neely, Carol Thomas. *Broken Nuptials in Shakespeare's Plays*. New Haven: Yale University Press, 1985.

Puckle, Bertram S. *Funeral Customs; Their Origin and Development*. London: T. W. Laurie, 1926.

Rogers, Daniel. *Matrimonial Honovr: or the Mutuall Crowne and Comfort of godly, loyall, and chaste marriage*. London: T. Harper, 1642.

Showalter, Elaine. "Feminist Criticism in the Wilderness." *Critical Inquiry* 8 (1981), 179–205.

Stone, Lawrence. *The Family, Sex and Marriage in England, 1500–1800*. New York: Harper and Row, 1977.

Williams, Penry. *The Later Tudors: England, 1547–1603*. Oxford: Clarendon Press, 1995.

9

Over Ophelia's Dead Body

[Princess Diana] told me never to give up because she never
would.
          —Marija Yakic, 15, of Tuzla, Bosnia, who
          lost both legs after stepping on a land mine.
          Newsweek, September 15, 1997, 21

At the beginning of the play, Ophelia is a happy, energetic young woman of fourteen or fifteen. She speaks with strength and wit to her brother as he leaves for Paris, and for some time she has been caught up in a love affair with Hamlet, a man twice her age. Agency, desire, and a sense of self are developing quickly. To use the play's imagery, Ophelia is an "infant of the spring," a "tender bud" enjoying "the morn and liquid dew of youth" (1.3.39, 41). However, as the play progresses she declines to melancholy and madness, and then, though we don't see this, she kills herself, the youngest person in the play to die. As this decline nears its end, her sense of self disintegrates. She withdraws into infantile, ritualistic behavior. With a collage of associative lyrical fragments ("snatches of old lauds" [hymns]), she tells the traumatic events of her life the only way she can, but no one on stage cares to understand echoes that carry "but half sense." As we watch this disintegration, and its tragic aftermath, we must ask: What causes Ophelia's suicide? Why

J. Hayter and W. H. Mote, *Ophelia*, from *The Heroines of Shakespeare* (1862–64). Courtesy of the Davidson Library, University of California, Santa Barbara.

does she give up? As critics, we may also ask: Why did Shakespeare put a suicide in this play?

To ask why Shakespeare included Ophelia's mad scenes and suicide in *Hamlet* is to ask why he developed a minor character who is present in only one scene of *The Hystorie of Hamblet* (see Chapter 7) into a major character. As do the other adolescents Shakespeare added to his source, Ophelia creates a *contrast* to Hamlet by closing out an option Hamlet could have taken, but does not. Ophelia and the other adolescents also reveal a *similarity*. Try as they do to escape the lethal triangle of patience, revenge, or suicide, each ends up dead. The point of this multiplication is to make sure the audience realizes that Shakespeare is addressing a general problem, not just an individual one. Moreover, he is addressing this problem at a time in early modern history when suicide rates were rapidly escalating, and "suicide was punished more severely than ever before or afterwards" (MacDonald 1981, 75).

In much the same way that Chapter 3 examines the forces that cause Hamlet to effect a lethal compromise between opposed parental demands, this chapter analyzes what Ophelia does in the face of an equally impossible demand. However, to understand why she kills herself, we must first get beyond circumstances that, though they obviously contribute to her suicide, do not cause it. The cause is not the loss of her former king, her brother, her lover, and finally her father. These losses are devastating; nonetheless, they are only contributing circumstances, since not every teenage girl who suffers losses of this magnitude or greater commits suicide. Likewise, the cause of Ophelia's suicide is not the fact that, with Polonius dead, Hamlet out of reach, and Laertes in Paris, the men who are (allegedly) her "head" have left her without any rational source of control. Though attractive to many male critics, this "woman who can't make it without a male authority-figure" analysis of Ophelia's situation is deeply sexist, not to mention false, given that Claudius, and later, Horatio are present, but to no avail. Nor is the cause of her suicide the fact that she is a woman. Though patriarchal societies have long maintained that female fragmentation, ambiguity, and chaos constitute a natural and sufficient explanation for why women go mad and commit suicide, surely this is a self-serving cover for the actual reasons. Ophelia's death is also not caused by her fear of being shamed and dishonored for having slept with Hamlet, or by the fact that, possibly pregnant, she has been abandoned by her lover, though shame, rejection, and the likelihood of further humiliation are also contributory circumstances. Nor is her suicide caused by the melancholy, despair, and madness that follow in the wake of loss, rejection, isolation, shame, and fear. Contrary to conventional belief, melancholy and madness do not cause suicide; rather, all three are the effects of a prior cause. That is, melancholy and madness, like loss and rejection, are the symptoms, the wobbles and lurches, a train manifests before it jumps its track, not the cause of these wobbles, lurches, and track jumping. Nor is her suicide caused by demons come from hell to lure her to eternal damnation, though conservative early moderns would have thought no less. Nor, finally, is Ophelia's suicide caused by a desire to escape unbearable social restraints and thereby gain a brief flight of ecstatic freedom as an independent, though mad woman. To be sure, madness allows her "an emotional intensity and scope" not available to proper women in early modern culture; in fact, it "enables her to assert her being; she is no longer enforced to keep silent and play the dutiful daughter" (Charney 1977, 451, 456). But as true as it may be that madness is perhaps the only way a young woman can be independent in a society as rigid as Ophelia's, such an unconscious acting out of feelings and desires too powerful to remain repressed or denied any longer is also not the cause of her suicide, though it is a temporary by-product. Surely such self-destructive forms of rage and honesty, of emotional intensity and independence cannot be powerful, long, or significant enough to be worth the price of a life. Though indeed, the public presence, the released ability to say anything in "unshaped" fashion, the opportunity to force everyone to look at and fear one's "winks and nods and gestures," not to mention the chance to disobey patriarchal law and be oneself in the brief moments madness provides before one kills oneself, are clearly better than the alternatives Ophelia and millions of suicidal women like her face who have no better way to acquire power and freedom.

It is often asserted that suicides "require a minimum of 'two' parties (someone who wants to die and someone who wants him or her dead)" (Napier 1978, 184). This bold claim is true enough, but, as it is merely the beginning of an adequate analysis of suicide, it is first necessary to turn to the present, and to look at the daunting problems connected with suicide in our own time before going back to Ophelia and the past: (1) the enormous numbers of persons each year who kill themselves, (2) the appalling lack of attention societies pay to this problem relative to other problems, and (3) the limited resources with which cultures cope with suicides, despite the fact that as Colin Pritchard, a modern British sociologist/psychologist, writes, suicide, "in resource and impact, is a far more serious social problem than *all* kinds of homicide." In the most recent figures available for the Untied States, "30,232 people died from suicide in a year, *more than 500 per week*"—almost twice the American homicide rate, "which is the highest in the world" (1995, 2). Moreover, "suicide is the second highest cause of death in young people in every developed Western country" (3) and these statistics are conservative since they do not include the millions of suicides that are reported each year as accidents, or the deaths that result from long-term substance abuse.

Given this monumental, generally suppressed, and hopelessly undersolved social problem to which cultures have been heir, it is no wonder that, at the end of the last century, theorists began dissolving the mystifications promulgated by dominant and residual understandings of suicide by placing it in a "context of relationships in which [it is] comprehensible . . . as the product of factors, as something that has become what it is or has been made what it is, as [an] element in a process" (Marcuse 1959, 65). In other words, those who radically retheorized suicide did so by reopening the question of *causation*, and by offering two brilliant but contradictory sets of answers: sociological ones following Émile Durkheim's *Suicide* (1888) and psychoanalytic/psychological ones following, in the main, Sigmund Freud's "Mourning and Melancholia" (1917).

Breaking away from the traditional practice of viewing suicide as a phenomenon caused by isolated, individual selves acting alone, Durkheim argued that society causes suicides, thereby making the act of suicide a product of the social order, its law, logic, and economics rather than individuals or forces marginal to or outside this order. Durkheim's limitation, however, was that he then developed his argument in a way that fails because, as we shall see, he substituted effects for causes.

Durkheim's argument may be presented by means of an analogy. Society, let us say, is an extremely large ocean-going ship. If there is not enough social *integration* on board this ship and it meets

rough water, some people will jump off one side (egoistic suicides); if there is too much integration, others will jump off the
other side (altruistic suicides). If there is too much *regulation*,
certain people will jump off the stern (fatalistic suicides); if there
is too little regulation others will jump off the bow (anomic suicides). (Anomic suicides tend to occur when, due to economic
crises or domestic losses, individuals are unable to satisfy their
aspirations.) Hence, concluded Durkheim, the solution to suicide
is to produce exactly the right combination of integration and regulation that will cause few, if any, to jump ship.

There are two fundamental problems with Durkheim's theory,
and the brilliant methodological insights of Michel Foucault's *History of Sexuality* (1976/1990) will enable us to isolate them. First,
Durkheim assumed that society simply *is* (that it is unitary, that in
the main societies are generally alike, and that they only need fine
tuning). Foucault recognized, however, that societies, far from being unitary wholes, are conflictual arrays of various interlocking
power structures (patriarchal families, businesses, professions).
Second, Durkheim argued that society's excesses, errors, and ex-
tremes cause the damage, even though this erroneously substitutes
society's excesses for society itself. However, it is not the errors or
excesses of a given social structure that produce suicides (e.g., an
incompetent ship captain or helmsman); rather, it is a society's
fundamental institutions of power, its central and sustaining truths
and virtues, its exclusion, negation, and exploitation of women and
minorities, its periodic programs of purgation and purification
(among numerous other constitutive practices) that do so. We cannot, as Durkheim did, displace the cause of suicide from the center
of society to its margins. Rather, we must recognize that patriarchal
societies produce suicides, that to survive they must do so, and
that even the patriarchal laws that prohibit suicide are part of the
dynamic by which patriarchies generate suicides. Socially speaking
then, suicide is a form of cultural work that certain individuals are
constructed to do and which they must do for patriarchal cultures
to exist, though like spies caught in the act, suicides are seen, by
the societies they serve, as having acted "entirely on their own."
If one has trouble accepting this, why, we may ask, doesn't one
have trouble accepting the corollary assertion that societies construct heroes, particularly heroes willing to die for their country.
What Herbert Marcuse argues concerning the general function of

death in patriarchies—"that a society perpetuates itself through the death of individuals" (74)—is as true of suicides as it is of any other form of death. In sum, suicide is a necessary and purposeful, never an accidental or inadvertent technology.

To illustrate this point, let us return to the earlier analogy. The situation is not that under certain stormy conditions the ship of state veers off its normal integrative and regulative course and *accidentally* loses people over the sides or ends. Rather, the situation is that in the face of certain threatening situations, patriarchal social structures *purposefully* veer off course, heightening or lowering their mechanisms of integration and regulation just enough to create that degree of too much or too little that will push certain people overboard. Thus, the more patriarchal and the more threatened a social structure is, the more suicides (or other forms of death) it will necessarily have to produce to stay afloat. To put this in context, let us realize that just as cultures control child mortality rates, interest rates, and college graduation rates, so do they also control suicide rates, though perhaps less consciously. The gravediggers in act 5 of *Hamlet* are quite clear on this point: "if the man go to this water and drown himself, it is will he, nill he, he goes, mark you that, but if the water come to him, and drown him, he drowns not himself; argall [therefore], he that is not guilty of his own death, shortens not his own life" (5.1.15–19)! The terrible irony of the term, *suicide*, then, is that it is never just a "self-killing"; rather, suicide is a social vocation, a job (however unknown this may be to those killing themselves), though not a particularly remunerative one given that one's compensation for doing this job is to be misrepresented as a sick or evil aberration over which society has little or no control. Patriarchies manifest contempt for suicides because, of the people they exploit, suicides are the most subjected to their needs, the most given over to doing their dirty work. Thus, one reason that no one in the past, except marginalized emergent thinkers like Shakespeare, came anywhere close to an adequate understanding of suicide was that for centuries, suicide was so necessary to those in power that they could not afford to identify its cause, or solve what to them was not a problem to be solved, but a solution to a problem.

Now we may understand what led Durkheim's account of suicide awry. He assumed that suicide was a cultural problem, a site of loss, and an unwanted byproduct of power. Thus he did not see that for patriarchal societies, suicide is a gain, a solution to problems they cannot otherwise solve, and thus a necessary and desirable relation of power. In short, Maurice Bloch's anthropological insight—that "death, rather than being a problem for the social order, is in fact an opportunity for creating it" (1982, 219)—is particularly pertinent to suicide.

If we were now to ask what patriarchal structures do to prevent suicides, the answer is simple: little or nothing. Despite rhetorical attacks, legal prohibitions, barbaric burial practices, and/or strategic feints in the direction of pretending to prevent them, such societies do not in fact go out of their way to prevent suicides (or, for that matter, many other forms of death) precisely because they can't do without them. Moreover, because they need suicides, they become quite good at producing them. In the face of this fact, our next question surely is, "But why?"

In formulating an answer it is helpful to return to *Hamlet* and ask why the fictive, onstage Danish partriarchy embodied in Hamlet constructs Ophelia as a suicide. First, two distinctions, the first between *suicide* and *chosen death*. A chosen death kills a body to keep a self from collapsing into a failing body's incapacitating, incurable pain—that is, chosen death, like euthanasia, gives death to a no longer functioning biological body, but an unwanted death to a self that desires to go on living. Suicide, however, kills a body to obliterate an unwanted self. The second is a distinction between *active* and *passive* suicides. Active (or heroic) suicides are committed by individuals like Romeo and Juliet or Antony and Cleopatra who seem to have their wits about them, whereas passive (or abject) suicides are committed by individuals like Ophelia who seem not to have their wits about them. What follows below deals only with passive suicides.

Why then does the patriarchy Hamlet represents need to produce Ophelia as a suicide? To answer this question, observe that at the beginning of act 5, there is an open grave in the middle of the stage. Ophelia is brought in and laid in this grave with scant, forced honors. Laertes and Hamlet jump into the grave, argue and gesticulate, and then jump out as the scene changes. To understand what we have seen, the relevant questions are: (1) What symbolic actions are taking place in Ophelia's grave? and (2) Why do these actions have to take place in the grave of a suicide?

One answer is that patriarchies use suicide to purge women who individualize themselves and, since Ophelia seeks to do this, she must be dumped in a grave. But why rely on such an indirect technology as suicide to get rid of such threats to male dominance? Why not murder/execute transgressive women the same way Polonius and Claudius are murdered/executed? For several reasons:

1. Because the blood of such women would pollute patriarchal hands;

2. Because it is taboo to take up phallic arms against women in Hamlet's father's culture;

3. Because from a patriarchal perspective all the women in this play must die, it is useful to let both of them kill themselves: who (a man can then ask) can be held responsible for the actions of deranged women?;

4. To make women prove—by committing an unforgivable mortal sin—that they are the demonic "things of nothing" patriarchal men take them to be, and thus to prove as well that their suicides, technically capital felonies, are self-executions and thus are forms of justice; and

5. Among other reasons, to solve the problem of gender *sameness*. When women threaten to become too much like men, suicide is an effective mechanism by which to reestablish an allegedly unbridgeable difference. To be sure, wealth, power, education, mobility, and status establish such difference, but these mechanisms are notoriously fickle, subject to reversals, not to mention subject to appropriation by women. Suicide has the advantage of creating irreversible difference because, in its passive or (allegedly) female form, it displays *difference* as painful depression, chaos, psychosis, and eventually as death. Over such abject and dead selves, patriarchal men and women feel superior, powerful, and immune from death. They feel that their world is no longer out of joint if only because someone else's world is thoroughly and permanently disjointed. In short, Ophelia's role as a dead woman is (to borrow a line from Judith Butler) to "be" precisely what Hamlet is not—that is, dead (1990, 45).

A second answer to the question of why patriarchies construct suicides is that once Ophelia's grave is opened in their midst, a number of onstage Danes will be able to use this aperture into the void as a bottomless pit to dump any toxic-waste product they feel they must eliminate to survive, be happy, excel, or escape punishment. In Luce Irigaray's terms, Ophelia and her grave function "as a hole" (1985, 71). Think, for example, about the sorts of toxic waste Hamlet is dumping into Ophelia's grave, and thus how necessary this hole is to his program of self-purification.

1. All those *suicidal feelings* Hamlet has been soliloquizing about. All that "to be or not to be" *melancholia* which has been paralyzing his patriarchal identity, delaying his phallic action. Notice that it is not until he dips himself into Ophelia's open grave and as it were, washes himself clean in the bathtub of her grave, passing to her the dirt of *his* suicidal tendencies, that he is able to feel that his psychic diversity is healed, and that he can act, at last, as a unitary and phallic man—as "Hamlet the Dane."

2. That *antic disposition* which has marked *him* as mad in the eyes of the court. Having progressively had this antic disposition transferred onto her from the beginning of the play, Ophelia now *is* mad, and Hamlet becomes sane at the very moment that he drops the last of his anxieties, doubts, despair, and manic-depressive vacillations into the void of her grave, this second lethal orifice opened up by Ophelia's body, her female "nothing."

3. Hamlet is unloading whatever remains of what he sees as *woman* in himself (to use David Leverenz's insight [1980])—all of his precious, effeminate pathos, all of his too intense sensibility— all the alleged toxic effeminacy (or one could say, humanity) that keeps him from being a "strong-in-arm" phallic exemplar like Fortinbras.

4. Hamlet dumps several *crimes* into this patriarchally constructed garbage truck just before *she* passes into oblivion. Consider, for example, the erotic subtext: Initially Hamlet loves Ophelia, and she him. But in his mind she betrays him because her father and her king use her as a piece of bait, and in her mind he betrays her because he sleeps with her on false pretenses, and then violently and abusively rejects her—"then up he rose and donned his clothes / And dupped [opened] the chamber door, / Let in the maid, that out a maid / Never departed more" (4.5.51–

Benjamin West, *Elsinore—King, Queen, Laertes, Ophelia & c.* (1802). Courtesy of the Davidson Library, University of California, Santa Barbara.

54)—leaving her to twist in the wind, without father, without brother, pregnant and husbandless, shamed and humiliated, her reputation and future going up in flames. "Quote she, 'Before you tumbled me, / You promised me to wed.' " He answers: " 'So would I'a' done, by yonder sun, / And thou hadst not come to my bed' " (4.5.61–64). Ophelia tells us this story (to use Alice Miller's phrase) "in the only way she can" (77), *symbolically*, singing songs and plucking phantasmtic flowers—rosemary, pansy, rue— from the air and handing them to the people she still imagines might help her, acting out (among other things) her deflowerment by compulsively and repetitively "deflowering" herself: "There's fennel for you, and columbines, there's rue for you . . . there's a daisy" (4.5.177–80). But king and queen do not, cannot, meaningfully translate these symbols. Thus, lacking any other way to objectify herself, any other way to use her imagination and the work of actualization to extend her sentience into the world of objects and others, any other way of keeping her disintegrating self from collapsing even further into her body (to use Elaine Scarry's terms), Ophelia terminates a body in pain (1985, 125). And when she is silenced, "the rest" of the story concerning the two of them that Hamlet does not want known or told also becomes silence, since the only witness to these crimes is now in a place "from whose bourn / No traveller returns" (3.1.81–82). In short, Hamlet produces Ophelia as *abjection*—the "abject" (as Julia Kristeva has taught us) marking that which has been expelled from society, discharged as excrement (1982, 65).

Once Ophelia's grave is constructed as a waste dump, anyone can exploit it—Gertrude, for example. Consider the beautiful yet self-serving story she tells Laertes of his sister's death:

> There is a willow grows aslant [across] the brook,
> That shows his hoary leaves in the glassy stream,
> There with fantastic garlands did she make
> Of crowflowers, nettles, daisies, and long purples,
> That liberal shepherds give a grosser name,
> But our cold [chaste] maids do dead men's fingers call them.
> There on the pendant boughs her coronet [garlanded] weeds
> Clamb'ring to hang, an envious sliver broke,
> When down her weedy trophies and herself

Stephano Cusamano, *Ophelia* (1970). Collection of the Tweed Museum of Art. University of Minnesota, Duluth, Patrons and Subscriber's Fund Purchase.

Fell in the weeping brook, her clothes spread wide,
And mermaid-like awhile they bore her up,
Which time she chanted snatches of old lauds [tunes],
As one incapable of her own distress,
Or like a creature native and endued
Unto that element, but long it could not be
Till that her garments heavy with their drink,
Pulled the poor wretch from her melodious lay [song]
To muddy death.   (4.7.137–54)

How, one may ask, does Gertrude know any of these facts about
the manner of Ophelia's death? Surely she is not present when
Ophelia lies drowning in this brook, and no one reports this scene
to her, since, had she or anyone else been present, they would
have done something to save Ophelia, or their efforts to do so
would be part of this report. But obviously neither Gertrude nor
anyone else was present, and this account (apart from the fact of
death by drowning) is a fiction. But why such an elaborate one? Is
the objective to create a beautiful memorial? To erase what Gertrude fears happened, and substitute in its place what she wants
to believe happened? To create a quasi-legal representation proclaiming Ophelia's death an accident, not a suicide—a representation needed to gain Ophelia at least the remnants of proper
burial, and/or to prove the power of royalty to construct the reality
it desires? Yes, all of these, but despite recognizing a multiplicity
of motives, such an analysis does not adequately explain the excesses of this eulogy, the seemingly gratuitous references, for example, to "long purples," "grosser name," "dead men's fingers,"
sexual euphemisms hardly vital to the work of mourning, denial,
exoneration, and containment. So what else fuels this eulogy? One
answer is Gertrude's personal need to exonerate her *self*, not with
respect to Ophelia's death, but with respect to her love for Claudius. Gertrude's report is designed to allow an unconscious trans-
fer of her own situation onto Ophelia's. Thus, as it is not Ophelia's
fault that her garments, "heavy with their drink," pull her to
muddy death, so it is not Gertrude's fault that her body's desire
drew her to "batten" on that "long purple" of Claudius's body
which "liberal shepherds give a grosser name," a greedy feeding
which has made Gertrude "incapable of her own distress." Clearly,
the toxic waste Gertrude needs to have Ophelia absorb, act out,

and cart away are her repressed fears and negative feelings about her fall from Hamlet Sr.'s "hyperion curls" to Claudius's "mildewed" embrace, the sexual thirst that brought her to his "long purple," and the as yet unacted scene of her story when, cup in hand, she will become heavy with the drink Claudius has poisoned for Hamlet just before she is pulled to her own muddy death.

We may turn now to the question of *how* patriarchies construct suicides. What technologies do they employ to produce abject persons willing to kill themselves, and thus remove themselves and whatever gets attached to them from the public sphere? Again, Ophelia's life as it unfolds, is instructive. In scene after scene powerful men refuse to give, and make it impossible for Ophelia to get, the knowledge and resources, and thus the individual subjectivity and sociality she needs to maintain an independent self. In short, her suicide, like all passive suicides, is produced by repetitive deprivations that force her to say, "I do not know, my Lord, what I should think," and "I shall obey" (1.3.104, 136). To use the argument of Simone de Beauvoir, a twentieth-century feminist, Ophelia is forced "to abdicate"—to "bury her childhood, put away the independent and imperious being that was she, and enter submissively upon adult existence" (1952, 335, 365) as a creature wholly dependent on brother, father, lover. Mary Pipher underlines this point in her recent best-seller, *Reviving Ophelia: Saving the Selves of Adolescent Girls* (1994): "I believe, as Alice Miller, Margaret Mead and Simone de Beauvoir believed, that pathology comes from failure to realize all one's possibilities. Ophelia died because she could not grow. She became the object of others' lives and lost her true subjective self" (292). Marginalized to the point of madness, and marked as a scapegoat, it is an easy matter then, when a crisis arises and her prince needs her to carry away death, to trigger her suicide by yet another massive and sudden withdrawal of her few remaining resources. At this point, clinging to the ocean liner's railing and unable to climb back on deck, is it not inevitable that she will let go and drop into the sea?

Deprivation is not, of course, the only technology patriarchies use to construct suicides. Of several others, two must suffice. One particularly effective technique is to create a social system in which women can access financial and social resources only by being wholly dependent on men—that is, women are fed and cared for if they are in their proper places as wives and "culture mothers," but are left homeless and destitute if they are not. To make this economic binary even more effective, patriarchies reinforce it with a rigid psychic binary, placing rational order on one side, madness and chaos on the other, with no middle ground between. Thus, if Ophelia isn't an ideal obedient daughter, then she's "nothing," and she must be punished by killing herself. In short, rigid ethical codes indelibly brand her as worthless for being a sexual and perhaps a pregnant young woman. (This is not to say that all teenage pregnancies are a good thing; rather it is to say that there are better ways to deal with such pregnancies than abuse, shame, insanity, and suicide.)

What deprivation, financial dependency, and rigid ethical binaries tell us, then, is that patriarchal culture's suicide-production technologies are ancient, well-practiced, extremely effective, often virtually invisible, and ubiquitous.

To commit suicide, then, is to do what one is constructed to do, to do what one is ordered to do. As the modern French philosopher Gilles Deleuze writes, one "is already dead when [one] receives the order-word" (1987, 107). Thus, though suicide is conventionally misrepresented as an act of transgressive disobedience, it is in fact an act of obedience that like revenge and patience, makes one's desire the desire of an authoritative other (e.g., a parent), though in many cases the unconscious desire of this other. Thus, the second worse thing about Ophelia's (or anyone else's) suicide—the first being the waste of a human life—is that by committing suicide Ophelia sustains the system of power that needs her to kill herself, not to mention empowering those in this system who want her dead. Suicide then, is no better, but it is also no worse a solution to melancholy than are patience or revenge, since, from the perspective of the play, all three of these forms of obedience lead to death.

We are now in a position to suggest a solution to the problem of suicide. If passive suicides are one of several ways patriarchies remove those who threaten their power, violate their codes, and/ or fail their expectations, then there are only two solutions to the problem of suicide. The first is to create nonpatriarchal spaces where individuals whom patriarchies have produced as "abjects" can find resources for new self-objectifications; nonpatriarchal spaces, that is, that do *not* function as zones of deprivation where

"death [is] the only way out" (Janov 1975, 273)—precisely the sort
of spaces that were *not* available to Ophelia or Gertrude, or, for
that matter, to novelist Virginia Woolf, poet Sylvia Plath, or the
billions of nameless suicides caused by the powerful patriarchies
of the past and present. To alter somewhat the classic formulation
of the feminist film theorist Laura Mulvey, the solution is to create
spaces where melancholic persons can learn to become makers of
lives, rather than suicidal (or patient or revengeful) bearers of
someone else's death; spaces where potential suicides could realize that to kill themselves is to empower the system that constructed them to do its dirty work; spaces where a previously abject
individual like Ophelia would understand that the patriarchy that
empowers itself by systematically removing her reasons to live empowers itself even more by her decision to die.

The second solution is, of course, to continue those programs
of political activism that are designed to put patriarchies permanently out of business—programs that rid sociocultural spaces of
those discourses and technologies that give—and cannot not give—
the gift of death to persons like Ophelia.

The important point to make is that both of these solutions were
well under way in England at the end of the sixteenth century.
Popular public theatres like the Globe were one such nonpatriarchal space, and productions of plays like *The Tragicall Historie of
Hamlet* were one such activist program.

Though it is a social system that kills a young woman like Ophelia, such women can fight back, as to be sure, many of them did,
and as many are doing—"roaring girls" then and "riot girls" now,
if you will. Like Princess Diana and Marija Yakic, young women do
not have to give up, and, if society is going to become less tragic,
these young women can't give up, even if, as in the case of Marija
Yakic, patriarchal land mine technology has blown both one's legs
off. The crucial thing to remember is that Ophelia does not commit suicide because she is insane, though this is what one sees in
most modern productions, and it is what many people want to believe. Rather, Ophelia is driven insane and commits suicide because men representing an altogether different way of life than the
one she desires want her insane and dead. It's not then, that
Ophelia is a capable young woman who destroys herself; it is
that as a capable young woman Ophelia is not allowed to be anything other than dead because Hamlet and her brother could not

otherwise create themselves (to use Elizabeth Bronfen's phrase) "over her dead body."

The following excerpted materials deal with (1) English customs and laws relating to suicide, (2) a contemporary case study, and (3) Ophelia's flowers.

EARLY MODERN SUICIDE LAW

In the year 1000, a canon attributed to King Edgar reiterated an earlier 672 canon prohibiting normal funerals for suicides: "It is neither lawful to celebrate mass for one who, by any diabolical instigation, hath voluntarily committed murder on himself, nor to commit his body to the ground with hymns and psalmody or any rites of honourable sepulture." At the same time, an exemption was made for mad persons. In Bracton's later *Of Pleas of the Crown* (1250–56), we find: "But what shall we say of a madman bereft of reason? And of the deranged, the delirious and the mentally retarded? or if one labouring under a high fever drowns himself or kills himself? *Quaere* [inquire] whether such a one commits felony *de se* [a felony against the self, i.e., self-murder]. It is submitted that he does not, nor do such persons forfeit their inheritance or their chattels, since they are without sense and reason and can no more commit an *injuria* or a felony than a brute animal" (1968, 424).

FROM MICHAEL MACDONALD AND TERENCE R. MURPHY,
SLEEPLESS SOULS: SUICIDE IN EARLY MODERN ENGLAND
(Oxford: Clarendon Press, 1990)

The combination of government pressure and religious change explains why the law of suicide was so rigorously enforced in the sixteenth and early seventeenth centuries. . . . The crown disciplined coroners and juries who blatantly defied the law, and coroners were probably especially anxious to avoid prosecution. And yet the behavior of coroners' juries went beyond mere compliance. They often returned verdicts of *felo de se* when it was impossible to prove with certainty that a suicide had occurred. Over one-third of all the deaths that were classified as self-murders were drownings. Frequently there was no physical evidence (an eyewitness, a note, or a pile of folded clothes, for instance) to prove that a death had been a suicide. . . . One authority has suggested that up to one-half of all the suicides by drowning could just as plausibly have been returned as accidents. There was plenty of scope for mercy, had juries been inclined to construe the evidence narrowly. . . . There was another way in which juries could have behaved more mercifully, had they wished to do so. Fewer than 2 per cent of suicides were found to have been insane when they killed themselves. . . . This is an unbelievably low figure, even given a very rigorous definition of insane behaviour (56–57).

In this context much that is puzzling about the graveyard scene in *Hamlet* becomes clear: why Gertrude or Claudius have to demand "enlarged" though still "maimed [burial] rites," why the gravediggers debate Ophelia's culpability, why a Doctor [a Priest] refuses to sing, and why Laertes demands that he sing "a requiem" (5.1.222). Had Ophelia's death been ruled a *felo de se*, she would have been denied the usual rites of mourning—as the play's "shards, flints, and pebbles should be thrown on her" (5.1.213) suggests. Her body (to paraphrase MacDonald and Murphy 1990, 47) would have been interred in the dark, without a coffin and the garlands that might have accompanied it. If folk custom prevailed, John Weever wrote, she would have been buried at a crossroad with a stake driven through her body "to terrify all passengers, by that so infamous and reproachfull a burial, not to make such their final passage out of this world" (1631, 22).

DEATH, INQUEST, AND VERDICT IN
SIXTEENTH-CENTURY ENGLAND

Eight days before Christmas in 1579, the body of a young girl was found in the river Avon, a mile east of Shakespeare's hometown. Her name was Katherine Hamlett, and she had made her living as a spinster, meaning that she spun wool (not that she was, as the word came to mean a half century later, an elderly unmarried woman). Eight weeks later her body was disinterred from its burial place for an inquest. Since inquests usually followed immediately after the discovery of a corpse, there must have been a suspicion concerning the cause of her death. Had she been of sound mind? Or, since illicit pregnancies and the not infrequent subsequent rejections by lover and family were strong motives for suicide, perhaps Katherine's death was not accidental. But whatever the cause of the delay, the inquest reached a verdict of death by accident, perhaps because someone with power, as in Ophelia's case, influenced the decision. As his later use of Katherine's family name indicates, Shakespeare, fifteen at the time, seems to have been deeply impressed by this young girl's tragedy.

FROM *MINUTES AND ACCOUNTS OF THE CORPORATION OF STRATFORD-UPON-AVON*, Vol. III
(1577–1586; Public Record Office, *Ancient Indictments* 652, Part 2, 262; Trans. Richard Savage, London: The Dugdale Society, 1926)

11 February, 1579/80
Inquest at Tiddington on the Body of Katherine Hamlett

Inquisition . . . taken at Tiddington in the County aforesaid on the eleventh day of February . . . before Henry Rogers, a coroner of the said lady the Queen . . . on a view of the body of Katherine Hamlett . . . spinster [a woman who spins], found there dead and drowned, on the oath of [the jury members]: Who say on their oath that the aforesaid Katherine Hamlett, on the seventeenth day of December in the twenty-second year of the reign of the aforesaid lady the Queen, going with a certain vessel, in English *a pail*, to draw water at the river called Avon in Tiddington aforesaid, it so happened that the aforesaid Katherine, standing on the bank of the same river, suddenly and by accident slipped and fell into the river aforesaid, and there, in the water . . . by accident was drowned, and not otherwise nor in other fashion came by her death. In testimony whereof both the coroner aforesaid and the jury aforesaid have set their seal to this inquisition . . . on the day, in the year, and in the place abovesaid.

OPHELIA'S FLOWERS, HERBS, AND WILLOW

In Chapter 9, Ophelia's act of handing imaginary flowers to members of the Danish Court—"There's fennel for you, and columbines, there's rue for you, and here's some for me, we may call it herb of grace a sundays, you may wear your rue with a difference, there's a daisy" (4.5.177–80)—was read as a way Ophelia can act out the story of her deflowerment by symbolically "deflowering" herself in public. Had there been space, various other significations of this action would have been included. In addition to (1) the argument above, and (2) the values Ophelia herself assigns these floral symbols (e.g., "There's rosemary, that's for remembrance"), critics have found (3) moral meanings for these herbs and flowers, particularly a sense of guilt (e.g., rue stands for sorrow and repentance). They have recognized (4) that Ophelia is caught up at times in an phantasmic scenario in which she is "larding" [garnishing] her father's grave with flowers to compensate for the lack of a proper burial. And they have seen (5) that, in keeping with the play's earlier use of flower imagery, Ophelia is trying to regain, Proserpina-like, that earlier time in her life when she was still an innocent flower. Later scholars working with renaissance herbals and early modern folklore have also identified (6) various erotic and/or sexual meanings for these floral signifiers (e.g., columbine symbolizes cuckoldry; fennel, fickleness in love). Other scholars working with classical and medieval medical treatises on contraception and abortion have identified (7) several of these flowers as commonly prescribed abortifacients (abortion-inducing agents), particularly fennel and rue. For example, one fifteenth-century English medical text "contains a number of recipes 'for that sickness which is in the womb' [an unwanted pregnancy]. . . . The recipes contain many of the familiar herbs such as this one: 'Take rue and sage and drink it with water' " (Riddle 1992, 155). Also commonly used to abort unwanted pregnancies were the leaves or branches of the white willow Ophelia seems to have in her hands when she is found dead. For example, one medieval treatise writes: "willow leaves drunk prevent conception [*prohibent conceptionnem*]," while another states that the leaves of the willow tree "*per se vero ex aqua conceptionem potu adimunt* [remove conception as a drink by themselves with water]" (Riddle 1992, 132, 147). Moreover, given that the term, "flowers," was a conventional early modern term for menstruation, it seems (8) that Ophelia's interest in rosemary, a powerful emmenagogue (agent to induce menstruation), is a way of convincing herself that her "flowers" are back on schedule. Handing out flowers to everyone at court visually demonstrates, so to speak, that she is "having her period," and that she cannot therefore be pregnant. Finally, (9) given that rue was said to make a man impotent, and that Ophelia makes much of this herb—"there's rue for you" and "you may wear your rue with a difference" (4.5.179)—she may be handing this herb to Hamlet *in absentia* to prevent a situation that is now perhaps unpreventable. In short, Ophelia's "flower" scene, which many, including Gertrude, wish to understand as a beautiful pastoral reminiscence, a pious act of contrition, or, like Claudius, a sign of insanity, seems, like her later interest in willow leaves, to be a desperate attempt to act out the wish that "prescribing" flowers for herself and those around her will magically prevent conception or abort its effects (Painter and Parker 1994, 42–44). Her flower discourse, then, like her mental state, is a chaotic hodgepodge of meanings that are understandable if the various threads of its "half sense" (or its multiple senses) are teased out.

If then, as Gertrude implies, Ophelia's dead body was found where "a willow grows aslant [across] the brook," it is likely, given the traditional lore summed up by the following passage, that Ophelia was "clamb'ring" on a willow tree to find a remedy for an unwanted pregnancy, rather than seeking a place to hang "fantastic garlands" of flowers (4.7.137 ff.).

FROM CAROLUS MUSITANUS, *DE MORBIS MULIERUM*
(Colonial AlloGrogum: Chouet, 1709; Cited and translated by
Norman E. Himes, *Medical History of Contraception*. New York:
Schocken Books, 1970)

Chpt. IV: De sterilitate

Many are the drugs which dispose of or impede semen, or cause the abortion of the foetus. Amongst those which destroy semen and prevent conception is willow, which does not weaken the appetite of small women so much as poisons do, for which reason it mitigates excessive salacity, if first, truly tender willow shoots are cut off, from this there flows a liquor; when it is shaped into a little lump and drunk by a woman it is efficacious, so that never is love deemed stronger, but if a potion of willow be drunk by a woman on an empty stomach several times it induces sterility.

STUDY QUESTIONS

1. When does Ophelia realize that men in her world have virtually all of the power? What kind of power, if any, does she get by consenting to become their submissive object?

2. What are the demands Ophelia is struggling to meet? Are these demands possible to meet? If not, why are impossible demands being placed on her?

3. In what ways is Ophelia herself deeply fragmented long before her speech and behavior become obviously so?

4. Why does Ophelia collapse after a scene filled with the wild energies of song and flowers? Is this collapse inevitable?

5. Why does Ophelia have such a difficult time telling her story? Why can she tell it only in a complicated, indirect, fragmentary, and symbolic fashion?

6. Why, from her point of view, is getting pregnant both a solution to her problems and the cause of her problems?

7. In what way is Ophelia putting on a female disposition in order to survive in her culture?

8. In the conflict between Ophelia's need to explore the world, take risks, and make mistakes on the one hand, and Polonius's need to protect and control her on the other, who wins and why?

9. In addition to those mentioned in Chapter 9, what technologies do patriarchal societies use to construct individuals as suicides?

10. What kept Princess Diana's bulimia, depressions, and suicide attempts from ruining her life? How was she able *not* to give up—not to follow the script pushing her over the edge?

11. Why, when going mad, does Ophelia get closer and closer to nature (flowers, herbs, willow tree, water)?

QUESTIONS AND TOPICS FOR WRITTEN AND ORAL DISCUSSION

1. One of the initial speeches in Ophelia's mad scene (4.5.7–13) is spoken by an anonymous Gentleman. Why is this speech important? Why create a new character to speak it (In the Folio, unlike the "good" Quarto, this speech is given to Laertes)? What demand does it make on a theatre audience?

2. Starting with Ophelia's promise—" 'Tis in my memory locked / And you yourself shall keep the key of it" (1.3.85–86)—analyze what, in

addition to the advice Laertes has just given her, it is that Ophelia is locking up. Why does giving the key to Laertes, among other men, prove fatal? What effect does locking things up have on Ophelia's desires and sense of self?

3. How much agency (ability to exert power and make significant choices) does Ophelia have at the beginning of this play? How much of this agency is left by the end? What erodes it?

4. Is what Claudius says about Ophelia—"poor Ophelia / Divided from herself, and her fair judgment, / Without the which we are pictures, or mere beasts" (4.5.80–82)—a helpful way of thinking about her problem? If so, why? If not, why not?

5. In light of his "conception" speeches (2.2.183, 185–86) and his "Get thee to a nunnery" speeches (3.1.122 ff), discuss Hamlet's intentions/ objectives with respect to Ophelia. Do not restrict nunnery to either its dominant or its transgressive meaning (convent, and brothel).

6. Discuss why many critics refuse to accept as true anything Ophelia says in her mad scenes about being seduced, compromised, rejected, and abandoned by Hamlet. Discuss, too, how the problems involved in reading Ophelia's accusations are related to society's difficulty concerning children who accuse parents and others of sexual abuse, and/ or women who allege sexual harassment by public officials or employers.

7. Nine ways to understand Ophelia's flower scene are offered above. After reading the following passage from Simone de Beauvoir's *The Second Sex*, construct a tenth: "But, above all, the lie to which the adolescent girl is condemned is that she must pretend to be an object, and a fascinating one, when she senses herself as an uncertain, dissociated being. . . . The very face becomes a mask: spontaneous expressions are artfully induced, a wondering passivity is mimicked; . . . the eyes no longer penetrate, they reflect; the body is no longer alive, it waits; every gesture and smile becomes an appeal. Disarmed, disposable, the young girl is now only an offered flower, a fruit to be picked" (1953, 358).

SUGGESTED READINGS AND WORKS CITED

Beauvoir, Simone de. *The Second Sex*. Translated by H. M. Parshley. New York: Knopf, 1953.

Bloch, Maurice. "Death, Power and Women." In *Death and the Regeneration of Life*, edited by Maurice Bloch and Jonathan Perry. Cambridge: Cambridge University Press, 1982.

Bracton, Henry de. "Of Pleas of the Crown." In *On the Laws and Customs of England (1250–56)*. Vol. 2. Translated by Samuel E. Thorne. Cambridge: Harvard University Press, 1968.

Bronfen, Elizabeth. *Over Her Dead Body: Death, Feminity and the Aesthetic*. New York: Routledge, 1992.

Butler, Judith. *Gender Trouble: Feminism and the Subversion of Identity*. New York: Routledge, 1990.

Charney, Maurice and Hanna Charney. "The Language of Madwomen in Shakespeare." *Signs* 3 (1977), 451–470.

Deleuze, Gilles. *1,000 Plateaus*. Minneapolis: University of Minnesota Press, 1987.

Durkheim, Émile. *Suicide: A Study in Sociology* [1898]. Translated by J. A. Spaulding and G. Simpson. London: Routledge and Kegan Paul, 1952.

Foucault, Michel. *The History of Sexuality. Vol. I: An Introduction* [1976]. Translated by Robert Hurley. New York: Random House, 1990.

Freud, Sigmund. "Mourning and Melancholia" [1917]. In *A Standard Edition of the Complete Psychological Works*. Translated by James Strachey. London: The Hogarth Press, 1957.

Irigaray, Luce. *Speculum of the Other Woman*. Ithaca: Cornell University Press, 1985.

Janov, Arthur and Michael Holden. *Primal Man: The New Consciousness*. New York: Crowell, 1975.

Kristeva, Julia. *Powers of Horror: An Essay on Abjection*. Translated by Leon S. Roudiez. New York: Columbia University Press, 1982.

Leverenz, David. "The Woman in Hamlet: An Interpersonal View." In *Representing Shakespeare: New Psychoanalytic Essays*, edited by Murray M. Schwartz and Coppélia Kahn, 110–128. Baltimore and London: The Johns Hopkins University Press, 1994.

MacDonald, Michael. *Mystical Bedlam*. Cambridge: Cambridge University Press, 1981.

MacDonald, Michael and Terence R. Murphy. *Sleepless Souls: Suicide in Early Modern England*. Oxford: Clarendon Press, 1990.

Marcuse, Herbert. "The Ideology of Death." In *The Meaning of Death*, edited by Herman Feifel, 64–76. New York: McGraw-Hill, 1959.

Miller, Alice. *The Drama of the Gifted Child*. New York: Basic Books, 1981.

Napier, Augustus Y. and Carl Witaker. *The Family Crucible*. New York: Harper and Row, 1978.

Painter, Robert and Brian Parker. "Ophelia's Flowers Again." *Notes and Queries* 41 (1994), 42–45.

Pipher, Mary. *Reviving Ophelia: Saving the Selves of Adolescent Girls*. New York: Ballantine, 1994.

Pritchard, Colin. *Suicide—The Ultimate Rejection? A Psycho-Social Study.* Buckingham: Open University Press, 1995.

Riddle, John M. *Contraception and Abortion from the Ancient World to the Renaissance.* Cambridge: Harvard University Press, 1992.

Salkeld, Duncan. *Madness and Drama in the Age of Shakespeare.* Manchester: Manchester University Press, 1993.

Scarry, Elaine. *The Body in Pain: The Making and Unmaking of the World.* New York: Oxford University Press, 1985.

Showalter, Elaine. "Representing Ophelia: Women, Madness, and the Responsibilities of Feminist Criticism." In *Shakespeare & The Question of Theory,* edited by Patricia Parker and Geoffrey Hartman, 77–94. New York: Methuen, 1985.

Weever, John. *Ancient Funerall Monuments.* London: T. Harper, 1631.

Conclusion

> What would he doe
> Had he the motiue, and the cue for passion
> That I haue?
>
> Hamlet (2.2.560–61)

Now that the play is over, let's review what we've seen Hamlet do. Though it may seem that he is merely procrastinating before blundering into death, it is clear, in retrospect, that throughout the play Hamlet is hard at work dealing with the melancholia created by the loss of his father, his father's world, and the place he expected to have in it. It is also clear that to deal with this melancholia he creates a ghost, ventriloquizes a revenge imperative, and puts on an antic disposition to suspend himself between opposed parental worlds. When this solution fails, stronger measures negate his mother's initiatives, construct Claudius as a tyrant, use Ophelia's suicide to cart off toxic waste, and, in the end, purge every woman and every man tainted by woman to create in Denmark a purified version of the patriarchal space he inherited from his father.

From the perspective of his father's world these accomplishments are necessities, and Hamlet is a hero because, by purging Gertrude's (alleged) contagious rottenness, he solves the problem of the life threatening "dram of eale" that has put himself if not his paternal world out of joint. From this perspective, in fact, the dead bodies Hamlet piles up at the end of the play write a brilliant comedy. Thus, to the question posed by the epigraph above of what the traveling player ought to do "had he the motive, and the cue for passion" Hamlet has, the answer, from this perspective, would be: Exactly what Hamlet does!

But if purging woman and purifying patriarchal space writes a comedy from the perspective of Hamlet's father's world, such actions write a tragedy from the perspective of Shakespeare's *The Tragicall Historie of Hamlet*. From this later perspective, Hamlet's actions, though regarded as necessities in an archaic past, are shown/seen to be present crimes. Hamlet is not a hero. His purge and purify option is tyranny. His use of Ophelia's suicide is obscene. His destruction of his mother's initiatives absents everything on stage that is truly alive. And, since bloody carnage and repetition of the past perfected are Hamlet's only accomplishments, he is a colossal failure—in fact, he himself is the chief obstacle in the way of (he is the "dram of eale" that is poisoning) Denmark's emerging future. To the question then, of what the player should do "Had he the motive, and the cue for passion" Hamlet has, the answer from this perspective, is: Nothing that Hamlet does! In other words, Shakespeare's literary tragedy implicitly raises for its audience the question of what Hamlet would have had to do to generate an emergent comedy instead of a tragedy. Shakespeare's *Hamlet* raises the question of what these six adolescents—Hamlet, Laertes, Ophelia, Rosencrantz, Guildenstern, and Horatio—have to do if this play is to end with a Denmark full of vital, spontaneous people happily engaged in productive and pleasurable lives. And since melancholy, madness, and suicide won't do, and patience won't do, and revenge won't do, and purge and purify won't do, what, then, will do?

First, these six adolescents, and especially Hamlet, would have to get completely out of Hamlet's father's world. They may respect this world, they inevitably will repeat aspects of it, but in the main they must let it die, bury it, and, more important, keep it buried along with its codes and practices, among these most particularly its melancholia, suicide, patience, ghost, revenge, and blood purgation/purification technologies. They also have to end this world's marginalizing and negating manner of constructing, representing, and exploiting women, not to mention its parallel suppression and repression of archaic feelings. In short, these six adolescents, if they are to write a modern comedy, have to get the old play they are in, the script they are following, and the roles they are playing permanently off the stage of their lives.

Second, they have to improve significantly upon Hamlet's mother's world. Though her dominant world is far, far preferable to the residual world of Hamlet's father's past, Gertrude's society in and by itself is not adequate enough to insure comedy if only (1) because, in Elizabeth I's early modern version of this world, a code of patience is finally a hopeless option for young Elizabethan men in Hamlet's position (the earls of Essex and Southampton, for example) to cope with their losses and melancholy, (2) because this world lacks adequate roles for, though it offers better roles to, women, and (3) because this world proved vulnerable to a Scottish king from the north who, like Hamlet, destroyed many if not most of Elizabeth's initiatives after her death in 1603.

Finally, as a way of becoming independent of these parental worlds and the limitations of each, these six adolescents need to invent new skills, ones altogether absent in their paternal past and missing to too great a degree in their maternal present. Denmark is not out of joint because Claudius killed Hamlet Sr. (royal murders of this sort were an inevitable and well-known feature of monarchy); rather, Denmark is out of joint because it lacks a wide range of these new skills. What skills then, must these adolescents invent if they are not going to write tragic deaths for themselves?

1. As we saw in Chapter 4, they need to invent mourning. They need to know how to replace melancholia with the work of mourning. Where malancholia encourages them to hang on to a lost object forever, refusing to let it go, turning it into a ghost, vision, or memory, and letting it shape their lives as a repetition of death, the work of mourning would allow them to let go of such lost finite objects, replace them, and go on living. In time, mourning would allow Ophelia to replace abjection with strength, just as it would allow Hamlet to get rid of his guilt, suicidal fantasies, ghost hallucinations, revenge obsession, antic disposition, and purge/purify behavior.

2. The independence mourning generates would then let these adolescents get beyond the obedience demands insisted on by both parental worlds—Gertrude's patience demand, as well as Hamlet Sr.'s revenge or suicide ones. If these adolescents are to construct better social formations than the ones that presently exist, they must discover how to *unlearn* much of what they have been taught, how to *disobey* parental imperatives creatively and successfully, and thus how to escape the double binds which such limited knowledge and such contradictory demands invariably create.

3. Ophelia and her peers must in turn learn to revise the status of the limited and limiting culture in which they presently live. Instead of regarding either the father's or mother's society as natural, inevitable, God-given, or ideal, they need to recognize that society is a *construction*—an object built by people like themselves—however natural their culture may seem to be simply because they grew up in it. They also have to learn not to underestimate the strength of such constructions, nor the number of adults whose invested interests require them to keep such constructions (the status quo) exactly as they are.

4. They must also learn that as persons, they too, are constructions, and that it is possible and necessary, though difficult, for Hamlet and Laertes to reconstruct themselves as post-patriarchal men, and for Ophelia to reconstruct herself as a strong woman independent of patriarchal men.

5. Then, having gotten themselves in positions of independence by abdicating many of the roles appointed for them by their parents, these six adolescents need to begin creatively rewriting the world in which they live, imagining new options, drafting new social blueprints, creating new plays and stages that will offer increasingly better lines, roles, costumes, and sets.

6. These adolescents then need to set about figuring out on their own how to actualize these new blueprints in a non-violent manner—to restructure the society in which they live as a representative, democratic society, a social formation which, for them, has never existed.

7. Finally, they need to invent ways of working in groups to make these changes. Rather than a tragic concerto in which a figure like Hamlet battles the rest of the group into a

grave, or an isolated fugue which removes Ophelia permanently from the group, Denmark needs to be a space where
alliances can prosper.

If the question then, is what the player ought to do had he the
motive, and the cue for passion Hamlet and the other five adolescents have, the early modern emergent answer is that, if he wants
to write a comedy, he would have to invent these skills and use
them.

What might these new blueprints contain? What new options
might six Danish adolescents invent who are free to be creative?
What sociocultural changes might they institute were Ophelia a
strong, empowered woman, and Hamlet and Laertes postpatriar-
chal men? Let us imagine various options Hamlet might have pursued using materials already available in his world. Consider his
relation to theatre. Instead of prostituting a group of traveling players to the contents of his suspicions by turning one of their plays
into both a mouthpiece for his ultraconservative values and a piece
of litmus paper to test a king, Hamlet could have gone to work
helping found an independent popular public theatre in Denmark
that would have gone a long way in making Claudius's "greatness
familiar." Or, think of Hamlet's relationship to women. Instead of
trying to browbeat Ophelia and Gertrude back into the confining
roles and scripts of the patriarchal past, Hamlet, if he wanted to
be a modern hero, would have understood and supported the
early feminist lifestyle his mother was inventing and Ophelia was
beginning to follow. Or, in the case of Ophelia, instead of helping
deprive her of an adequate education, and instead of sleeping with
and rejecting her, and then killing her father and ignoring the consequences of both his "wild oats" and his murderous violence,
Hamlet could have helped her invent romantic love, intimacy, social mobility, subjectivity, sociality, and the like. Moreover, he
could have worked with her to insure that young women would
get an adequate education as well as the opportunity to use their
intelligence and abilities in any way they might choose to do so.
Or, he could have worked with Ophelia and others to set up ther-
apeutic spaces to counteract the sociocultural inadequacies that
were driving men like himself to the madness of violent purgation/
purification and women like Ophelia to the madness of depression
and suicide. Or, consider Hamlet's relation to Claudius. Instead of

plotting in a totally impotent and futile fashion to expose a royal criminal, Hamlet could have thrown his energies into inventing forensic science and a strong parliament, forms of new knowledge that might have secured sufficient evidence with which, and a place in which, to prosecute a king. Or, like Junius Brutus, and unlike Hamblet, Hamlet could have worked in other ways to replace absolute monarchy with a form of representative government supportive of the initiatives outlined above. Or, these six adolescents could have used their freed-up energies to invent any number of other institutions their Denmark lacks: a judicial system that is separate from the royal court, a local university separate from the church, the beginnings of banking and trade, viable professional vocations, or new forms of music and dance among many other new modes of pleasure and self-empowerment. Obviously, a list of the new doors these adolescents could have opened in the prison that is their confining culture goes on and on if we think not just about what they could have done, but about what had to be done if Denmark was to bury its past and generate the political and cultural necessities that, among other things, allow us, as its audience (modern or early modern), to sit in a public theatre and watch this Denmark act out its brief and painfully dysfunctional social life on a stage before us.

Hamlet is a tragedy, not because Claudius kills Hamlet Sr., but because Hamlet's father's Denmark lacks every institution a civilized culture needs in order to prosper; because his mother's Denmark is in the process of losing those few it has recently created; and because the brightest, best educated, and most promising of Denmark's adolescents are trapped in options that destroy them and any chance of their bringing a more adequate culture into existence.

We are now in a position to ask why Shakespeare staged Hamlet's failure to be an emergent hero for his early modern audiences. Presumably *The Tragicall Historie of Hamlet* was produced

1. To show its early modern audience what they themselves had left behind, and what they could *not* resurrect as ghost, revenge, patience, suicide, or violent blood purgation/purification if they wanted to go on living.

2. To show this audience that they would still be living in Hamlet's father's world if people like themselves had not

invented and used the skills listed above, and that persons in the past like themselves—apprentices, servant girls, wives, artisans—had done this work almost entirely by themselves. To show ordinary people that their ancestors—ordinary people like those who accompany Laertes to Elsinore to topple Claudius from power, but who do not even get onstage (though they are heard in the wings)—had successfully figured out ways of getting an increasingly larger say about how the culture was to be designed and what roles they would play in it.

3. To show this audience that they can't expect, or wait patiently for a prince like Hamlet to help them create a better culture for themselves because, in such a prince's mind, what is better for them is worse for him, thus making him one of, if not the worst, obstacle in their way.

4. To show this audience that the violence, contagion, and death that erupts and destroys Hamlet's Denmark comes not from the lower levels of the culture (women, adolescents, ordinary people) but from the upper levels that are supposed to be the source of order, right, truth (prince, fathers, king, courtiers).

5. To show this audience that it was neither accidental nor inevitable that their present culture takes the form it does, and that at any moment a reactionary backlash like the one Hamlet generates onstage could reduce it and them to a pile of dead bodies.

6. And perhaps, to show this audience what an actor's life in theatre was like before public professional theatres came to be established in London, and how limited theatre was when traveling groups of players had to serve the desperate wish and will of local aristocrats like Hamlet.

For Shakespeare to stage *The Tragicall Historie of Hamlet* is to show his audiences why they had created and had to keep creating a better world, the obstacles they had overcome in doing so, and what they had given up to do so. Like the ordinary people at the gates of Elsinore whom we hear but never see, those Elizabethans acting in and watching Shakespeare's play in 1599 had experienced radical loss and disempowerment. They had tried revenge, suicide, patience, and/or purgation and purification. But, to varying degrees, they (unlike the adolescents in the play) had abandoned such hopeless options, had gotten seriously into the business of creating a viable culture, and, among other things, had created the professional public theatre in which they were presently acting and sitting. Instead of a revenger like Laertes, a suicide like Ophelia, a stoic like Horatio, patsies like Rosencrantz and Guildenstern, a sleight of hand man like Claudius, or a "minister and scourge" like Hamlet, these early modern audience members and their predecessors had produced (among many other things) a playwright (Shakespeare) who understood Hamlet's failure and its consequences, a player (Richard Burbage) who could act this failure, and audiences who could benefit from observing such a failure. So, although those onstage do not write a comedy, those in the Globe definitely had written and were continuing to write one, and *Hamlet* not only unequivocally articulates the difference between these on- and offstage activities, but celebrates the difference.

To bring the purpose of playing *The Tragicall Historie of Hamlet* closer to home, let us briefly hold Shakespeare's dramatic mirror up to the American South rather than an archaic Denmark. In this version of the play, Hamlet's dead father epitomizes the worst and best of the white supremacist apartheid system of power that was dominant in the Old South. After her husband's death, Gertrude, wanting to live in a more tolerant and less bigoted culture, marries a southern white man sympathetic to her desire to increase equality between whites and blacks as well as between men and women. After vacillating between these conflicting parental worlds, Hamlet chooses to be a reactionary remnant of the bigoted and sexist system of the past, and in time violently destroys (somewhat as George Wallace did in Alabama) the racially more equal society his mother is trying to establish. As spectators watching this southern version of *Hamlet*, we are a racially mixed audience that is *not* on the side of apartheid if only because we wouldn't be in this theatre watching this play if we were. What then, as black and white theatregoers do we learn from this play? We learn that disenfranchised members of the old white power structure will destroy us if they can; that neither patience nor suicide will get us anywhere; that to turn to revenge or purgation/purification is not so much to copy but to concede victory to our adversaries; and that we must employ whatever nonviolent strategies we can devise to support and develop the kind of culture Gertrude is trying to bring into existence if we are ever going to be free, happy, and safe from endless insult, humiliation, abuse, exploitation, and murder in our daily lives.

Why, we may now ask, does Hamlet fail? Who or what is to blame for the fact that, given "the motive and cue for passion" he has, he does nothing of significant value except delay the destruction he eventually visits on Denmark—that he does nothing to develop an emergent culture?

One answer is that since he doesn't (and in his mind, can't) leave his father's world, he gets infected by it. Just as Polonius blasts the infant buds of Ophelia's spring, so Hamlet's father's world destroys Hamlet by pouring its poison in Hamlet's ear. In the world of Denmark, the river of custom sucks all of these adolescents down no matter how powerfully they try to keep their heads above the world they live in. Despite its strength, however, this answer to why Hamlet fails will not do. It explains why our sympathy lies with these victimized adolescents, but, as an answer, it is too easy. Heroes always live in worlds corrupted by their parents or other forces, and emergent heroes are heroes precisely because they solve problems, not because they succumb to the disease that caused such problems. So a better explanation of why Hamlet fails is needed, and a second answer is that he does so because he lacks a decent Denmark; he is deprived of everything one needs to succeed. He has no love, no allies, no adequate education, no satisfying sex life. The place he lives in is so impoverished, he is so completely on his own, and so without resources, that it is no wonder he fails. He wants and needs Ophelia to be loyal, Gertrude to be a ideal mother, no one hidden behind an arras (tapestry), and a world that is filled with something other than loss and corruption. Had he such a lover, mother, situation, he would have been a hero! But obviously this explanation of why Hamlet fails also fails to suffice. An emergent hero is a hero precisely because, when he finds himself in such a space of absence and loss, he does something significant to remedy this lack. If Denmark were a space of cornucopian resources, it would not be out of joint and would not need a hero. So, to argue deprivation is again to beg the question.

As we saw above, Hamlet fails because, in a situation of paternal infection, deprivation, and loss, he does nothing significantly different. From an emergent perspective *Hamlet* is a tragedy of failed creativity—a failure on Hamlet's part, among others, to get from there (onstage Denmark) to here (Elizabethan England and beyond). Who, if not Hamlet and these other adolescents, could create such a new social order? And if not Hamlet, then perhaps it is (and was) up to those offstage ordinary Danes we do not see onstage—those unseen people like Shakespeare and his audiences—to rewrite cultural history! To go back to our southern *Hamlet* analogy, if George Wallace is a hero from the perspective of the South's racist past, only those numerous blacks and those few whites who created a more equal Alabama are heroes from an emergent perspective.

In the end then, Hamlet fails because he relies on the *best* that his father's culture has to offer him, never seeing that this best is what is responsible for the infections and deprivations that are destroying Denmark. Like a doctor who bleeds patients to cure them, Hamlet, unable even to begin imagining doing otherwise, is an anachronism trapped by a technology of power that condemns him with the name of his father, a son who fails (from his audience's emergent perspective) precisely because he becomes nothing more than "Hamlet the Dane."

What is fundamentally at issue in *The Tragicall Historie of Hamlet* is the kind of world we are going to live in, the kinds of people adolescents are going to be, and the tasks their energies are going to perform. The answer Shakespeare's literary masterpiece gives us is that if these energies go into the options available in its onstage Denmark everyone will soon be dead. Thus, it would be far better if these energies were put into nonviolent creative options instead, given that the best things about early modern culture were not built, nor are they going to be improved upon, by patient obedience, suicide, revenge, or bloody programs of purgation and purification. In sum, *Hamlet* was written to ask its audiences, and it became increasingly more famous because it kept on asking its audiences, whether they were going to invest their passion in repeating the residual past, in maintaining the dominant status quo, or in making a significant emergent difference? In other words, *Hamlet* asks you to consider what you will do when you have "the motive, and the cue for passion" that Hamlet, Ophelia, Laertes, Horatio, Rosencrantz, and Guildenstern have. Understanding *Hamlet* in this sense is to know the option you yourself will take when you are next confronted by the infections, deprivations, traumatic losses, and the lack that (in Philip Levine's phrase) will inevitably "burn on the tongue and spill into the small valleys of our living" (1976, 34).

STUDY QUESTIONS

1. What options did Diana, Princess of Wales take when she "had the motive and the cue for passion" that one or another of the adolescents in the play have?

2. What is Prince Charles doing with his energies while he waits in the wings to be king?

3. What did Martin Luther King, Jr. do when he had a "motive, and [a] cue for passion"?

4. What did Timothy McVeigh do?

5. What is the difference between transgressing parental law, and learning to disobey it in an emergent, creative fashion? How does transgression help sustain and strengthen the status quo?

6. What options other than revenge, patience, or suicide do you have if you are up against bigoted police officers who do to you what a number of Los Angeles police officers did several years ago to Rodney King, or what several New York City policemen did to Abner Louima, a Haitian immigrant?

7. A Shakespeare critic has argued that revenge is the only course of action Hamlet could have taken to secure justice. Is this true?

8. Why does Hamlet take his father's side against his mother? What would have to happen, what conditions would have to exist, for a son like Hamlet to be able to take and improve on his mother's innovations? How would such conditions come into being? Who would create such conditions?

9. What could Gertrude have done to keep her new world from being destroyed by her son?

10. Who is the onstage playwright Shakespeare most identifies with—Hamlet, or Gertrude?

11. At present, does our culture have an adequate repertoire of options available for its members, particularly its adolescent members, to follow?

12. In addition to imagination, what do adolescents need in order to be creative, and what conditions do they need to be able to actualize new ideas? Who creates these resources and conditions if they do not already exist?

13. What persons or groups in American society are acting in Hamlet-like fashion to purify America by destroying the representative institutions that make America free and democratic?

QUESTIONS AND TOPICS FOR WRITTEN AND ORAL DISCUSSION

1. Develop this concluding chapter's argument in terms of Britain's House of Windsor and Diana, Princess of Wales. That is, if a hero is someone who solves a life threatening problem for a given constituency, what problem did Diana solve from the point of view of those who consider her a hero? As reported in the press, what was Queen Elizabeth II's and/or the House of Windsor's point of view on this matter? What is Prince Charles's role in all of this? What does he see as the problem? What could he have done (what did he do) to be a hero in this situation? And, finally, what will Princes William and Harry have to do to be heroes from these opposed perspectives, and how can they possibly satisfy such conflicting expectations and/or demands?

2. Describe a personal situation of lack or loss in which you gave up on the options of depression, patience, revenge, suicide, and/or purging/purifying, became nonviolently inventive, and succeeded in creating a new life for yourself. Compare this to a situation in which you gave up on these options and yet failed to get anywhere. What made the difference?

3. A Shakespeare critic has written that there is "finally no action that can be commensurate with [Hamlet's] grief, not even the killing of a guilty King." How would you respond?

4. Discuss what it would take for members of urban street gangs to give up their revenge code and create new options for themselves.

5. Why is independent, popular professional theatre a crucial part of any significant effort to remodel a fixed finite culture, and why is this sort of theatre such a threat to anyone who monopolizes or wants to monopolize power?

6. Discuss how urban street gangs, the Mafia, or other groups destroy or monopolize theatre.

7. Could it be said that literary tragedy, at its roots, represents a culture's fear that its children will only imitate their parents—that they will not be inventive?

8. Imagine a relationship between two people. Why isn't patience enough to make it work? When does patience invariably run out? What generally takes its place? What new knowledge (options) have modern cultures invented to replace patience and/or whatever takes its place when patience fails?

WORKS CITED AND SUGGESTED READINGS

Eagleton, Terry. *William Shakespeare*. Oxford: Blackwell, 1987.

Greenblatt, Stephen. "General Introduction." In *The Norton Shakespeare*. New York and London: W. W. Norton, 1997.

Jorgens, Jack L. *Shakespeare on Film*. Bloomington: Indiana University Press, 1976.

Kamps, Ivo. *Shakespeare Left and Right*. New York and London: Routledge, 1991.

Laroque, François. *The Age of Shakespeare* [illustrations]. Translated by Alexandra Campbell. New York: Harry N. Abrams, 1993.

Levine, Philip. *The Names of the Lost*. New York: Atheneum, 1976.

McDonald, Russ. *The Bedford Companion to Shakespeare: An Introduction with Documents*. Boston and New York: St. Martin's Press, 1996.

Pape, Walter and Frederick Burwick, eds. *The Boydell Shakespeare Gallery* [illustrations]. Essen: Peter Pomp, 1996.

Parsons, Keith and Pamela Mason, eds. *Shakespeare in Performance* [illustrations]. London: Salamander Books, 1995.

Schoenbaum, Samuel. *William Shakespeare: A Compact Documentary Life*. Rev. ed. Oxford: Oxford University Press, 1987.

Taylor, Gary. *Reinventing Shakespeare: A Cultural History from the Restoration to the Present*. New York and Oxford: Oxford University Press, 1989.

Wells, Stanley, ed. *The Cambridge Companion to Shakespeare Studies*. Cambridge: Cambridge University Press, 1986.

Index

About the Author

RICHARD CORUM teaches English at the University of California at Santa Barbara. His field of expertise is English Renaissance literature, especially Shakespeare, on which he has published essays on *Henry V* and *Love's Labour's Lost*. He has also published an essay on Milton's *Paradise Lost*.

The Greenwood Press "Literature in Context" Series